Crack Cocaine Users

Crack cocaine users have significant health problems, and place a significant burden on social services, the criminal justice system and drug treatment agencies. Among policymakers, professionals and the wider section of society, they are the most poorly understood drug-using group and have the worst retention rate in prison drug programmes and community drug agencies.

This book is about their addictions and the realities of their lives. Based on ethnographic research (observation and interviewing) conducted in south London, it aims to highlight their day-to-day struggles as they attempt to survive in a violent and intimidating street drug scene while trying to make changes to their lives. The book unpacks the myths and stigma of their drug use, highlighting their fragile position in society in an effort to better understand them. With the help of several key characters, the book uses their words and experiences to take the reader on a journey through their crack addiction from a life in and out of crack houses, their experiences with law enforcement and welfare agencies to their life aspirations.

The findings have important policy implications, and are relevant and accessible to academics and students in the field of criminology, sociology, psychology and research methods. The research is equally relevant for central and local government policymakers, and frontline healthcare and drug agency staff.

Daniel Briggs is a Senior Lecturer in Criminology and Criminal Justice at the University of East London. He works with a range of social groups – from the most vulnerable to the most dangerous to the most misunderstood. His work takes him inside prisons, crack houses, mental health institutions, asylum seeker institutions, hostels, care homes and hospices, and homeless services. His research interests include social exclusion, culture and deviance, and late modern identities. He has recently undertaken work in Spain on gypsies and youth risk behaviours while on holiday and is currently undertaking research on youth gangs.

Routledge Advances in Ethnography

Edited by Dick Hobbs
University of Essex and
Geoffrey Pearson
Goldsmiths College, University of London

Ethnography is a celebrated, if contested, research methodology that offers unprecedented access to people's intimate lives, their often hidden social worlds and the meanings they attach to these. The intensity of ethnographic fieldwork often makes considerable personal and emotional demands on the researcher, while the final product is a vivid human document with personal resonance impossible to recreate by the application of any other social science methodology. This series aims to highlight the best, most innovative ethnographic work available from both new and established scholars.

Crack Cocaine Users

High Society and Low Life in south London

Daniel Briggs

Routledge
Taylor & Francis Group

LONDON AND NEW YORK

First published 2012
by Routledge
2 Park Square, Milton Park, Abingdon, Oxon, OX14 4RN

Simultaneously published in the USA and Canada
by Routledge
711 Third Avenue, New York, NY 10017

Routledge is an imprint of the Taylor & Francis Group, an informa business

British Library Cataloguing in Publication Data
A catalogue record for this book is available from the British Library

Library of Congress Cataloging in Publication Data
Briggs, Daniel.
Crack cocaine users : high society and low life in South London / Daniel
Briggs. -- 1st ed.
     p. cm.
     Includes bibliographical references.
     1. Cocaine abuse--England--London. 2. Drug addicts--England--London--
Biography. 3. Drug addicts--Rehabilitation--England--London--Case
studies. 4. Addicts--England--London--Services for. I. Title.
     HV5840.G7B75 2011   362.29'8094216--dc23
     2011022786

Typeset in Times New Roman and Gill Sans
by Bookcraft Limited, Stroud, Gloucestershire

ISBN 978-0-415-67133-0 (hbk)
ISBN 978-0-203-15415-1 (ebk)

Printed and bound in Great Britain by the MPG Books Group

Contents

Acknowledgements

This book is only possible because of the people involved in the crack scene in south London. I am completely indebted to Dawg, Blood, Fam and, in particular, Cuz. You and others spoke about your life experiences, dilemmas, worries and ambitions. You also allowed me into your lives and I hope what I write conveys your experiences to a broad section of society. Thank you to the professionals who participated in interviews and the local Drug Action Team (DAT) who also added direction to the project. Thanks also to Galahad Substance Misuse Solutions. I am extremely grateful to the editors of this series – Emeritus Professor Geoff Pearson and Professor Dick Hobbs. Geoff, in particular read numerous chapter drafts at short notice. Initially, Brian Willan contracted me to undertake this work and his daughter, Julia, who now works at Routledge, has provided immeasurable support and guidance.

In my early university days, lectures from Professors Jock Young and John Lea provided impetus for me to further my career. I learnt much from Professor Roger Matthews with whom I later worked at London South Bank University. This book is based on my PhD fieldwork, so credit is due to my supervisors Professor Tim Rhodes and Dr Linda Cusick. Over this period, Dr Jo Kimber, Dr Chris Bonnell and Dr Cicely Marston also provided important guidance and feedback. Thanks also to experts in the field of substance use – Dr Mike Shiner and Professor Joanne Neale – who helped me develop the conceptual insight into this work. I called on the advice and wise words of Emeritus Professor Howard Parker, Professor David Moore and Professor Philippe Bourgois. More recent guidance and friendship I have gleaned from Tim Turner, Dave Cudworth, Dr Axel Klein, Dr Sébastien Tutenges, Dr Jennifer Fleetwood and Toby Dodson.

My friends and family have offered endless support and painstakingly helped me through the editing process of this book. Mum, your curiosity and ability to talk to strangers was infectious, and you always told me to believe in myself. Dad, you always told me to 'try again' and 'think laterally' in the face of defeat – losing is definitely part of winning. Lastly and most importantly, my wife, to whom this is dedicated – thank you. You are my influence as my inspiration. You believed in me and, despite the demands of your own schedule, were always there when I left on fieldwork days and were there waiting when I returned late at night. I'm sorry you were worried when I left you with only an address and instructions what to do if I didn't return.

Glossary

Before you start this book, do familiarise yourself with these slang terms, acronyms and other phrases or words which are used:

ABC   Anti-social Behaviour Contracts precede the use of ASBOs as a warning that, unless behaviour changes, an ASBO will be sought.

ASBO   Anti-social Behaviour Orders are court-imposed bans from certain behaviours/people/places.

Bag (of heroin)   An amount of heroin.

To be bailed out   An advance of crack or/and heroin.

To bang it up   Smoking and, in some contexts, injecting crack and/or heroin.

To talk bollocks/bollocks   To talk rubbish/substandard.

Booting   Smoking crack/heroin.

Brown   Heroin.

Buzz   A good feeling/experience from substances.

CARAT workers   'Counselling, Assessment, Referral, Advice and Throughcare' workers identify drug users in prison, give them advice and refer them to other welfare services on release.

Clipping   Pretending/proposing to offer sexual services but instead stealing from prospective clients.

Clucking   Suffering physical withdrawals from heroin/crack.

Copper   Policeman/woman.

Crack head   Subjective label for someone who uses crack.

DAT   Drug Action Team. This team is responsible for drug prevention and treatment in the local area.

DF118   Dihydrocodeine, which is an opioid painkiller.

Go/act digi   Crack use resulting in facial muscle spasms.

Dirty hit   Injecting with dirty equipment, which results in intense sickness.

Dog end   Cigarette butt.

DTTO   Drug Testing Treatment Order.

DVT   Deep vein thrombosis.

E   Ecstasy.

End(s)   *Crack house(s)* although the term has different meanings in other social contexts.

Fag   Cigarettes.

Fix/fixing   Most commonly associated with injecting crack and/or heroin but can mean to take drugs.

Flush   A flush is undertaken after the vein has been found and the syringe is withdrawn and blood fills the syringe before this process is repeated a number of times.

On the foil   Smoking crack or/and heroin on foil.

Gear   Mostly used to mean heroin but can also mean drugs or even crack and heroin.

Geezer   Person.

Graft/grafting   Making money for crack or/and heroin predominantly through criminal activity such as theft, robbery, etc.

A grand   One thousand pounds.

HCA   High Crack Area

HCV/Hep C   Hepatitis C.

HIV   Human immuno-deficiency virus.

Lick   Smoking/getting a hit off a crack pipe.

Nick   To steal; also means prison.

One-on-one   Known as one bag of heroin and one rock of crack. Some dealers offer 'two-on-two's – two crack rocks and two heroin bags and/or 'two-on-one's – two crack rocks and one heroin bag.

PCSO   Police Community Support Officer.

Ponce/poncing   A person who begs/begging or to beg off someone. It may also mean hassling depending on social context.

Prang or **Wired**   A state of paranoia and high anxiety when or after using crack.

Punter   Client – normally used in the context of sex workers.

Rehab   Residential rehabilitation service.

Rock   An amount of crack, usually valued at between £10 and £20.

RSL   Registered social landlords.

Runner   Someone delivering/dealing drugs (most likely to be crack and heroin).

Scag/scaghead   Heroin/someone who uses heroin.

Score   To make an exchange for crack and/or heroin.

Skin pop   Jabbing the skin without finding a vein to inject.

Smack   Heroin.

Speedballing/Snowballing   Using crack and heroin together (most commonly in a syringe but also in pipes and on foil).

Spliff   Form of roll-up cigarette which may include drugs like cannabis, crack, etc.

STIs   Sexually transmitted infections.

Stone   An amount of crack; denominations vary.

TB   Tuberculosis.
Tenner   £10.
Touch   A moment or run of good fortune.
Weed   Cannabis.
White   Crack.

Chapter 1

Introduction

Obviously there are things that I don't know what I'm talking about but if you asked me something that I didn't know I'd sit there and admit that I didn't know what to say. But on this sort of subject – crack cocaine – I do know what I'm talking about and it's something that I can stand up and get a microphone and speak it because I really do want my voice to be heard. Do you understand what I'm saying? I really do want people to understand what this [crack cocaine] is all about. It's not a fucking joke – put it that way. It's serious and I want people to realise. Do you know what I mean? [Gritting his teeth] And it is time for these people [starts pointing at people around the café] to understand that, as I said, it ain't a joke. Ok you can say 'Well, they're doing it themselves. It's self-inflicted', but at least you've got to give them some sort of help because the help we've got now is all bollocks.

(Cuz)

Introduction

Crack cocaine users ('crack users' hereafter) have significant health problems and place a major burden on health and social services, the criminal justice system and drug treatment agencies. They are responsible for significant levels of crime, have the worst retention rate in prison drug programmes and community drug agencies, and remain the most poorly understood drug-using group among UK policymakers and professionals, the media and wider society. This book is about crack use and the realities of users' lives. It is based on ethnographic research – observation and interviewing – conducted over the course of 2004 and 2005 in one south London borough, which I refer to as 'Rivertown'. It aims to highlight crack users' day-to-day struggles as they try to survive in a violent and intimidating street drug scene while trying to take some steps toward making changes to their complex lifestyles. I write this book because this particular drug-using group is the most heavily stigmatised in the UK context.

The chapter that follows this gives you more about the structure of the book but, for now, I would like to try to put you, the reader, in the quagmire that is the world of crack users. Chapter 1 is a reflexive account, using field notes, which contextualises the main players of this book: Dawg, Blood, Cuz and Fam.

Dawg's crack house and early introductions

> We came up in the lift, which stank of urine. I stood crammed in the lift with Dawg, Big T and JC. We walked out across the landing and Dawg fumbled for his key. He apologised in advance for the mess. I guess he felt embarrassed that someone who didn't take drugs was coming in. I felt privileged, as he said he wouldn't normally do this unless someone had crack for him. The toilet was on the right hand side as we went in. There was a fish tank in the hallway because for some reason Dawg thought he might one day have fish. The floor was tiled but hadn't been swept for months. JC and Big T went straight into the living room, on the right as we walked in. Dawg politely showed me his bedroom, which was on the left from the hallway. It was made up of a single bed in the corner, which was white with yellow stains on the mattress and duvet, a broken mirror and a cupboard. The living area was a rubbish dump. There was sawdust everywhere and some pornographic magazines lying around. There was no distinctive smell. The crack-smoking area was around a decrepit sofa Dawg had been given by a church charity. There were small crack wrappers and some crack pipes on the little table near the sofa and a television propped up in the corner. The kitchen, which had no flooring, was bloodstained in areas.
>
> (Field notes)

After several days hanging around in the streets with Bones, JC and Big T, I was finally invited to Dawg's crack house. While Dawg always denied his flat was a 'crack house', his crack-using associates felt otherwise. They had reason for this because Dawg invited all sorts of strangers to smoke drugs in his flat at all hours. When not in his flat, Dawg lingered outside Connections North (a drug service) asking around for loans of crack or money. This was because he couldn't 'graft'. Reflecting on their 15-year crack-smoking relationship, Bones described how awkward Dawg was when they were 'grafting' for money for crack:

> That's just him [Dawg], he knows that he can't do anything [cannot make money for crack] and I do all the work. I walk with him so he can give me a bit of smother, block the view so people can't see what I'm doing [shoplifting], pretending to talk to him, but I am just going in the shop pretending to see who is about. But Dawg isn't going to do anything. I am going to put this stuff in my bag and walk out. Nothing is going to happen to him, even if he did walk out and they grabbed him, he can just go: 'Fuck off, I don't know that boy'. Even though there is no danger to him whatsoever, he will still act robotically.
>
> (Bones)

Because of his inability to earn money, Dawg bartered out his flat to allow people to use crack in the flat in exchange for a 'rock or two'. The flat regulars were Blood, who had met Dawg in a hostel; Big T, a large man in his 50s who had spent time in prison for murder; JC, who, in his late 30s, suffered from a rare lung condition but continued to inject crack and a variety of prescribed drugs; and Bones – the thinnest of them all – an adept shoplifter from Ireland. Big T and JC only came to Dawg's on occasions but Blood and Bones spent long over-night spells, making their money for crack and treating him to a few pipes. What amazed me the most was when Dawg broke into unpredictable, never-ending narratives about his life experiences after smoking crack.

> Normally, a £15 crack rock would last Dawg about an hour as he didn't like to smoke it all at once and normally preferred to have a Valium 10–15 minutes before smoking crack. If Valium wasn't available, heroin would do. It took him 15 seconds to smoke his first pipe and Dawg went into verbal overdrive, reflecting on imperial times of racism and slavery. He then made another four pipes although he said this was 'greedy' for him. He carefully broke off '£2.75 of the rock' he said, crushed it as much as his shakey hands could, then got the back-end of a knife and continued to reduce the size of the rocks. Once he had done that, he sprinkled the cigarette ash on the foil of the crack pipe so the small crack rocks wouldn't burn too quickly and fall down the little holes in the foil, which was wrapped around the crack pipe. He put it to his lips and inhaled while burning the crack with a cheap lighter. His verbal overdrive continued about incessant 'everythings and nothings' about slavery and racism. He started to perspire slightly and his nose became runny; he left it dripping to start with but then just wiped it off with his hand. His eyes became very wide and kept darting in all directions as if he were searching for something. His hands started shaking again and when he got up, his left leg went into a slight spasm every now and then, as if someone had a remote control and was operating his leg without his knowledge. He began to walk around and pick up things that didn't seem to need picking up and put them about an inch away from where they originally were placed. Three times, he picked his coat from the seat only to deposit it back in the same place. While describing a Turkish girl he liked, he proceeded to describe a mole she had on her face and even went looking for a pen and paper to draw me a life-size shape of it. Every time he took a pipe he did the same, walked around picked up things put them back in their original place; looking in the drawers several times for no reason. He was talking so articulately about some things, which I didn't have the first clue about. He did this for ten minutes or so. Reflecting on his pipe yesterday, he said Blood had spoilt it because he interrupted his 'buzz'. With only heroin available to minimise potential depression while coming down from the crack high, he kept saying to himself: 'I wish I had a Valium'.
>
> (Field notes)

Dawg had grown up local to the area, but suffered the loss of his father at a young age. It was difficult for the 39-year-old to hide several large scars on his face received from violent exchanges with drug dealers, but he compensated for it, he argued, by dressing smartly. This was important for him because it countered his drug-user image. He said that a stammer and severe dyslexia compounded his problems at school and, soon after leaving with no qualifications, he struggled to find work knowing that his mother and his brother would lend him money 'here and there'. His early experiences with drugs in his twenties included marijuana and LSD, but he moved on to experiment with benzodiazepines before heroin. He had been using heroin for ten years before trying crack in his council flat in the north of Rivertown. As his frustration increased at his lack of achievement and lengthy unemployment, so did his crack use, and the flat started to attract more people. His abilities to fund drug use were limited and crack dealers quickly heard about a potential flat to exploit. The police raided his flat in 2002 and he was evicted and moved to hostel accommodation. Perhaps because of his vulnerable 'mental health conditions' and 'suicidal thoughts', he was re-housed again in council accommodation early in 2004.

Throughout September and October 2004, Dawg's flat seemed to be the busiest flat on the floor, yet he was always worried that the neighbours would be curious about his out-of-hours social life. However, it wasn't only Dawg who tried to deter community attention. There were also two crack dealers on the lower floors. They rarely left the flat and instead sent out young drug runners on the local streets. On many occasions, I came face to face with the runners on their new BMX bikes. They offered me crack in the estate grounds and seemed to be amused by this; perhaps they assumed I was 'on the white' and 'brown', because they had seen me while they were doing hallway drug deals with Blood. Dawg and Bones, however, had no association with these dealers or runners. Neither party seemed to want to draw attention to their activities of crack dealing or crack taking. Yet, Blood persisted in dealing directly at their doorstep in attempts to save precious money by avoiding the cost of a call to a dealer. The risk may have made sense. The motivation for many crack dealers to meet people like Blood, for small purchases such as £10 crack rocks or even a £15 'one-on-one', was generally minimal. Indeed, this seemed to be why many dealers and runners were frequently unreliable, inconsistent and late for drug deals – because it simply wasn't good business for them.

Early street days

With the experience of spending time in Dawg's flat, I took to the streets. Early street experiences were clumsy. A drug dealer pulled a knife on Dawg and me while we were on a drug deal following a visit to Dawg's mother to borrow money. In a hallway drug deal a few days later, Blood was thrust up against the wall when he laughed at one of the drug runners. This gave me some perspective on how they were treated in the crack scene. On one occasion, Dawg and I walked into a shop for some milk and cigarettes:

People are looking twice at us: Dawg with the scar down his face and striped shirt and black jeans, me with my messy hair, unwashed and smelly jeans and scruffy jumper. As we walked into the shop, two men from the front desk start circulating themselves around the shop as if we are about to steal something. Dawg started talking really loudly and asked the shopkeepers about where things were at every opportunity so as not to cause suspicion, but it seemed to do the opposite.

(Field notes)

These experiences seemed to compound Dawg's emotions because he was frequently seen as weak. The only person who seemed to suffer as a result of these feelings was Blood. Indeed, Dawg grew increasingly angry with Blood because he brought attention to the flat and jeopardised what Dawg considered to be his 'non-drug-using reputation' with the neighbours. For this reason, he lost his patience with Blood and, on occasions, often banned him from the flat for short periods. It was during these times that Blood sheltered in what he called the 'crack house squat'.

Blood was 18 years old at the time of research. Of African origin, he had moved to the UK when he was 14 for a better life, away from the civil war in his home country. He had no experience of alcohol or drugs in Africa. He said he first lived with his aunt in 2000 and joined the Territorial Army (TA). After two years in the TA, aged 16, he left his aunt's house after a dispute. He then moved in with his sister but, with no qualifications or work experience, he struggled to find money to pay rent. He left and managed to get himself into hostel accommodation while he awaited housing. There he met Dawg who introduced him to crack and heroin. When Dawg received accommodation, Blood got impatient and left the hostel to stay with Dawg, and consequently lost his place in the housing waiting list. Between stints at Dawg's flat and making small amounts of money for crack and heroin, Blood slept rough in squats and on the streets. He found salvation in what he called the 'crack house squat' which was sandwiched between two arches of a bridge. Blood frequently referred to it as his 'home'. My field notes recorded the physical realities of entering this setting:

We [Blood and I] had to climb a wall near an old train bridge under some barbed wire and then almost jump down into what I think used to be a garage. It was slippery because it had been raining. I nearly fell, slipping on the bricks and wood. In the yard there were old tyres. There were flies buzzing around, and a strong smell of piss and shit. As we walked over the broken bricks and wood into the downstairs room, I saw a mattress in the corner and loads of fag butts on the floor. We went upstairs, or tried to, as there were stairs missing and you had to almost jump up. We pulled ourselves up with the help of a rope. Blood warned me to watch where I stood as there were needles and syringes everywhere. It was so dark, I could hardly see where I was going. We pulled ourselves to the top of the stairs;

a bird flew out of a hole in the roof. I looked to my left and there was what looked like a bedroom, a couple of mattresses and sofas – half upturned, half torn. The piss and shit smell became stronger. We walked through a narrow corridor to the right and came into what looked like the main room. There was piss, shit, syringes and semen stains all over the mattresses and sofas. Under each step I took, I could hear the crunch of syringes. I was glad I was wearing my heavy-duty boots. I was invited to sit down by a squat regular who was well practised in the art of bike theft. I looked at the sofa, and carefully perched on the arm. The place lacked everything – light, water, electricity, warmth, and it was right under the railway so I don't know how people slept here. Blood had spent the last two nights there since Dawg kicked him out. Now he had lice.

(Field notes)

In the months after my visit, the location was raided under the Rivertown police's crack house protocol and the eight residents were emptied out on to the streets without the offer of treatment. Some months later, I spotted some thoughts poignantly written on a wall by a former resident: 'Please respect my home and u [you] will all be welcome'.

Increasingly, I spent more time on the streets and, after spending some time with outreach workers, I was reunited with Cuz who I had met two years previously in prison while I was conducting another study.

Venturing out with Cuz

Cuz looked a young 37 and talked of a complicated past. Originally from Cyprus, his family was involved in the importation of heroin consignments from Turkey and Cyprus. Having abandoned school at an early age, he had little idea of work other than the family business. He worked for them up until the age of 25 and, although he had periodic employment with various manual contractors, he also worked for his family on these imports. When he started to experiment with heroin, his family ostracised him. He continued to get temporary work and started experimenting with crack. However, as his crack use increased, he continually lost ad-hoc jobs, then his tenancy and became homeless in south London. The years that followed were composed of prison sentences for robbery, burglary and shoplifting and several drug-free spells in prison. He had also attempted to 'get clean' and had attended several rehabs: he was accused of theft and disqualified in one and relapsed several times in others. This had severely dented his faith in these establishments and had made him angry. When he had subsequently tried to engage with community drug services in Rivertown, he was excluded after missing three appointments. He was made homeless again in February 2004, and started injecting crack and heroin before gaining access to hostel accommodation in July 2004. We had much to talk about:

I didn't recognise him at first as he was skinny and his eyes seemed to have sunken into his head. His skin looked glazed and plastic. He had lost a ton of weight but somehow he recognised me. He told me how he had been home-less, had lived in a crack house for months, was thrown out of rehab and, because he was in rehab, how he had to give his flat back to the council.

(Field notes)

On learning about the research I was undertaking, he started making prom-ises about accessing potential interviewees and about ensuring my safe entry into crack houses. Indeed, without Cuz, I could not have broadened the sample. He quickly introduced me to hostel life, where I met BA – an airline engineer who started using heroin and then crack after his son was murdered in Scotland – and Deaf – a tall thin Irishman, who required 'translation services' from Cuz, because no one could really understand what he said. They had all met through the hostel and relied on each other for money, drugs and paraphernalia. My involvement with Cuz grew quickly and he was quite happy for me to accompany him on crack deals.

Cuz and I walked down the high street. When he reached the junction on the right hand side, he phoned his dealer, who ran a car park business but also sold crack. Cuz phoned again and waited another ten minutes. We seemed to be in very similar kinds of dilapidated estates to those where I had previously accompanied others on street deals in the north of Rivertown. We were told to wait in the 'normal place', which to me looked too open; then, after another phone call, the drop location changed. Cuz thought that because the dealer was taking his time it meant he would attend in person. However, as we reached the new location behind a café on the high street, a boy no older than 12 or 13 emerged, smoking a spliff, and went behind the garage. We followed and the deal was done in seconds just as someone walked past. Cuz scored two white (£15) and one brown (£15) but got the lot for £25 as he had known the dealer for some time. Cuz said the dealer didn't like to make public his crack business and had never run a 'crack house' as it were. As we walked back down the high street, Cuz started to question whether the boy he had met was the dealer's runner. He started unwrapping the crack on the street to make sure it was crack. It was the real deal, but he struggled to wrap it up correctly and put it back in his mouth (to hide it). This seemed to make him nervous. Even though we were walking, my bike somehow got a puncture and Cuz suggested we go to a nearby pub. He pointed out the King's Head pub which, he said, until a few years ago, was a notorious place to buy crack. Last year, it was raided by police and Cuz said crack dealers had moved behind the nearby post office. We went in and bought a drink, and Cuz went to the toilet. There were large cubicles and he locked himself in there for 20 minutes while he smoked crack and heroin on a piece of foil. On his return, he said was finding it difficult to control the 'buzz' but was somehow keeping it together. We drank our orange juice and he went down to smoke again. He came back and didn't even finish his drink. When we left, he reflected how several years ago he would have been 'buzzing and walking fast' but, over time, he said he could 'appear normal'. I didn't notice any difference in the way he spoke or how fast he was walking; he seemed to be, essentially, controlling the drug.

(Field notes)

Some days later, outside the social security office, Cuz introduced me to Jack the Lad: he was only 26 and had used crack and heroin for ten years. Presentations like this continued, although Cuz took it upon himself to introduce me to inter-view candidates regardless of the social situation. On one occasion, I found myself crouching on the steps of the social security office with Bombshell:

Bombshell [40] [was a] very chatty woman who had smoked crack for 17 years. She wasn't involved with [drug support] services but said there were times when she had wanted to approach them but they had been closed. She wanted to quit crack but had no idea how to start. She carried her own crack pipe around with her and showed me – it was in her top pocket.

(Field notes)

Cuz's enthusiasm for the research continued. He recommended I speak to a young girl staying in his hostel, but her boyfriend wouldn't let her leave for the interview. Cuz said he was 'slapping her around'. Cuz, however, had other connec-tions and soon after I interviewed Gums, a tall figure with a ponytail who had recently finished a short stint in Brixton Prison for burglary. Gums had good rela-tions/links with dealers in neighbouring boroughs, so it was no surprise to learn that that was where we were going for a 'score and smoke': the epic journey on foot climaxing when he and a few others ended up smoking crack in a churchyard.

My street adventures with Cuz reduced my contact with Dawg, so I dropped in to catch up on events. When I arrived, Dawg was out but Blood welcomed me in, clutching his stomach as he was withdrawing from crack and heroin. He was in debt to the dealers in the lower blocks and begged to use my mobile phone to ask for more drug credit. He had already ventured out to see if anyone would lend him money and asked for a 'bail out' from another dealer. The dealer just hung up on him. Indeed, many crack users I met seemed to be last on the priority list yet were the first to improvise with clothing and equipment:

It was about 1.30pm. Cuz, Scruff and I walked under the flyover and Scruff made the call – in fact, several calls – to the dealer, who was a Rastafarian guy and was taking his time as well. We waited outside the supermarket car park and it must have looked pretty obvious who we were and what we waiting for. However, there was an odd paradox: Cuz seemed to be taking more care of his clothes and appearance and didn't look as bad as Scruff or myself. Scruff was dressed in a hood, leather jacket with various tears and holes in, and jeans that were about ten sizes too big for him held up by some improvised rope which acted as a belt. He had blood-stained shoes and said he couldn't even wear socks because of the DVT he had. One of his shoes was shoelaceless because he said he traded it for a crack rock so someone could use it as a tourniquet to get a vein to inject. We moved away from the car park and called again. It was about 3pm, and we had been waiting about 30 minutes after repeated assurance that the dealer would come at any minute. Scruff went off to meet the dealer then came back five minutes later after scoring and we walked to the flyover for a quick pipe. We stopped in the public alleyway – there was no one around. Scruff rummaged around in a bin for an empty soda can while Cuz hunted around for cigarette butts. After success on both mini missions, we huddled around to shelter ourselves from the wind otherwise the crack and ash would blow away. Scruff then snapped off the lid of the soda can and slightly dented the side. He pierced six holes in a circle in the dent and tried to place the ash on top of the holes. I found a drier cigarette butt and sprinkled the ash on the can for him. He broke off a bit of crack from the £20 stone – it looked small compared to the ones I had seen for £15 but looked whiter than others I had seen. Scruff smoked the pipe they were supposed to share and Cuz started to get impatient.

(Field notes)

I was disappointed when Cuz didn't meet me the following day but, having met Gums, I was invited to score crack with him. Never had I seen an exchange of hands so quick under the surveillance of CCTV and visible street policing. I was even more impressed with his crack pipe improvisation with a soda can and a chocolate foil wrapper. We retired to the side of an old community hall while he had a smoke.

Later that day, I rendezvoused with Sneaks to hear what he had to say about the crack scene:

So, in the end, there are opportunities for relationships to be formed, but it's about yesterday I had the most money and today I have no money. Yesterday I looked after you now I demand you look after me; and it's when it's not reciprocated, then it's like people feel hard done by.

(Sneaks)

I felt confused in the days that followed because, after promising to meet me several times, I couldn't locate Cuz. I started to suspect he had been arrested but he appeared some days later in the hostel, boasting about how he had manipulated money and drugs from Black Eyes; a vulnerable young schizophrenic man who was constantly bullied in the hostel. That afternoon I spent in the company of Dawg, Blood and Bones. They seemed entertained by the recent high volume of women who had been sleeping in Dawg's flat. In the short space of time since our last contact, his flat had been raided by the police under the Rivertown crack house protocol. Indeed, several 'crack houses' were raided in the same tower block in the same month, but without any arrests. The only person who was arrested was Blood. He had been granted bail and was awaiting trial on suspicion of supplying Class A drugs, even though he said the police only found one 'bag of heroin' on him. It was difficult to assess whether this was the case, but he was no big-time dealer. Blood felt his arrest was to put some gloss on a failed police operation. In the process of the raid, neither Blood nor Dawg said they were offered any help or treatment. Blood was to stand trial in the New Year.

It was Halloween when Cuz introduced me to Fam, a 44-year-old crack user with dreadlocks and a high-pitched voice. Fam had managed to keep his flat and avoid another visit to prison despite breaking the conditions of his Drug Treatment and Testing Order (DTTO) on several occasions. He regularly swapped his positive urine tests – to test for drugs – with someone else's at the DTTO offices, while limiting the number of people who knew about his crack operations to a minimum. Somehow, Fam had got to the top of the housing list in just over a year, after sharing a hostel room with Twitch, who was 37 and also lived with him. They had certainly seemed to have reaped the benefits, as I was to learn.

After what was my introduction to Fam, I met Cuz back at the hostel. Black Eyes and Jack the Lad were back and forth, in and out of people's rooms, attempting to muster money for crack while Cuz, Gums and I sat around discussing how many dealers there were in the local area. I was becoming a regular around the hostel and had got to know other residents: there was Bottle, who had a reputation for leaking blood from his groin when he walked – made possible by the frequency with which he injected crack and heroin in the same site – and Bradda, a Portuguese man who denied using any drugs but was often seen in the park smoking crack and talking to himself.

The risks of my entry into this scene were always present. The next day, Cuz told me that Gums had spread rumours in the hostel that I was an undercover policeman. He suggested this might be because Gums was envious of Cuz's role as 'the contact'.

However, this did not deter me from continuing to use Cuz's connections and, later that day, I listened to Lady Di describe her recent ordeal after her release from prison with no accommodation or drug treatment support. Indeed, her situation typified many in the sample. I left with Cuz and he scored crack in some college grounds, where we met another hostel resident, Brummie. His furious groin itching concerned me so I asked what was wrong. He pulled his trousers down and displayed three large, sore-looking holes either side of his groin where he had been persistently injecting crack and heroin. After Brummie's public groin display, I returned to a café to interview Roman, 35, who said he was sexually abused when he was 11, and he said his father blamed him for 'telling tales'. Spending much of his younger years in care, he became homeless, started taking drugs and was introduced to heroin and, shortly after, crack.

In addition to the urban myths that were being spread about me, I was also encountering new social situations. Awkwardly, one winter morning, I was outside the social security office with Cuz, when The Duke, Lady Di's abusive boyfriend, came over to talk to us:

> What was meant to be a ten-minute process turned out to take about an hour [getting Cuz's social security payment]. I was waiting around outside and The Duke, who Lady Di had said was beating her up, came up to us. At first, he ignored me but talked to Cuz. It was only when I started to loosely ask The Duke questions that he started to talk to me but wouldn't look at me. When I wasn't looking at him, I could feel him look at me. I was glad Cuz was there because I knew The Duke had asked about me.
>
> (Field notes)

While Cuz was influential in introducing me to locations and people, at times his bluntness with social interaction both frustrated and amazed me. Indeed, when visiting Fam's crack house for the first time, he didn't hesitate to treat it as a data-gathering opportunity. Fam was 41 at the time of research. He lived in Jamaica until the age of 24 but came to the UK after witnessing the violent death of his mother. Without other work options, he started dealing cocaine and crack but quickly became depressed and started using cocaine and cannabis. He started a family and had a son, but family relations broke down when the pressure grew to 'go legit'. By the time he had tried crack, he separated from his wife and son – at the age of 30 – and as he became more depressed his crack use increased. He served a series of prison sentences for various offences including armed robbery and burglary before starting to use heroin with crack in his late 30s. He struggled to hold on to accommodation because of consecutive prison sentences, persistent crack use and mounting unpaid council tax and utility bills. Nevertheless, after a year in hostel accommodation, he was allocated a flat in 2003 in a respectable area of Rivertown. After a few chance meetings on the streets, Cuz and I were invited to his crack house.

> It was an old Victorian house. We arrived just after 1pm. The TV was on and Twitch answered the door. She was welcoming. She was wearing a white bathrobe and looked so thin, I thought her legs were going to snap. She checked cautiously down the street. As I walked through the hallway, there was no carpet but it didn't have that decrepit feel like some other places had. The air was not stale but fresh. We walked past the front room on the right. The curtains were drawn and it was filled with boxes of merchandise. There were brand new clothes all stacked up in the room but I didn't ask about them. The place was well kitted out with furniture and the bathroom was stocked up with expensive toiletries, shampoos, aftershaves, perfumes and at least ten toothbrushes. To my surprise, the toilet was clean. Fam was in the bedroom in a vest and trousers. I sat down and Cuz immediately asked if

> I could put the tape recorder on. I was annoyed that he asked, but Fam and Twitch allowed me.
>
> (Field notes)

Fam had something very valuable in the crack scene: safe accommodation. Moreover, unlike Dawg's, there were only a select few who knew about it. They were Cuz, Twitch (Fam's girlfriend), Mary and Tiny. Mary and Tiny came most days from a nearby street. Mary also spent time at Fam's smoking crack and heroin: she came from a nearby area most days and was on probation. She didn't seem to show much emotion when revealing that her 17-year-old sister was now smoking crack. The operation of Fam's credit-card scams had broadened to include them because Mary's boyfriend, who also used crack and supported her crack use, had been imprisoned.

Fam's crack house appeared to offer decent sanctuary from the chaos of the crack scene. There seemed to be a shared understanding among the unit: that 'whatever came in' went around to whoever was present. Essentially, Fam stole the credit cards and members of the team ran the cards 'dead' in various shops and retail outlets. He had about 10 to 15 'live cards' and kept them in the top drawer under the TV and DVD player. This sharing philosophy was spearheaded by Fam, whose calm demeanour appeared to filter down to his workforce. His tranquil disposition also appeared to defuse the potential for explosive disagreements over crack:

> Then, 20 minutes later, Mary walked in – she was about to go grafting with the credit cards Fam had stolen. She was wearing a white jumper and looked very thin. Her teeth were yellow and she avoided smiling. She told me she wasn't into the white that much and she had a brown habit more over the white. Although Mary was banned from driving, they left in her car to score from a dealer. They returned 30 minutes later and Mary immediately went into the bedroom to smoke heroin and Twitch had to beg for her share back as Mary was suffering from heroin withdrawal. Fam just sat there and waited for everyone to share it out – Twitch wasn't allowed to share out the crack as Fam said she would share it 'unfairly'. It didn't seem to matter because she definitely had more pipes than Fam – two over his one and when she was piping, she kept the lighter on for longer and hovered it over the ash on the pipe to collect every last crumb. Mary stayed very quiet while she smoked crack on the foil. As Cuz and Twitch had done, she dented the foil tube to collect the residue and then smoked the foil tube. The conversation drifted towards politics: Bin Laden, Bush and terrorism then the film *Bad Boys* caught their attention.
>
> (Field notes)

The effectiveness of the management was evident in the desire to keep a 'good thing' going, knowing that they were working undercover in a Victorian house, on a reasonably well-to-do street where the police seemed to have little interest.

Indeed, Fam's main concern was ensuring that the cards were not used inside the 'grafting area' – he meant not in London. A typical day would see them get up early, travel out of London, 'run the cards dead', stop at a local dealer and return to smoke crack and heroin. Cuz was vocal in warning Fam about jeopardising his accommodation:

> Before Cuz had even started to smoke his crack, he was telling Fam not to 'fuck this place up' [jeopardise the tenancy] and how he should be grafting in the 'far away places' first, so as not to arouse suspicion or bring heat [attention from the police]. Fam knew this and had made some adjustments to his lifestyle. He had, for example, made sure when he did use the cards, he also bought food as well as cigarettes and alcohol to reduce suspicion [of their being stolen].
>
> (Field notes)

My time with Cuz continued. At the hostel the next morning, he was publicly boasting about his newfound wealth after shoplifting a bag of DVDs from a Museum. Some days later, I was introduced to Bruv and Cuddles, who were both crack smokers. Cuddles introduced me to MRS, a young woman who had been tempted by her boyfriend's private crack use. Later that week, Cuddles started some sort of relationship with Tooth. She had taken it upon herself to house him and shelter him from the police, as there was a warrant for his arrest.

Meanwhile, my relationship with Cuz continued to strengthen. Reflecting on meeting me again, he said he preferred to spend time with me because it kept him out of the hostel where people pestered him for drugs. The next day we met another of Cuz's 'friends', Shake. Shake had been released from prison in November 2004, after getting clean, and described how he had been plunged back into the 'madness' of the crack scene. We sat down for an interview after he had 'booted up' crack and heroin in a side alley. In the following weeks, I met Shake's girlfriend who Cuz said he had 'rumped' [had sexual relations with]. I got the impression that Cuz wanted to appear as if he were a success with women. However, if this was the case, I was surprised how Cuz and Shake managed to sustain any relationship, given that Shake said he had caught Cuz in bed with his girlfriend and threatened him with a knife.

Had we not met Shake outside the bank and chatted in the café, we would not have met Babe and Dawn who recognised Shake talking to us in the window of the café. Dawn stumbled in claiming it was her 'first can [of high-strength beer] of the day', but she had already smoked several 'rocks' that morning. She was wearing a new t-shirt, jeans and new trainers. She admitted she was quite fat for a drug user, but explained that liver cirrhosis affected her body weight. Babe was 36 years old and said she had just got 'clean of the brown' a few months ago. She still smoked crack and was on a methadone and DF118 prescription. Her eyes were slightly sunken in her face and her cheeks hugged the thin bone structure of her jawbone. Nevertheless, she made a big effort for public appearances, fashioning both exotic make up and new clothes. This was because she said she wanted to feel 'normal' – or as normal as possible.

The relationship between Cuddles and Tooth, however, perplexed me and I spent a day or two with them. Tooth said he wanted to 'look after her' and make sure she took her medication for her severe depression each morning. She was mentally vulnerable and was collecting £240 of state benefits every two weeks, which they spent together on crack. They escorted me to a car park where I met 27-year-old Mr Lee, who had been homeless for the past six years, every night of which he had slept in the same car park. When I met him, his face was completely hidden in the long hair, long beard and dirt. He didn't say a word, just nodded and shook his head to my questions.

Cuz and Babe seemed to become closer, and we decided to try to access one of the local drug services; it was closed for a staff conference. It was on the steps of the drug service that we met Frank, who was also trying to get help from the same place. Frank told us that, some months previously, he had been stabbed in the head by his ex-girlfriend and was rushed to hospital. Large metal staples had been inserted in his head to aid the healing process. Although they had been taken out, he still looked as if he had holes in his head. He was there with his grand-mother waiting for the drug service to open in the afternoon. He reasoned that the presence of his grandmother was the only protective factor that would deter his ex-girlfriend's two brothers who were out to 'do him over'.

It had been some weeks since I last saw Scruff, but while I was cycling around at midnight on a Saturday, I saw him begging for money. I stopped to talk to him and I was introduced to Silencer, his 'using associate', as he described him. There we spent the night, talking while they smoked crack near some garages.

Fam and Dawg revisited

Over the winter months, gaps started to appear in my contact with Cuz, and he became increasingly elusive. Feeling that I had neglected Dawg over the last month, I called in but a stranger answered the intercom and did not believe I knew Dawg: my access was denied. Instead, I continued contact with Fam. Although the fundamental operation of Fam's unit had continued over the next month, there had been some slip-ups. This all seemed to stem from the release of Mary's boyfriend from prison. Once he had resumed his car-smuggling business, Babe and Tiny reduced their appearances at Fam's flat. This meant that Fam had to drive the car on 'grafting days'. However, he had a signifi-cant number of previous convictions, most of which were driving offences. Conscious of the danger of Fam being stopped by the police, they had started to use the credit cards more locally. However, this disrupted the routine of the longer journey and the close proximity of crack dealers made it a little too tempting to just 'have a quick pipe' then go to another shop. It was during this period that Fam's crack use seemed to escalate once again. In addition, while he was adept at skilfully evading awkward moments in PC World when using stolen credit cards to buy expensive laptops, it seems he had difficulty in being a father to his young son:

> Fam's 14-year-old son was staying over. Fam spent the first few minutes telling me about how his son's mother was wrong about bringing him up preventing him to do things for himself. I listened as Fam seemed quite keen to ask me about whether I agreed with him. His son lived in another borough and, according to Fam, he was an angel and never took drugs. When I spoke to Twitch after she had managed to drag herself up from the bed, she told me she was due in court tomorrow for breaching her DTTO and not going to the [help] groups. I tried to encourage her to make the effort but she didn't seem too bothered. When I had arrived, there was no electricity, the floors looked in a worse condition and there was hardly any food. I sat down in the bedroom and Twitch got some heroin out as she was clucking while Fam paced up and down and told me about his son. After 30 minutes Twitch told me that Fam got arrested when they used some strong heroin and fell asleep at the wheel of his car. The police saw them illegally parked but found him in possession of crack worth about £40. He was also due in court. I was not sure what would happen to both of them but it didn't look like they wouldn't be at their place for much longer. His son then came in and stood before us, and I introduced myself. He looked quite shy but never looked his dad in the eye and kept looking at the ceiling.
>
> (Field notes)

After telling his former wife that he wanted more of a role in his son's life, Fam was now trying to be a 'model father' but was instead exposing his son to the realities of his drug-using lifestyle. Moreover, these events had brought uncertainty over the future of Fam's flat. The early-morning trips into the suburbs to run up hundreds of pounds on credit cards were replaced by extended mornings indoors, in a quandary over their escalating situations.

Cuz, meanwhile, explained that he had been 'stressed out' and that his elusive behaviour was linked to a threatening letter from the hostel that read 'you have 14 days to clear your belongings and leave'. The letter was really a contract under which he needed to agree to pay his mounting rent arrears, but he had misinterpreted the wording, which looked too punitive in any case. I met the manager of the hostel in an effort to explain how the wording of the letter made Cuz panic, leading to increased crack binges. The next day, despite the fact I helped to arrange some other way to pay the hostel back, Cuz told me he had a doctor's appointment and didn't answer my calls. A fellow hostel dweller, Canon, said Cuz was with Babe. I cycled down to locate him in the usual places but couldn't find him. Instead I met Shake who was about to score crack.

Over Christmas, Cuz disappeared off my fieldwork map and I spent more time with Scruff and Fam. When I finally met Cuz towards the end of the year, he had lost weight and looked ragged. He put this down to crack binges with Babe.

He had also got into fights in the hostel, and had consequently been evicted. On our way to the hostel, we met Bottle, who had clearly had some better luck. He had been in hospital and, although he looked yellow, was looking considerably healthier than when I interviewed him some months earlier – he had had two operations on his groin. With some effort, I persuaded Cuz to meet the next day to re-establish our contact. Once more, and possibly feeling ashamed that he didn't answer the last time, he disappeared from contact again.

The New Year saw Scruff experience some mysterious fortune. Amazingly, albeit suspiciously, Scruff said his 'aunt' had given him £5,000 in cash and he checked into a local hotel. He had cut his hair, shaved and bought new clothes, but still smelt badly. I was invited into his hotel room where there was a young woman sitting on the bed. Pix, just 19, said she had used crack and heroin since she was 14, and had been selling sex since she was 16. It wasn't long before she recounted other aspects of her past. The previous year she said she had been raped by a gang of dealers and, as a result, had a child who was in the care of her mum. Homeless and vulnerable, she had met Scruff at the bridge where she said he had 'promised' to look after her. I saw fear in her eyes as there seemed to be another story to the relationship:

> When Scruff left the room, Pix started crying and told me that she was under-appreciated. She said he never treated her to any crack and felt she was treated like absolute shit. She went on to say he ordered her around, insulted her, and persuaded her to make money from prostitution to fund his crack use.
>
> (Field notes)

Scruff's high life did not last for long. Later that month, he was to be rushed to hospital with vein problems from injecting crack, and he was on the streets again soon after. I was even more surprised to see Cuz in the same week. He was walking along the high street with Babe. Eager to hear recent events, we deviated to a nearby café. Having lost his hostel accommodation, and fearing arrest by the police, Cuz said he had moved in with Babe. He was thinner and had not shaved, but was parading new smart clothes that he wore to avoid the attention of shop-keepers and store detectives when shoplifting.

When I next visited Dawg's flat, the whole scenery of his life had changed. Over the next week, we reacquainted ourselves and caught up with recent events. He had somehow accumulated new furniture but the flat still suffered from odd odours because of the blocked drains. He had started some sort of relationship with a woman and, in need of more intimate time with her, had asked Blood to move out. On the other hand, however, he had been excluded from Connections North and his methadone prescription had been withdrawn from the chemist. He was also facing a court appearance for non-payment of rent arrears of over £1,000. With £25 being deducted from his benefits every two weeks, he was receiving less than £50 a fortnight. Nevertheless, these quite significant events did not seem to be pushing any 'self-destruct' buttons as similar ones seemed to have done in the past. Could his new relationship be offering something to stabilise him?

Appropriately, I finally met Dawg's new lady on Valentine's Day. I only stayed an hour or so; her hands rummaging up his jumper while he was shaving seemed to suggest she wanted a little privacy. She had clearly had some impact and Dawg's life appeared to be stabilising. Over the coming weeks, she persuaded him to attend his court appearance, where he discovered the £1,000 he thought he owed was actually only £109. Because of conflict between the two neighbouring boroughs over the payment of the rent, there had been a serious error in the tax calculation. This removed a great weight from his shoulders because mounting bills and a court case had contributed to increased crack use in the closing months of 2004.

Blood, however, looked more ragged. His tracksuit trousers had cigarette burns, his hair was dirty – even though he hid some of it with a cap – and he looked very different from the young man I had first met five months ago. He was due to face a court case for possession of Class A drugs from the police raid. Some days later, I saw Blood over by the hostel. My excitement to see him was premature and led me into interrupting the dynamics of a drug deal:

> As I cycled up to meet Bradda by the park, there were two other Portuguese guys nearby. I was surprised to see Blood mixing with this group. I directed my attention to Blood and went straight up to him but I was invading a drug deal. Blood and Bradda were crossing the road over to the entrance to the park while the two Portuguese guys waited on the other side of the road. I cycled up to Blood and Bradda and the dealer said: 'Who the fuck's this?' – Bradda told him I was a mate and told me to wait over the other side of the road. I was oblivious to this until I crossed the road. I guess I was so happy to see Blood alive and well – well, alive anyway.
>
> (Field notes)

Bradda and the Portuguese crew went off to smoke, while I spent the day catching up on events with Blood. We walked to the hospital where he showed me another paraphernalia-laden squat where he had been sleeping and taking drugs. We then left for Dawg's to collect Blood's benefit papers, where he received a frosty reception. Dawg thought Blood was now developing a 'reputation' in the area because he had 'stung'[1] several other drug users. In addition, Blood had missed his first court appearance and, although I attended his second, he didn't show up. There was a warrant out for his arrest and his case had been forwarded to Crown Court for a February hearing. Two days later, our paths crossed. He had been 'hanging around' the estates after the 'crack house squat' had been raided.

The following week I spent with Fam during and between all-night crack sessions. The flat's merchandise seemed to have been replenished and Fam was modelling a new Nike jumper. Cuz, however, seemed to have damaged his relationship with Fam. Fam and Twitch claimed that Babe (Cuz's girlfriend) had not been fair in distributing the proceeds of a planned handbag theft. They also said Cuz had invented a story to account for our lack of contact which had been fed to other street drug users. This story, according to Fam, involved my persistence in 'demanding to listen to his psychologist's tapes', which, of course, was not true. I felt stupid, cautious and paranoid. The next day, I saw Cuz for the last time on the high street. Despite my efforts to hide my disappointment at his allegations, the conversation didn't last long – he seemed stand-offish. My time was later spent with Blood and two of his using associates while they smoked crack and heroin in a hospital squat. In the days that followed, I spent more time with Fam who had somehow persuaded his ex-partner that he was able to look after his son from 'time to time' at weekends in an effort to be a 'responsible father', as he said. The flat remained full of food, clothes and toiletries from suburban shops.

Towards the end of the fieldwork period, my focus turned to interviewing professionals and drug service representatives and less time was spent in the crack scene.

In the few weeks I was absent from the scene, however, the hostel population, which I had come to know quite well, appeared to have shifted significantly and half of the people I asked around for no longer lived there. When I asked for reasons, the staff said 'we can't give you that information'. I was fortunate to meet Bail, who I had met once or twice in the early fieldwork period. Bail was Scottish and had started using heroin aged 29 and has been using crack for the past five years – he was now 40. I had trouble convincing some of the new hostel colleagues of my identity and it felt like I was starting the research from scratch. Tall Guy was particularly sceptical, despite reassurance from Bail and from several other drug users in the area. While discussing drug transactions, my knowledge of local dealers made Tall Guy suspicious that I was a police officer. The following week, my relationship deteriorated with Bradda because I refused to lend him money. Bail managed to get funding for a detox and left the hostel and, with few solid relations at the hostel, my time switched again to Fam's crack house.

Once again, Fam's carelessness behind the wheel and hasty scoring abilities had put him in trouble. In March, he was stopped in the car by police and was arrested again for driving while banned. This offence was added to a court case that had been set for April 12. Shortly after, he was caught in possession of crack and heroin while in the car and this charge was added to the court date. In the days preceding the case, Fam was nervously anticipating a custodial sentence. He said they were 'silly offences' which he could not believe he got 'nicked for'. I, too, was confused because they didn't seem to reflect the skill he applied to his credit-card operations. Regardless of Fam's patchy appearance at the DTTO and failed attempts to get a prescription to reduce his drug use, the whole operation, the flat and his relation-ship with Twitch appeared to be again in complete jeopardy:

> I arrived at Fam's in the afternoon. He had been acting quite strange with me on the phone. When I arrived the whole place had been carpeted and a lot of the shit (mostly stuff bought from credit cards) had been moved and stored.

He said that he and Twitch had been arguing and she said she was leaving him (but hadn't yet). He felt she was dragging him down and this was the reason that he wasn't able to keep a straight head on anything [grafting]. I wasn't so sure. I felt something was up and he told me he had been arrested again for driving whilst banned. He said that he was taking Twitch to the hospital because she was sick and had to drive. His court case was in April and he had been told that he was looking at a prison sentence [because of previous arrests, missed DTTO appointments, etc]. The authorities told him if he could show himself in a positive light on the 12th, that is if he could do something to show the court that he had good intentions, then he may not get a prison sentence. He had been arrested two weeks ago and his case was in a little over a week. He had done nothing [to show himself in a positive light]. I suggested getting a prescription but he had already booked appointments at the chemist but not turned up four times to collect it and consequently lost the prescription.

(Field notes)

In the days preceding the case, he was nervously anticipating a custodial sentence for driving while banned. However, when I went to court after inter-viewing Prince Shakka about his crack use and disturbingly violent past, Fam was back in the dock. In a miraculous turn of events:

The solicitor's argument seemed honest: Fam had done this before but the seriousness of his offences had reduced over the years and it would need time for him to adjust to a 'crime-free life' – he also played on the fact that prison would not be a suitable answer although it seemed like the inevitable punish-ment. The judges then said they would retire and we all had to stand up. Fam looked at Twitch and me, and pointed a thumb down as if to say he was going to prison. Ten minutes later, at just after 1pm (we had been in there for about 20 minutes) the judges came back and commended the Probation Officer for his report. To my astonishment, they said that this really was his last chance and sentenced him to 100 hours community service, an 18-month driving ban and a compulsory driving course 'Think Drive' (or something like that). The Probation Officer came out and couldn't believe it – the solicitor said 'what-ever you do, don't get in a car'.

(Field notes)

One hour later in Fam's flat:

Fam seemed happier and had a schoolboy bounce to him. He had done it and I too felt a sense of elation, too. He said he was going to score crack and to meet us back at his flat. We arrived at Fam's and I made a drink while Twitch went straight to have a boot [of heroin] because she was clucking [from the withdrawal]. Soon after Tiny appeared at the door; his hair was longer and he hadn't shaved. He started saying how he was fed up with grafting every day for drugs and said he might give up soon – he had a very bad cough which he said was down to the crack. He had some Iranian Rias which he had taken from someone's bag which were worth around £100. I turned the tape recorder on when they both started talking about drug treatment. Tiny mentioned Subutex and said it interested him. Fam then came in with a large rock [of crack] and laid it out on the bed and shared it. Minutes later, there was a call on Fam's phone – it was Twitch's brother trying to sell him a stolen car for £100. She relayed this all back to Fam – he nodded but looked pained. I thought to myself what would happen now and asked who would drive and Twitch said she would – I wasn't so sure.

(Field notes)

The next day, he bought the car.

In the final days in the research field, Fam introduced me to Rem; who smoked crack, made a £100 a week through sex work and lived with and cared for an elderly man. I continued, when I could, to maintain a presence outside the benefits office with outreach workers. Jack the Lad was still injecting crack: he looked rough as he limped around. A few months prior, he had had a hostel place, a phone and reasonably clean clothes. Now he was homeless and was waiting for a little fellow called Blackbeard, whom I had met in the car park, who owed him money. Blackbeard turned up but didn't recognise me and they went off to score together. I left with Mr Lee, a 44-year-old Jamaican who had been using crack for the past seven years to meet up with his 'civilised crack-smoking colleagues'.

Conclusion

This introductory chapter presents crack users in Rivertown. It gives you the background of the main players of this book and some clues to the potential themes that arise in subsequent chapters. In particular, the narrative highlights how the key players of the book are involved in complex interactions which often affect the decisions they make (Chapter 5). The chapter also shows that, even as a researcher, attempting immersion in this group is problematic. Now that you have some idea of what goes on in this scene, I focus on how we got to this situation in Chapter 2.

Chapter 2

How did it get to this?

Any group of persons – prisoners, primitives, pilots or patients – develop a life of their own which becomes meaningful, reasonable and normal once you get close to it, and a good way to learn about any of these worlds is to submit oneself in the company of members to the daily round of petty contingencies to which they are subject.

(Goffman, 1961, ix–x)

I mean, coming to me because I mean then most people on the street, who would be writing down this and writing down that, would not come near me. A person is not going to go up to them who uses drugs, you know. I mean 'cos, I'm doing drugs which is a mind alterating thing, you know. You coming to me, you know, I think that's terrific, and if more people approach drug users, I think they would get more results in a way.

(Mr Lee)

Introduction

To understand why crack is considered to be a problem – in both Rivertown and the UK – we must consider the various historical, political, social and structural processes that play a part in its current availability. Indeed, these same forces play both direct and indirect roles in crack users' daily lives. This chapter synthesises the available literature on how cocaine came to the UK, and where and why crack markets evolved. It also describes how crack is made and its effects, criminal and health consequences, patterns of use and crack careers. It reviews UK governmental and treatment policy responses to 'the problem of crack' and the development of drug services for crack users. In doing so, I also consider why crack users are generally thought to be the most hard-to-reach drug-using population, or, as some describe them, 'the marginalised among the marginalised'.

Cocaine and the development of crack

After cannabis, cocaine is the second most trafficked illicit drug in the world (EMCDDA, 2007). In 2005, global seizures of cocaine totalled 756 tonnes, with the largest quantities exported to the US and Europe from Colombia, Peru and Bolivia (UNODC, 2007). Agar (2003) shows in *The Story of Crack*, that the flood of cocaine, together with decline in demand among affluent white US users because of adverse publicity in the early 1980s, dented the attraction of cocaine (Reinarman and Levine, 1997). This created a market crisis for cocaine producers and resulted in innovative marketing responses by entrepreneurs. Dominican, Jamaican and Los Angeles gang networks innovated the market in poor urban communities where social and economic suffering was endemic. 'Crack', it seems, was a good and rare business opportunity in a time of extreme social and economic decline, especially among marginalised minority ethnic communities (Agar, 2003; Reinarman and Levine, 2004). Moreover, many of these communities were also exposed to a growth in the culture of need and greed (Young, 2007). Competition ensued between local gangs and this fuelled the level of violence among these communities, resulting in greater media attention (Reinarman and Levine, 2004), harsher law enforcement policies (Bourgois, 1995; Wacquant, 2002) and increased arrest and imprisonment rates of predominantly poor, minority ethnic populations (Provine, 2006; Sherman, 2004; Wacquant, 2004).

Unlike cocaine powder, which enjoys both 'party drug' and 'high-class' status, crack quickly became associated with US inner-city crime, violence, broken communities, deprivation and marginalisation, and minority ethnic groups (Adler 1985; Fischer and Coghlan, 2007; Fryer *et al.*, 2005; Goldstein *et al.*, 1989; Venkatesh and Levitt, 2000; Williams 1990). Crack use in these areas was bolstered by intense media attention, moral panics, political rhetoric and anti-drug use policies that declared 'crack's potential to destroy communities' (Belenko, 1993; Boland, 2008; Garland, 2008; Reinarman and Levine, 1997, 2004). Subsequent crime control policies – developed primarily in US ghettos – became increasingly punitive and contributed to the tripling of the prison population from 1980 to 1994 (Wacquant, 2002, 2004).

For already at-risk populations, such as the homeless, sex workers, drug users, immigrants, and populations otherwise outside formal social systems (Bourgois, 1989; Dunlap *et al.*, 2006; Tourigny, 2003) crack became preferred drug of abuse (Agar, 2003; Singer, 2001). Such populations tended to 'have fewer bonds to conventional society, less to lose, and far fewer resources to cope with or shield themselves from drug-related problems' (Reinarman and Levine, 1997: 47). So: 'For these individuals, crack was a new and convenient method for obtaining a quick, powerful cocaine high at low cost from a substance with which they were already familiar' (Golub and Johnson, 1996: 229).

Golub and Johnson (1996: 222) also note that 'crack was introduced within the hard-drug-using population and spread as result of contact between crack users with other hard-drug users'. They observed that 'not all were equally enticed' by crack but that members of pre-existing drug subcultures 'particularly heroin injectors, cocaine snorters and cocaine freebasers' were most likely to initiate crack use (also see Bourgois, 1995). Consequently, crack disproportionately exacerbated the conditions of those who were already suffering from systematic poverty, social exclusion, racism and discrimination (Bourgois, 1995; Bourgois and Schonberg, 2007), and this was intensified by the potential for compulsive consumption (Agar, 2003; Davis and Lurigio, 1996; Hatsukami and Fischman, 1996).

These populations were blamed for their poor decision-making and criminal predicaments (Reinarman and Levine, 1997) when the problem of 'crack', as some indicate, was a symptom of ongoing problems of hard-drug use and other persistent, underlying social and structural problems (Bourgois, 1995; Golub and Johnson, 1996; Reinarman and Levine, 2004). Indeed, the deterioration of US urban inner cities where crack flourished was set against the decline of urban manufacturing industries, weakening welfare support services, and widening income disparities (Agar, 2003) which saw a 'collapse of the official economy corresponding to the vertiginous growth of the informal economy, and especially the drug trade' (Wacquant, 2004: 103). The 'War on Drugs' that followed provided the perfect impetus for politicians, media and law enforcement agencies to use to the image of 'crack' to reinforce their political and budgetary interests (Adler, 1985) of crime control of the 'problematic populations' (Wacquant, 2002).

Cocaine's expansion to Europe gathered momentum following the US 'crackdown policies' ('War on Drugs'), which diversified market opportunities. Indeed, increases in cocaine prevalence rates were seen across Europe in the 1980s and 1990s (Shifano and Corkery, 2008), although they did not reach the same levels as in the US (EMCDDA, 2007). The UK was not exempt from this expansion (Seddon, 2006). As with other European countries, UK cocaine seizures rose year on year (GLADA, 2004) and five-fold (from 1636 to 7744 tons) between 1990 and 2003. Cocaine use and heroin use also steadily increased from 1975, and this was augmented in the mid- to late 1990s by the advent of crack use in the UK (EMCDDA, 2007; Shifano and Corkery, 2008). Very soon, as in the US, similar social and economic repercussions became evident. Research found that crack markets had evolved in 'urban disadvantaged communities', which, some suggest, resulted in increased neighbourhood crime and vandalism, drug dealing, family breakdown, poor educational attainment and disaffected young people (Child et al., 2002; Lupton et al., 2002; May et al., 2007). Yet most of these communities were already socially excluded (Parker et al., 2001). Already vulnerable populations such as sex workers (Gossop et al., 1994; Hunter et al., 1995), heroin users (Fountain et al., 2003; Gossop et al., 1994) and marginalised minority ethnic populations (Fernandez, 2002; Sangster et al., 2001) seemed to be worst affected (Parker et al., 1998).

What's the 'buzz' about crack cocaine?

Crack is a smokeable and injectable form of cocaine, which is made into small lumps or 'rocks' (Hasaan and Prinzleve, 2001). To make crack, cocaine is boiled in a mixture of water and ammonia or sodium bicarbonate (baking soda) until it forms lumps or rocks. Its name comes from the crackling sound it makes when being burnt (Chitwood *et al.*, 1996; NIDA, 2004, 2005). Crack can be smoked in spliffs and on glass pipes, as well as using makeshift devices such as aluminium cans, inhalers, or other metal or glass implements (Firestone *et al.*, 2006). Injecting crack is made possible by mixing it with an acid such as lemon juice or citric acid (Buchanan *et al.*, 2006; Ford, 2004).

In comparison to cocaine, the crack 'high' is said to be more intense (Ford, 2004). The 'effects of crack' are 'extreme and short-lived' and 'users are driven to obtain the drug repeatedly to avoid withdrawal symptoms' (Turning Point, 2005: 4). When crack is used, crack users 'feel more alert and energetic, confident and physically strong and frequently believe that they have enhanced mental capacities' (Ford, 2004: 2). Low and moderate 'hits' from crack produce euphoric sensations as well as increased self-confidence and reduced social inhibition (Al-Rahman *et al.*, 2007). Furthermore, crack can reduce fatigue and the need to sleep, while increasing vigilance, nerve and sexual activity (Gold and Millner, 1997; Marcos *et al.*, 1998). It can also lead to increased irritability, restlessness and paranoia resulting in psychosis – a state in which the user loses touch with reality and experiences auditory hallucinations (NIDA, 2004).

One characteristic way of managing the 'wired' effect[1] of crack is through the use of depressant drugs such as cannabis, heroin and alcohol (EMCDDA, 2007; Parker and Bottomley, 1996; Parker *et al.*, 1998; Usdan *et al.*, 2001; Zule *et al.*, 2003). This, however, can lead to dependence on such drugs (Falck *et al.*, 2007) and it is for this reason that some crack users have as many as four or five drug-dependence issues (Stitzer and Chutape, 1999). Crack is considered psychologically addictive (Brain *et al.*, 1998; Turning Point, 2005) and appears to have no physically addictive properties (Harocopos *et al.*, 2003).

It is often perceived that crack is instantly addictive and destroys the lives of its users (Garland, 2008; Provine, 2006; Reinarman and Levine, 1997, 2004; Williams, 1990). However, US research suggests that crack's pharmacological properties do not necessarily promote chaotic or continual use (Jackson-Jacobs, 2002; Morgan and Zimmer, 1997), because many who try crack do not remain regular users, much less 'lose control' and destroy their own lives (SAMHSA, 1995). Conversely, UK research suggests that the drug 'changes' people and that increased use leads them to use crack more 'chaotically'. For example, in a statement from the Home Office's *Tackling Crack: A National Plan* (2002: 8), the following is hypothesised:

> However, as their use increases, or crack becomes the predominant drug, their dependency and need for the drug may become more chaotic and desperate.

A primary crack user may thus have acute periods of almost constant craving where normal restraints on their behaviour are relaxed, but at other times show little obvious signs of dependency, sometimes going several weeks between purchases. At the height of a binge, they may be buying crack almost 24 hours a day for several days or even weeks.

UK descriptions of 'how one gets addicted to crack' and 'how crack is experienced' tend to discount emotional, social and structural factors which may have affected the individual, and these misperceptions also appear in UK local policy and local research literature. In this account from a project that informed local policy on crack use in one London borough, crack use is said to drive the individual to 'smoke more' because of a chemical imbalance it produces in the brain as a result of repeated crack use:

> Usually the first hit they have or the one at the beginning of the binge is the strongest and gives the biggest buzz. This is because the brain develops a tolerance to the crack and because of the depletion of dopamine and serotonin. Simply put, people only have certain amounts of these chemicals; the more people use, the less they have available to give them the high they are searching for. This explains why the high becomes less and less intense as the binge goes on and users are forever chasing this initial high.
>
> (Lindsell, 2005: 11)

Crack is described as continuously hitting the 'do-it-again' switch in the brain, thereby significantly challenging attempts to leave the drug behind (ibid, 2005). While these perspectives are useful, they do not tell the whole story. Indeed, as American researchers indicate, while crack has neuro-pharmacological effects, dependence and harm appear to be mediated by social factors that affect particular populations more than others (Agar, 2003; Bourgois, 1995). Some US commentators indicate that crack addiction is more about the social circumstances of the user (Morgan and Zimmer, 1997; Reinarman et al., 1997).

Crack: new social problems

There are societal, social and individual consequences from crack use. Firstly, crack users are considered highly criminally active (Bennett, 2000; GLADA, 2004; Lupton, et al., 2002). In 2008, at least one in eight arrestees – or 125,000 people – in England and Wales were estimated to be 'problematic' crack and/or heroin users, and between one third and half of new receptions to prison were problematic drug users (crack or/and heroin users) – equivalent to between 45,000 and 65,000 prisoners in England and Wales (UKDPC, 2008). Estimates indicate there are approximately 198,000 crack users in England (Hay et al., 2007), 140,000 injecting crack and heroin (Hay et al., 2006). In London, estimates suggest there are 46,000 crack users (Hope et al., 2005). The estimated volume of use also leads to high social and economic costs. Enforcing UK drug policies through various agencies such as the police, Courts, probation and the prison service has been estimated to cost £13.5 billion in England and Wales (Hay *et al.*, 2006).

Using crack, especially for long periods, carries a large number of health risks that can severely damage the individual's physical and mental health (Dackis and O'Brien, 2001; Fischer and Coghlan, 2007). These include high prevalence rates of:

- HCV (Bird *et al.*, 2003; Brewer *et al.*, 2006; Buchanan *et al.*, 2006; Faruque *et al.*, 1996);
- HIV (Booth *et al.*, 1999; Grella *et al.*, 1995; Johnson *et al.*, 2002; Latkin *et al.*, 1996; Sterk, 1988; Unger *et al.*, 2006);
- STIs (Booth *et al.*, 1999; Howard *et al.*, 2002; Inciardi, 1995; McMahon and Tortu, 2003; Ross, 2002);
- TB (Cohen *et al.*, 1994; Leonhardt *et al.*, 1994; Perlman *et al.*, 1995; Story *et al.*, 2008; Tortu *et al.*, 2004).

Both smokers and injectors of the drug are exposed to physical risks. Smokers, who mostly use makeshift devices such as tin cans, inhalers, or other metal or glass implements, regularly expose their lips and throat to high temperatures required for smoking crack (Faruque *et al.*, 1996; Ludwig and Hoffner, 1999) and this can result in oral cavity and facial burns (Haydon *et al.*, 2005; Porter *et al.*, 1997; Tortu *et al.*, 2004). Viruses such as HCV and HIV can also be transmitted via such open wounds in the oral cavity area (Edlin *et al.*, 1994; McCoy *et al.*, 2004).

Injectors also experience health risks. The odds of HCV and HIV infection transmission are elevated among crack and speedball injectors compared with heroin-only injectors (Hickman *et al.*, 2004). Crack is not readily dissolved for intravenous use and requires ascorbic acids to increase its solubility and allow for injection (Levine *et al.*, 1996) so crack injectors can develop problems because of the additive properties of the acids and also from the use of larger needles for the injection of solutions of crack (Hunter *et al.*, 1995). Furthermore, crack injectors are more vulnerable than heroin users to increased risks of abscess formation, cellulitis, DVT and other injection-site infections (van Beek *et al.*, 2001; Hickman *et al.*, 2006; Murphy *et al.*, 2001; Spijkerman *et al.*, 1996; Waninger and Thuahnai, 2008).

Crack injectors themselves report high levels of injection-site infections (Hope *et al.*, 2008). Rhodes *et al.* (2007) found that speedball injection and, in particular, crack injection are strongly associated with the rapid deterioration of veins at injection sites (also see Hickman *et al.*, 2006; HPA, 2008). Other physical complications associated with crack use are constricted blood vessels, dilated pupils, asthma, respiratory problems or failure, thermal airway injury, impairment of lung capacity, stroke, seizure, epilepsy, diabetes, brain seizures, gastro-intestinal problems, paralysis and heart attack (Ford, 2004; Hser *et al.*, 1997; Inciardi *et al.*, 1996; Laposata and Mayo, 1993; Ludwig and Hoffener, 1999; NIDA, 2004, 2005; Payne-James *et al.*, 2008).

Situationally, crack use can be associated with mental health symptoms such as fatigue, mood swings, depression, paranoia and depersonalisation as users 'come down' from the high (Carroll *et al.*, 1994; Ford, 2004; Payne-James *et al.*, 2008; Woods *et al.*, 2003). Users of the drug may also experience feelings of restlessness, irritability and anxiety, which can lead to more intense paranoid experiences, particularly after bingeing on crack (Ludwig and Hoffener, 1999). During binge use, crack users can experience crack psychosis, which has been compared to schizophrenia (Withers *et al.*, 1995).

Some commentators estimate that, over their crack career, lifetime crack injectors have twice the risk of a history of mental illness as injecting drug users who had not injected crack (Buchanan *et al.*, 2006). Long-term crack use can lead to personality disorders, psychiatric sectioning, suicidal thoughts and suicide attempts (Boyd and Mieczowski, 1990; Cornish and O'Brien, 1996; Falck *et al.* 2004; Fischer *et al.*, 2006; Harocopos *et al.*, 2003; Inciardi *et al.*, 1996; Webster, 1999). Some studies confirm that crack users are also likely to suffer co-morbid status – that is having two or more mental health conditions (Carroll *et al.*, 1994; Falck *et al.*, 2008; Kleinman *et al.*, 1990; Weaver *et al.*, 2002) – and have greater treatment needs and higher frequencies of treatment service use than other types of drug user (Kessler *et al.*, 1994; Kessler *et al.*, 1996). Some indicate that the high levels of mental illness among crack users are connected to social exclusion, high levels of poverty and homelessness (Logan and Leukfeld, 2000; Ottaway and Erickson, 1997; Page-Shafer *et al.*, 2002; Rhodes *et al.*, 2006). Therefore, because of the complexities of these conditions, they tend to seek treatment from a variety of agencies, across drug services, mental health services and primary healthcare (Kessler *et al.*, 1994; Kessler *et al.*, 1996; Regier *et al.*, 1993). However, because treatment for such conditions is not always available, crack users 'stabilise themselves' through the use of crack (Fox *et al.*, 2005).

Pathways into crack

Despite some understanding of pathways into crack use, current knowledge is not definitive. On one hand it is suggested that crack users experience a series of 'significant traumatic events' and/or are exposed to 'risk factors', and that, consequently, this catapults them into crack use. On the other hand, other studies locate pathways into crack use with participation in various social networks such as recreational drug scenes, social and peer groups, among the homeless, in temporary accommodation and sex-worker networks. Early literature on pathways into crack use stems predominantly from US studies (Boyd and Mieczkowski, 1990). More recently, Cohen and Stahler (1998) conducted 31 life-history interviews with homeless crack users in Philadelphia, US. They chart parallels in crack users' life histories and locate a number of similar life experiences which contributed to crack use, such as early-life disruptions, childhood trauma and interpersonal violence, street gang life and violence, and transitory and unstable employment histories. However, crack user narratives quickly descend into discourses of 'bottoming out' – a series of downward life events – and the analysis fails to consider how individual decision-making and social processes might contribute to pathways into crack use.

Collectively, US studies identify an extensive list of 'risk factors' that correlate with the use of crack. Typically, these studies show that initial involvement with drugs like crack results from peer pressure, drug availability or other risk factors in an individual's social or family environment and that involvement in crack is multifaceted (Crum *et al.*, 1996; Hawkins *et al.*, 1992). The studies are useful but refer to 'significant life events' without further qualification. In addition, they tend to apply statistical correlations that undermine the social process of events. There are some exceptions. For example, Boyd writes on crack use among women:

> Multiple factors contribute to a woman's addiction to alcohol and other drugs; a complex interplay among environmental, psychological and biological conditions appear to influence the initiation and maintenance of her substance use.
>
> (1993: 433)

Available literature in the UK shows that pathways into crack use are not well understood and the literature tends to apply deterministic analyses. The only exceptions are those undertaken by Howard Parker and his colleagues. These researchers attempted to examine the process by which people start using crack. Their initial study found that the 63 'crack takers' in North West England in the mid-1990s lived in poverty and socially exclusion, were typically in their mid- to late 20s, in receipt of benefits rather than working and tended to use other drugs alongside crack (Parker and Bottomley, 1996).

The follow-up study, which was composed of 50 of the original 63 crack users and 29 users new to crack all located in the same neighbourhoods, found that crack use had become available in the recreational drug scene, and that young people were trying crack from an earlier age – typically, for the new-using group, this was in their early 20s (Brain *et al.*, 1998). Although the demographics of the original sample remained roughly the same – 86 per cent without work – the proportion in receipt of sickness/invalidity benefit had risen from 5 per cent to 22 per cent. This, they hypothesised, represented important changes in the profile of people trying and continuing to use crack.

The second body of UK literature draws attention to pathways into crack use through participation in certain drug markets, social networks or/and drug-using environments. For example, pathways into crack use are linked to the convergence of the heroin and crack markets (Edmunds *et al.*, 1996; May *et al.*, 1999) and that, as a consequence, some heroin users also became crack users or poly-drug users (Arnull *et al.*, 2007; Ford, 2004; Gossop *et al.*, 2001; NTA, 2002). Similarly, a substantial amount of literature examines how certain established existing drug-using networks – such as sex workers, homeless, temporary accommodation and drug dealing networks – also offer the potential for pathways into crack use (Booth *et al.*, 1996; Briggs *et al.*, 2009; Cusick *et al.*, 2003; McClanahan *et al.*, 1999; Miller, 1995; Rhodes *et al.*, 2006; Small *et al.*, 2006). 'Risk factor' studies are also popular in the UK context. Similarities have been be found between the social backgrounds of crack users and crack dealers, such as disruptive, unsettled childhoods, experiences in a children's home, living with a foster family or not experiencing secure accommodation (Edmunds *et al.*, 1998, 1999; May *et al.*, 2005; Turnbull *et al.*, 2000). Yet, there is little clarity about how pathways into crack use evolve through social processes. We find similar gaps surrounding crack-using patterns.

Crack-using patterns

Crack-using patterns are not well established. Although research in both the US and the UK has attempted to disaggregate aspects of crack use, a recognisable model has not yet been determined. Studies addressing this issue appear to fall into two categories. First, those studies that attempt to allocate 'mean scores' to crack use across their respective samples – i.e. average crack use is 20 crack rocks per week and therefore the annual crack expenditure is £10,400 – thereby generalising crack-using patterns. This approach tends to neglect different crack-using groups and changes in crack-using trajectories – because, for most, crack use is largely unpredictable (Chapter 5). Furthermore, the 'crack binge' makes these analyses redundant since it essentially skews the real frequency of crack use. For example, Weaver *et al.* show in their careful analysis of 99 crack-using clients in contact with four specialist stimulant drug treatment services that:

> On average, clients used crack in the ten days of the 30 days before referral, spending in the region of £60 on those days, totalling £600 a month. However, there was clinically significant variability between the four services in terms of these measures of consumption.
>
> (2007: 3)

Such studies present a distorted picture of crack use patterns because they evenly spread crack use over the 'life course' of the crack career, and periods of reduction or abstinence and the respective reasons for this are sidelined (see Harocopos *et al.*, 2003).

Second, and of greater value, are those studies that examine specific patterns in more detail. These studies avoid placing crack expenditures into quantifiable boxes, thereby evading a downgrade to generalisable scores. However, such a consideration remains absent in the UK context. UK researchers instead seem preoccupied with 'typologising' crack users. For example, Ford (2004: 4) cites three main types of crack user: *recreational* who take the drug infrequently and in small amounts at social occasions with friends. If use increases, they are considered to be *binge* or *problematic users* who actively seek crack and will buy increased quantities, plan social activities to involve crack and establish a recognisable pattern of use, isolating themselves from others and using large quantities at one time. This pattern of use is potentially life threatening and such users often present for help. The last type of crack users is *chronic high dose* or *dependent users* who consume as much as possible and may demonstrate a life-threatening pattern of use. At this stage, relationships and work are affected or are non-existent, and there tend to be psychological and physical signs of use (also see Webster, 2001). The process by which crack users pass from stage to stage seems quite linear and is presented as if 'crack addiction' is the certain end result for those who try crack. In addition, the stage of recreational and chronic use seems unclear; however, the binge phase appears to be quite a specific period in the 'journey to crack addiction'.

Let us briefly examine 'binge crack use' in more detail. The binge, as Inciardi *et al.* (1996: 12) note, can be for 'days at a time', which results in crack users 'neglecting food, sleep, and basic hygiene'. While reasons for binges are generally under-explored (Waldorf *et al.*, 1991), some commentators indicate that the binge is confused with traditional notions of 'addiction' because of the irregularity of its patterns of use (Reinarman *et al.*, 1997). During binge use, the crack user displaces potential risks to personal health and welfare (Denison *et al.*, 1998; Inciardi *et al.*, 1996; Reinarman *et al.*, 1997) and this 'involves the drug user more often in the street economy' where 'the desire to obtain crack may supersede all other needs and obligations' (Ziek *et al.*, 1996: 223). However, there is a tendency in the literature to blame the drug for the binge and discard the social and emotional influences that may contribute to binge periods. McBride and Rivers suggest that crack users then enter a 'crash phase' which is:

> characterised early by agitation, depression, anorexia and high cocaine craving. These symptoms are followed by fatigue, depression, insomnia, paranoia, and exhaustion. If the crack user does not binge again soon, withdrawal symptoms often appear … which can result in an increased willingness on the part of crack users to act aggressively and in ways that will bring violence upon themselves.
>
> (1996: 407)

There have been one or two exceptions to the analysis of the 'binge'. Bourgois *et al.* (1997) suggest that binge drug use revolves around state institutions and their distribution of welfare cheques, which results in drug users making exchanges and favours which produce drug-taking risks that are not normally taken. There remains, however, little conclusive information about crack binges as no UK studies appear to pinpoint when they are likely to occur, what drives them and how they stop. Given that research suggests that this is a particularly vulnerable period for crack users, further examination is required in this area.

Crack careers

Longitudinal research in the US and UK indicates that crack-using careers are difficult to break. In the US, Falck *et al.* (2007) followed a sample of 430 urban crack users in a mid-western US city from 1996 to 2005. Commendable efforts were made to retain the initial sample. The follow-up rates ranged from 86.7 per cent (372 of 429) at six months to 74.7 per cent (292 of 391) at the final interview eight years later. The research confirmed that most crack users engage in crack use for many years without interruptions or even phases of abstinence. Similarly, Hser (2002) found 'at least weekly use' of cocaine/crack was higher compared to other drug users – such as heroin, marijuana and methamphetamine users – and that cocaine/crack careers tended to last longer than other drug careers (see also Brecht *et al.*, 2008).

While such a longitudinal analysis remains absent in the UK, some studies have attempted to capture the crack career. When Brain *et al.* (1998) interviewed the 50 crack users recaptured from their study two years earlier, only five had given up using illegal drugs ('the quitters'). Eight stopped using crack, in particular, and 15 took steps to reduce their crack use ('the reformers'). Almost half, however, (n=22) continued to use crack and other drugs heavily ('resolute rockheads'). While the authors accessed hidden crack users, questions remain about why and how crack users desist from crack use and why so many continued to use the drug.

Equally, UK studies that have tried to measure crack use and treatment outcomes also highlight the difficulty in breaking crack careers. Gossop *et al.* (2002) undertook five-year longitudinal research with 496 drug users from UK treatment programmes. While improvements in abstinence were seen among heroin and amphetamine users, crack users had less successful treatment outcomes. At intake, 67 per cent were abstinent from crack. This rose to 81 per cent in year 1, but decreased to 77 per cent in year 2, and 71 per cent in year 4–5. Those not using crack at intake were found to be using it in year 4–5. They were, however, not able to accurately conclude on the reasons why (see also Harocopos *et al.*, 2003). This raises important questions regarding why crack users, in particular compared to other drug users, use crack for such lengthy periods.

As it stands, there remain large gaps in our understanding of what shapes crack use throughout the crack career. Research on transitions between crack use stages has mostly focused on correlates, or risks and protective factors, and few studies have empirically investigated how critical turning points affect major shifts in the direction of crack-using trajectories.

Treatment policy responses to the problem of crack in the UK

The UK central government responded to these problems by establishing the National Treatment Agency (NTA) for substance use as a special health authority in April 2001. It accompanied the disbursement of new funding to support the expansion and enhancement of drug treatment and was coupled with increased investment in treatment, especially through diversion or referral from the criminal justice system. There has since been a massive expansion in the numbers of users in treatment; from around 88,000 in 1998 to 195,000 in 2006/7 (NTA, 2007). However, despite rhetorical commitments to rebalance UK drug policy spending towards treatment (Hellawell and Trace, 1998), the bulk of public expenditure remains devoted to criminal justice measures (Reuter and Stevens, 2008; Stimson, 2000). Some suggest there was a shift in the NTA's accountability from the practical matters of recovery such as housing, social care and benefit support, to an 'overemphasis on the treatment of addiction' (Audit Commission, 2004; Fox *et al*., 2005) at the expense of other key areas of drug policy, such as the prevention of drug-related deaths, viral infections, and/or reducing the social exclusion of drug users (Reuter and Stevens, 2008). Increasingly punitive measures for attendance into treatment were also introduced (Briggs, 2010) which meant that drug users, and in particular crack users, had fewer options for treatment and experienced stringent conditions and regulations as well as longer waiting times (Fox *et al*., 2005).

Service engagement

Despite ambitious efforts to get drug users into services, most drug support services do not successfully engage crack users nor meet their needs (Al-Rahman *et al*., 2007; Arnull *et al*., 2007; Becker and Duffy, 2002; Ford, 2004; GLADA, 2004; Lindsell, 2005; McElrath and Jordan, 2005; NTA, 2002; Parker *et al*., 1998; Sangster *et al*., 2001). Furthermore, there is little conclusive international evidence pointing to the superiority of any one treatment modality for crack users (Donmall *et al*., 1995; Sievewright *et al*., 2000). While there have been renewed calls to address this, the overall focus of drug treatment in the UK remains focused on heroin users (Fox *et al*., 2005; Parker *et al*., 2001; Sangster *et al*., 2001). Consequently, there are also high attrition rates among crack users in drug programmes (Turnbull *et al*., 2000; Turnbull and Webster, 2007; Weaver *et al*., 2007), and many relapse during or after intervention, unhappy with the level of specialist help (Fox *et al*., 2005; Parker *et al*., 2001). Those that do engage are often in 'crisis': often with complex social, financial and emotional difficulties (Harocopos *et al*., 2003; Morris, 1998), and have low levels of self-esteem and confidence (Al-Rahman *et al*., 2007; Fox *et al*., 2005). Many feel greatly ashamed of their crack use when they do engage (Ahern *et al*., 2007; Neale *et al*., 2006) and have trouble facing up to their 'spoilt identities' in treatment settings (Simmonds and Coomber, 2009). This is perhaps why they are labelled as the most hard-to-reach drug-using group (Bourgois, 1995; Cornish and O'Brien, 1996; Cregler, 1989; Fryer *et al*., 2005).

Crack users: the most hard-to-reach drug-using group

International studies show crack users to be the most socially disadvantaged drug-using group even when compared to other groups of street drug users such as heroin users. They are, as some say, the 'marginalised among the marginalised' (Agar, 2003; Bourgois, 1995; Fischer and Coghlan, 2007). They suffer from the highest rates of homelessness, extreme poverty or lack of basic subsistence, high degrees of discrimination from society and the highest barriers to social care or healthcare (Bourgois, 2003; Fischer *et al.*, 2005; Young *et al.*, 2005): a picture exacerbated by the fact that most crack users engage in their drug use for many years without interruptions or even phases of abstinence (Falck *et al.*, 2007; Gossop *et al.*, 2002; Hser, 2002). These long drug-using trajectories put crack users at a higher risk of physical and mental health risks (NIDA, 2005; Rhodes *et al.*, 2007; Small *et al.*, 2006) and risk behaviours (Darke *et al.*, 2001; Klee and Morris, 1995; Latkin *et al.*, 1996; Rhodes *et al.*, 2005), and expose them to specific risks in environments like crack houses, shooting galleries and general makeshift locations (Dovey *et al.*, 2001; Fitzgerald *et al.*, 2004; Rhodes *et al.*, 2007; Small *et al.*, 2006; Thorpe *et al.*, 2000).

Rationale for this book

The prevalence of crack use has increased in the UK and presents numerous problems for policymakers, criminal justice and frontline drug workers, as well as for those involved in these lifestyles. The current UK literature lacks a detailed account of pathways into crack use, crack-using patterns and how crack careers evolve. Furthermore, we lack significant data on how health problems develop, and where crack users end up as a consequence. We also lack an understanding of how they make decisions under these circumstances and find ways to navigate their predicaments. While we have some clues as to why crack service provision is inadequate, there is little understanding attached to the social and structural context of crack use which may impact on decisions and attitudes to make lifestyle changes. Such an insight is important so that appropriate measures can be taken to improve the situation. Taken together, this creates a strong impetus for ethnographic research on crack users in the UK.

The study

The ethnographic data in this book is taken from a study on crack users and crack houses funded by Rivertown's DAT from September 2004 to May 2005. However, my interest in doing this work evolved in 2003 when I had started to see policy shortfalls regarding crack users in work I undertook for the Home Office on prison and post-custody support services for 'problematic drug users'. When I initially approached two university ethics committees about an ethnographic study on crack users, they indicated the work was 'too risky' and would not support it. This is one reason why I sought employment with a private drug and alcohol research company to seek funding. Rivertown's DAT funded a 12-month study because there were gaps in knowledge about crack. The project aims were to examine the reasons why crack users dropped out of services, the service needs of crack users and the function of crack houses; and the link between crack and crime. Before I started the work, I signed an insurance liability waiver. My time was spent with crack users in crack houses, street-dealing locations, on council estates, derelict sites, car parks, parks, and streets and alleyways. Contact was made with 85 crack users and almost two thirds of the sample (63%, n=54) consented to one-to-one interviews. Conversations were also recorded in crack houses. The 31 crack users who were not formally interviewed provided explanations of their experiences and lifestyles through informal discussions.

Methods

Ethnographic methods were the primary research method. The ethnographic method examines the behaviour and interaction of groups in their natural settings using field observation and open-ended interviewing techniques with an emphasis on people and their behaviours; the meanings people attach to their actions; and the ways in which social processes emerge and change (Hammersley, 1992). Ethnography has come to be well regarded in drug research (Anderson, 1990; Becker, 1953; Bourgois, 1995; Brain et al., 1998; Briggs, 2010; Hamid, 1990; Preble and Casey, 1969; Rhodes et al., 1999; Rubin and Comitas, 1975; Williams, 1990). For example:

> It is exciting, unique and instructive to read raw observational accounts of the lifestyles and experiences of drug users and others forced to the margins of society. There are many examples of studies that have provided a rich vein of marvellously detailed data to add to our collective and historical base, in a way that would not be possible without an ongoing commitment to ethnography.
>
> (Power, 2002: 330)

Access

Entry and access to the sample was achieved through established contact with several known crack users (Bourgois, 1995; Inicardi, 1995) and local drug outreach teams (Bourgois and Schonberg, 2009). These contacts were influential to the expansion of the sample and provided important advice throughout the study. Street outreach through the local Crack Service and Cross Street Harm Reduction (see Chapter 3) helped to recruit potential users to the study. These workers also helped to reassure clients about the confidentiality of the research. While access was gained quite quickly, managing contact with close informants and potential interviewees was more difficult. Like most London boroughs (Harocopos et al.,

2003; Lindsell, 2005; Weaver *et al.*, 2007), crack users in Rivertown are a transient population and flexibility was needed to access them (Chapter 1). During the nine-month fieldwork period, close relationships were made with four crack users (Dawg, Blood, Cuz and Fam). I shared personal experiences as a researcher, as a student, as an outsider looking in, as a listener and as a friend.

Building relations

To be part of – and be accepted in – this culture, one needs to do favours, run errands, agree with things that one may wholehearted disagree with, go places where one would not normally go and offer an impartial ear. In some instances, I helped crack users – not because they necessarily needed it – but because I became emotionally attached to them and their circumstances. Indeed, once bound up emotionally in this world, as someone trying to make sense of it, it became even more difficult to understand and separate myself from it. In the end, I found it more of an obligation to help where I could as well as document what I could.

I joined drug deals and observed risky drug use practices to understand this particular culture. On numerous occasions, I turned down crack and other drugs, and although I didn't – and still don't – smoke or drink extra-strength alcohol, I opted instead for these forms of substance use on occasions to be accepted in some form by those around me. According to Agar (1986: 12): 'such work requires an intensive personal involvement, an abandonment of traditional scientific control, an improvisational style to meet situations not of the researcher's making, and an ability to learn from a long series of mistakes'.

In many of my early introductions with crack users, correct ways of what to 'say or do' were explored. Appearing calm and friendly, interested to talk and empathetic to life dilemmas was most useful in these instances. Despite social and cultural differences, ways of connecting our lives and experiences were found (Goodenough, 1967). In most contexts, neutral examples of heavy substance use were used. For example, this excerpt was taken from a recorded conversation that took place in Fam's crack house while I was in the toilet:

CUZ: *The good thing about it is he's [Dan] making these people know what it's really about. He told me that he went out with all these bankers – all these rich people – and they kept lining up in the toilet and he asked me why would they line up in the toilet. Taking crack – not crack – powder [cocaine], snorting it, and he said to me 'do you know how much money they were spending?' Hundreds of pounds. They've got it, these cunts. They've got it and they think we're bad because we take the crack. Them cunts don't know anything.*

TWITCH: *You get fucking judged by everyone.*

CUZ: *But if he was a copper – look at the questions he's asking – what's a crack house? And those sort of things. No way. I know for a fact he's a very nice guy.*

TWITCH: *Yeah, he seems a nice guy.*

CUZ: *No, he is. You know that Fam? He's safe, mate. He's the only guy I really know who doesn't take drugs.*

TWITCH: *Like you said, he is doing it properly* [through research]. *He is.*

Appearing curious put the emphasis on participants to explain aspects of their crack use and the cultural aesthetics of the crack scene. This allowed me to establish a bank of knowledge about the crack scene and the cultural practices associated with its operation (Chapter 5). Using ignorance with participants was also advantageous on occasions when faced with unfamiliar street terminology, unclear drug-using practices, and also among new social groups. Spending time with crack users meant exposing some part of my personal biography and appearance to the social context of the research. When with crack users on the streets, in crack houses and in various public settings, my appearance and theirs attracted attention. Not only was I with people who did not resemble the nicely-dressed, everyday person but also I rarely shaved, and I dressed in ripped and stained clothes that over the course of nine months had accumulated dirt and bad odour. Passers-by on the streets and the police often stared at us in disgust. Shopkeepers and security guards often considered us potential thieves and followed us round shops. Experiencing these situations first-hand with crack users appeared to strengthen my relationship with them.

Sampling

The sample was predominantly obtained by 'snowballing', which is one of the most practical techniques of building ethnographic samples. It is done through 'one who will vouch for you with others' (Polsky, 1969: 129). Two different types of sampling framework were used during the fieldwork: opportunistic sampling and selective recommendation sampling[2] – or purposive sampling. At the start of fieldwork, existing contacts were used and sampling was entirely opportunistic. This approach was bolstered through spending time with drug outreach services to gain some 'overall picture'. This method was used because it was often unclear as to whether contacts might play a role as an interviewee. Nevertheless, once contact had been established with close participants, greater consideration was given to recruiting. With the advice and assistance of four close contacts, selective recommendation sampling was used to recruit crack users who my informants described as 'good speakers' who 'wouldn't bullshit me'.

Sample demographics

Over the fieldwork period, I met 85 crack users, 54 of whom consented to one-to-one interviews. Table 2.1 provides the gender, ethnicity and age of the interviewed sample:

Table 2.1 Gender, ethnicity and age of the interviewed sample

Demographics	Male (n=33)	Female (n=21)	Total (n=54)
Age			
18–25	1	3	4
26–31	4	5	9
32–40	22	12	34
41–50	5	1	6
50+	1	–	1
Ethnicity			
White British	16	8	24
White Irish	2	–	2
Black British	3	3	6
Black Caribbean	5	4	9
Black African	2	–	2
Portuguese	3	–	3
Chinese	1	–	1
Greek	2	–	2
Filipino	–	1	1
'Mixed Race'	–	1	1
Italian	1	–	1
Unknown	–	2	2

Epistemological position

This ethnography uses a critical realist appreciation of knowledge construction. For critical realists, social phenomena can sometimes be understood, but not often – meaningfully – measured, hence a preference for qualitative methods. By using this epistemological position, I acknowledge my presence and interactions in the social dynamics of the crack scene and how this contributed to the construction of meanings (Atkinson and Hammersley, 1994). So the narratives of this book are co-produced from both the subjective experiences of crack users in the crack scene, and my ethnographic experiences with crack users at this particular time under these particular circumstances.

Theorising crack users

The theoretical framework I use in this book aims to highlight the socio-structural position of crack users; what shapes their decisions and interactions in their day-to-day lives; and, ultimately, what affects their motivation towards making life-style changes. I make use of theoretical perspectives from the management of identity, political economy, and risk and insecurity in late modernity. Throughout the book, however, I borrow on other perspectives. Below, I briefly indicate how and why these perspectives are relevant.

Management of identity

Crack users' activities are labelled as heavily stigmatised because such destructive drug use breaks various social norms and codes. This is why many try to remain clandestine about their movements and practices. For some time, symbolic interactionists have discussed this relationship in the context of the labelling that powerful dominant groups apply to groups of drug users such as crack users. Thus:

> Social groups create deviance by making the rules whose infraction constitutes deviance, and by applying those rules to particular people and labelling them as outsiders. From this point of view, deviance is not a quality of the act the person commits but rather a consequence of the application by others of rules and sanctions to an 'offender'. The deviant is one to whom that label has been successfully applied; deviant behaviour is behaviour that people so label.
>
> (Becker, 1963: 9)

In particular, crack users are vulnerable to what Duster (1970) calls 'a moral outrage against drug use', where society's vulnerable groups become the object of extreme hostility. In the context of drug taking, this may not necessarily be deviant or a social problem but deviant only to groups who condemn it or for those who wish to eliminate it (Taylor et al., 1973). The media, along with 'moral crusaders', experts and law enforcement agencies therefore play a lead role in initiating social reactions against drug users (Wilkins, 1964; Young, 1971). Such systemic opposition may have implications for crack users' identities.

Therefore, countering transformation into the 'important stigmas' such as 'prostitutes, thieves, homosexuals, beggars, and drug addicts' requires crack users to be clandestine about their illicit operations and potential failing in society (Goffman 1963: 93). For crack users, early on, denial of their position becomes integral to their sense of self. It is, as deviance sociologists argue, confirmation of their illicit/illegal actions which appears to act as catalyst for further identity shifts (Lemert, 1967; Maruna, 2001). Crack users, however, may make use of a façade which can show the conventional world that everything is under control (Goffman, 1963). This is done to deflect personal feelings of shame and guilt (Giddens, 1991) and avert personal responsibility (Sykes and Matza, 1957).

Indeed, how crack users start to see and evaluate themselves, their position and evaluate their movements rests heavily on notions of self identity (Chapter

4; Maruna, 2001) and their participation in the crack scene (Chapter 5). This is because the modern 'self' is a reflection of social participation that confirms who he/she is (Cooley, 1964). In the company of other crack users, the 'social self' likely identifies with these values and becomes 'one of them' (Holstein and Gubrium, 2000; Matza, 1969). Surviving in this world – and the practices associated with it – becomes part of the core identity of the crack user (Maruna, 2001; Preble and Casey, 1969) and this is reinforced through contact with criminal justice and drug treatment institutions (Chapter 8; Garfinkel, 1956; Lemert, 1967; Maruna, 2001; Ray, 1964). This has implications for the internal framework of the individual:

> Treating a person as though he were generally rather than specifically deviant produces a self-fulfilling prophecy. It sets in motion several mechanisms which conspire to shape the person in the image people have of him. When the deviant is caught, he is treated in accordance with the popular diagnosis of why he is that way, and the treatment itself may likewise produce increasing deviance.
>
> (Becker, 1963: 34)

These perspectives on identity have been more recently complemented by a broader body of research and theorisation around the role of macro processes in the formation of identities. Most poignantly, this is evident through Bourdieu's (1984) concept of 'symbolic violence'. Symbolic violence is generated through discourses and practices of cultural systems and is experienced through macro social forces such as discrimination, stigmatisation and poverty and reproduced in everyday lived experience (Bourdieu, 1984; Bourdieu and Wacquant, 1992; Connolly and Healy, 2004; Farmer et al., 1996; Rhodes et al., 2007). Some link the experience of symbolic violence with the internalisation of social suffering (Kleinman et al., 1997) through stigma (Parker and Aggleton, 2003) and psychological or emotional harms, such as fatalism, feelings of shame, worthlessness or powerlessness, and health risk behaviour (Farmer, 1997; Wilkinson, 2006). These are all relevant attributes associated with crack users (Chapter 1; Chapter 7; Chapter 8).

Such macro forces become embedded in everyday practices (Chapter 4) and interactions (Chapter 5; Chapter 7), and these are exacerbated by the sense of shame and degradation crack users experience when their drug use is publically exposed (Rhodes et al., 2007). Even then, crack users may also internalise feelings of shame and stigma in the environments in which they use the drugs (Duff, 2009; Parkin, 2008; Rhodes et al. 2007). This is important to consider in the context of crack users because it provides useful theorisation to consider how identity is built and shaped through interactionist processes (Chapter 4; Chapter 7), social and cultural (Chapter 5; Chapter 7) as well as structural processes (Chapter 6; Chapter 7). Macro forces are also important to consider for an understanding of the everyday practices of crack users.

Political economy

The political economic perspective considers how economic and political institutions produce and reproduce social and economic conditions that shape inequalities (Doyle, 1979; Navarro and Muntaner, 2004). This perspective shows how particular vulnerable groups, such as crack users, are exposed to macro forces that result in harm (Friedman *et al.* 1998). The perspective is useful to help us understand what shapes crack users' attitudes, decisions and practices, and, in turn, how they respond (Chapter 6; Chapter 8; Lemert, 1967). In the context of drugs, the political economy perspective is particularly illuminating to macro processes of social exclusion, discrimination and racism – all of which play a part in high levels of crack use and exposure to risk (Bourgois, 1995; Finestone, 1957; Marez, 2004). As Bourgois (2003: 32) notes: 'the pharmacological qualities of substances are virtually meaningless outside of their socio-cultural as well as political economic contexts'.

Political economy analysis has experienced a resurgence since the 1970s, especially since Western cities have become State-led targets as sites for the development of entrepreneurial and competitive practices. It is characterised by an expansion of governance mechanisms through a variety of public–private partnerships, infrastructure development as well as urban, social and cultural policies (Brenner 2004; O'Connor, 2004), and zero-tolerance policing (Chapter 6; Hall and Hubbard, 1998). However this is often at the political, economic and social disregard of certain populations (Wacquant, 2002) – such as crack users (Bourgois, 2003; Provine, 2006). The social consequences of these practices are often manifested in high crime rates and destructive levels of crack use (Reinarman and Levine, 2004). At the hub of this political and social abandonment are increasingly punitive attitudes and policies to crime (Aitkin *et al.*, 2002; Chapter 8) which are linked to political and moralistic motives to provoke fear and the perceived potential threat that 'problematic populations' pose to middle-class values and dominant political ideologies (Fitzgerald and Threadgold, 2004; Jayne *et al.*, 2006; Punch, 2005; Reinarman and Levine, 2004; Wacquant, 2002).

In particular, US crack ethnographies provide a useful indicator of the shortfalls of federal policies to alleviate crack problems but also help to understand the structural position of inner-city crack users. Bourgois (1995) has made a large contribution to our understanding of the social and structural organisation of the crack scene in New York. His work throughout the early 1990s examined crack dealers' relationship with mainstream society and their interaction with the legal labour market. For Bourgois, the crack dealers' main problem was not lack of skills, because they managed a complex system involving marketing, distribution of resources and human relations, but rather their lack of 'cultural capital' (see Bourdieu, 1984), literacy, savvy in handling city agencies, or the ability to switch between the street and white-collar worlds. Consequently, they survived in the underground economy. Thus:

The objective, structural desperation of a population without a viable economy and facing the barriers of systematic discrimination and marginalisation gets channelled into self-destructive cultural practices.

(Bourgois, 1995: 63)

On a daily level, victims perpetuate interpersonal violence, usually against their friends and loved ones, as well as against themselves (Bourgois, 2002; Chapter 7; Dunlap, 1995; Dunlap and Johnson, 1992). This form of structural violence is not only experienced individually, but also collectively as common forms of 'lived-oppression' or 'social suffering' (Bourgois *et al.*, 1997). Social suffering is said to be the result of the devastating injuries that social forces inflict on the human experience (Kleinman *et al.*, 1997). This 'traumatic stress disorder' is produced by the combined effects of being subject over time to intense social oppression such as racial hatred, sexism, class discrimination or homophobia, which is subsequently individually internalised into depression, stigma, self-hatred and a sense of powerlessness (Singer, 2001). Again, these are all social attributes associated with crack users (Chapter 1; Neale *et al.*, 2006). These experiences are further amplified against perceptions of 'social failure' in cultures of personal achievement (Agar, 2003; Bauman, 2007; Young, 2007). Consequently, Singer posits that both:

Social suffering and the hidden injuries of oppression are emotionally damaging and pressure the sufferers to seek relief. Drug use, in an action-oriented culture that forcefully emphasizes (through the media and elsewhere) instant gratification, pain intolerance, and chemical intervention, is a commonly selected solution.

(2001: 205)

Both macro political economic processes and micro symbolic interactionist practices have implications for crack users, their response to their circumstances and the composition of their identities. This reciprocal relationship is what Giddens (1984) terms 'structuration'; that is, the changing and interplaying nature of relations between structure and the agent. In this process, Giddens suggests, the self or the agent is not separate from structure nor vice versa. Instead, the two form a duality, meaning that 'social systems are both medium and outcome of the practices they recursively organise' (Giddens, 1984: 25). However, these macro and micro processes are increasingly constructed in unstable circumstances, in a time of risk, uncertainty and insecurity.

Risk society and insecurity in late modernity

The risk and uncertainty of late modern living is well catalogued: the breakdown of community, mass migration, globalisation, 'flexibility' of labour, instability of the family, rise in virtual realities, mass consumerism, individualisation, choice and spontaneity, loss of religion and decline in the attachment to tradition (Beck, 1992; Giddens, 1991). What was:

> a world of high employment, stable family structures, and consensual values underpinned by the safety net of welfare state, has now been replaced by a world of structural unemployment, economic precariousness, a systematic cutting of welfare provisions and the growing instability of family life and interpersonal relations.
>
> (Young, 2007: 59)

These features have particularly devastating consequences for crack users.

The disembedding of tradition and social systems, coupled with the loss of continuity of history, creates the search for psychic security (Lasch, 1985) and the need to balance ontological security (Giddens, 1991). Therefore 'potentially disturbing existential questions are defused by the controlled nature of day-to-day activities within internally referential systems' (Giddens, 1991: 202). These internal referential social systems lie at 'the reflexive project of the self'. Because there has been a decline in ritualistic activities in relation to major transitions of life, an increased lifespan that revolves around open experience removes an important psychological prop to the individual's capacity to cope with such transitions (Gidden, 1991). The self:

> establishes a trajectory which can only become coherent through the reflexive use of the broader social environment. The impetus towards control, geared to reflexivity, thrusts the self into the outer world in ways which have no clear parallel in previous times.
>
> (Giddens, 1991: 148)

The self becomes something to be reflected on. Coupled with increasingly reflexive biographies and identities, the more the individual internally references self identity, the more shame comes to play a role in the adult personality (Goffman, 1963). These days 'shame bears directly on self identity because it is essentially the anxiety about the adequacy of the narrative by means of which the individual sustains a coherent biography' (Giddens, 1991: 65). This results in a fear of inadequacy or failure that can 'haunt' people for life (Bauman, 2007: 58). Thus:

> Whereas illness, addiction, unemployment and other deviations from the norm used to count as blows of fate, the emphasis today is on individual blame and responsibility. [Consequently] your own life – your own failure. Social crisis phenomena such as structural unemployment can be shifted as a burden of risk onto the shoulders of individuals.
>
> (Beck and Beck-Gernsheim, 2002: 22)

For example, some argue that the 'responsibilisation of health' 'represents the extension of techniques of social regulation to an unprecedented extent' (Petersen 1997: 696). That is, in a society that expects its citizens to take care of their health, those who do not do everything they can for their health become 'irresponsible citizens' (Rimke, 2000). Such citizens might be accused of being in breach of a 'social contract of health' and, individually, they may experience this breach as a form of personal or 'moral failure' (Petersen, 1997). The social expectancy of groups like crack users, therefore, is that they should 'rise up', 'against all odds', and this is embedded in societal moral standards. Therefore crack users are responsible for their harms and the harm to others; it is not society's problem but the individual's problem if they cannot control/reduce their crack use (O'Malley, 2008).

The structure of the book

The chapters of the book are organised as follows. Chapter 3 provides contextual data on Rivertown's drug users and community drug support, and describes the operation of the local crack market. Chapter 4 highlights pathways into crack use, the development of crack careers and crack-use patterns. Particular attention is devoted to the role of shame and paranoia among the population. Chapter 5 discusses the social organisation of the crack-using environment – otherwise known as the crack scene. It uses a 'bottom up' approach to describe its cultural scenery, hierarchies and the mistrustful and violent interactions. Chapter 6 takes a political economy perspective to consider 'top down' how crack users' lives are influenced and shaped by macro structural forces. It discusses the role of aggressive social policies, law enforcement drives and the role drug support services play in shaping crack careers and crack-using practices.

Chapter 7 examines how crack users counter their low social status in the crack scene and the conflicting ways in which they deploy themselves across the arena of the crack scene. Chapter 8 uses case studies to consider how crack users attempt to make changes or seek a 'way out' and Chapter 9 draws on the literature, theoretical perspectives and research findings to discuss, conclude and make recommendations for change. Chapter 10 – the Epilogue – attempts to trace those crack users who have been met in the years since the study.

Chapter 3

Rivertown

The research context

Introduction

This chapter offers details on the research context: Rivertown. It first provides an overview of Rivertown's social demographics. Second, it examines the number of drug users, including crack users, in Rivertown. Third, it provides a basic description of drug support services. Last, it describes the operation of the local crack market. This data is important to consider for it helps contextualise the social and structural backdrop to crack users' lifestyles and practices (Chapter 5) and decision-making (Chapter 7).

Rivertown's demographics

Historically, Rivertown has very high levels of deprivation; it is among the most deprived boroughs not only in London but also in England and Wales. It has a high proportion of public sector housing (55 per cent) and a low proportion of privately owned housing (32 per cent) compared to London averages of approximately 27 per cent and 55 per cent respectively. Much of Rivertown's population is characterised by high levels of state benefits; relatively high levels of unemployment; low levels of educational attainment; low incomes; relatively poor health; a complex social mix – more than 100 languages are spoken in Rivertown; and high turnover in population (Rivertown DAT, 2003).

Rivertown has a population of approximately 240,000. The population increase over the past 20 years reversed a century-old trend of population decline and reflects the general inner-London renaissance – as well as high birth rates and increasing inward migration in the borough. The population of Rivertown is also relatively young and rich in ethnic and cultural diversity. Estimates indicate that there are 77,500 people from black and other minority ethnic groups resident in Rivertown. This represents 33 per cent of the total population of the borough – an increase of 8 per cent from 1991 – compared to the national average of around 5 per cent (Rivertown DAT, 2003).

Number of 'problematic' drug users

The number of 'problematic' drug users has remained difficult to capture in Rivertown. Data from the Regional Drug Misuse Database shows that from April 1999 to March 2001 there were 744 individuals engaged in 'problematic' drug use: 125 individuals for crack use in comparison to 465 with opiate use. Despite the commissioning of a small-scale study that recommended the development of a strategy to focus efforts to tackle increasing crack use in Rivertown, the process was complicated by the subsequent studies which presented conflicting information on the number of 'problematic drug users'. Although Child et al.'s (2002) report on Rivertown's substance users' treatment needs, drug users' views and experiences were discounted in favour of 'anecdotal' stakeholder perspectives and baseline statistics, their 'cautious estimate' of the number of problem drug users in Rivertown was around 4,000 with a modest drug expenditure of £200 per week. This equated to a total of about £800,000 per week and a total drug economy of £42 million per annum.

Yet, confusion over the numbers of crack users and their primary drug of 'choice' has continually been overlooked. In 2003, locally based research estimated that there were '1,593 problematic crack or cocaine users in Rivertown' (Rivertown DAT, 2003: 25) but no distinction was made between how many used crack and how many used cocaine, or indeed, what was meant by 'problematic'. In the same year, Rivertown's Safer Neighbourhoods Partnership undertook a needs assessment and found there to be 1,728 'notifications' from Rivertown drug support services – some notifications were double counted (Fox et al., 2005). The average age of the clients was 33; the male ratio to women was 3:1; two thirds were white and under a fifth were black; and the most common drugs used were opiates (73 per cent) compared to stimulants (18 per cent). This demographic picture of those presenting to agencies, however, did not match snapshot data taken from arrest data taken by the police. This data suggested the average age of arrestees was 22; that 45 per cent were black and 45 per cent were white; and the most common drug for which arrestees tested positive was crack – 71 per cent of men and 58 per cent of women (Safer Rivertown Partnership, 2004b). Later that year a GP commissioning document estimated there to be 2,300 illicit and problematic drug users in Rivertown (Rivertown Primary Care Trust, 2004). However more recent research shows that there are 4,836 (3,707 men and 1,129 women) 'problematic heroin and crack users' in Rivertown (Hay et al., 2006).

The existing framework of drug support services in Rivertown

There are seven main services that crack users can access in Rivertown; only one of them is a crack-specific service or Crack Service (see Table 3.1). There are two prescribing services in the borough: Connections Central, located in the centre of Rivertown, supervises the consumption of prescriptions, and Connections North, in the north of the borough, oversees prescriptions, but allows some service users to withdraw weekly supplies of medication. Many crack users felt that such services, however, were generally aimed towards opiate users and tended to have rigid opening times and appointment systems. There was also a distinct lack of provision to the south of the borough.

Despite this, the need for urgent 'stimulant user treatment' provision was recognised as early as 1994 (Dale and Perera, 1994). Even in 2003, when Rivertown was branded a High Crack Area (HCA), there were 'no services in Rivertown

Table 3.1 Main drug support services for crack users in Rivertown

Service	Services offered
Rivertown Referrals	Housing information; employment training; support for those leaving prison; rapid prescription and counselling; escort from prison to services and rehabilitation service; outreach to client's address when concern about engagement.
Crack Service	Development of a therapeutic relationship with service users. Services include: motivational interviewing; cognitive behavioural therapy; counselling; drop-in and outreach facilities; advice and onward referral to temporary accommodation; surgeries in community centres and social services and job centres.
Cross Street Harm Reduction	Registered national HIV and HCV charity working with former and current drugs users, commercial workers, people living with and at risk of HCV and other blood-borne viruses. Services include: access to social services and job centres; visits to hostels and temporary accommodation.
Connections Central	Advice and information; needle exchange; clinic for pregnant women; dual diagnosis assessment; hepatitis B vaccinations; acupuncture; substitute prescribing; onsite supervised dispensing; community scripting; community and inpatient detoxification; methadone maintenance.
Connections North	Concurrent harm minimisation; health education; brief intervention; relapse prevention and other drug counselling approaches; methadone maintenance.
St Peter's Drop-In	For substance users and those with mental health issues. Services include: Brief Intervention Team; advice; drop-in; counselling; Wet Centre Team (for alcohol users); outreach team; training team (education and training); DTTO programme; street-based outreach; and flats for tenancy support.
Temple House Rehab for women	Residential rehabilitation service for women, specialising in support for pregnant women and women with small children. Services include: counselling; one-to-one therapies; various day activities.

where problematic crack users can receive an integrated package of care which adequately responds to their complex and varied needs' (Rivertown DAT, 2003: 8). High numbers of crack users were processed through the criminal justice system, yet often failed to attend first appointments and dropped out of treatment programmes. For example, in 2003/04 Rivertown Referrals reported that of the 186 referrals they received, nearly a third (n=58, 31 per cent) failed to attend their first appointment. A significant proportion of their clients (n=166, 89 per cent) were crack users. From 2002/2003, Rivertown issued 45 DTTOs, as part of the government's aim to coerce drug users into treatment. However, in the same year, only five completed their order. From 2003/04, 12 of the 67 receiving the same sanction completed the order (Safer Rivertown Partnership, 2004a).

In addition, statistics from the Rivertown Drug Intervention Programme (DIP) database indicated that from April 1 2004 to March 31 2005, Rivertown Referrals and Connections Central assessed 578 crack users, 291 of whom said crack was their 'drug of choice'. Data from the same source showed that almost a third of crack users (n=185, 32 per cent) assessed in services disengaged from them (Fox *et al.*, 2005). There were also long waiting lists. In December 2003, problematic drug users such as crack users – and including heroin/poly-drug users – could expect to wait on average eight weeks and three days for in-patient treatment; three weeks for rehab; 11 weeks for specialist prescribing; four weeks for structured day care; and five weeks and two days for structured counselling. These timescales often were subject to conditions of engagement through the criminal justice system. The longest waiting times of around 25 weeks were through accessing services by self-referral in the community.

The increase in caseloads in drug services appeared to be linked to a higher number of referrals through the criminal justice system. However, high proportions of crack users continued to drop out of services. This has, for some years, been considered a major problem which has not been matched with sufficient resources.

The dimensions of the crack market in Rivertown

The local crack market in Rivertown operates a mixture of open and closed market selling (Burgess, 2003; GLADA, 2004). Open market selling is characterised by a crack dealer selling to anyone in a variety of social spaces, whereas the disposition of a closed market is a crack dealer selling to known buyers only (May *et al.*, 2007). Research and policy documents indicate that as a result of increased law enforcement on heroin and cocaine markets during the 1990s, modes of selling drugs in London shifted to accommodate these pressures (Chapter 2). In the context of crack, the mobile phone changed the nature of the organisation of the cocaine/crack market as more covert operations took place in different locations thereby reducing detection (Burgess, 2003; GLADA, 2004). These are also the market conditions for this study. Similarly, crack dealers place responsibility for their deals with younger men who act as 'runners' to avoid detection (May *et al.*, 2007). It is similar young men who are often sent out to make the face-to-face exchanges with crack users in this study. Most crack users do not like these interactions because, for some, it reasserts their low status among the social strata – even in the crack scene (Chapter 5).

Dawg left his mum's at about 4.45pm and we walked up the road and started to bump into familiar faces. Dawg started asking around for a couple of nuggets [pounds] to round his £8 up to a £10 for a rock. The first guy he approached managed to give him a pound, the second had nothing. We waited by the phone box. Someone was making a phone call. As we waited, we could hear the conversation and the guy was making arrangements for a street drug deal. He then ran out and another guy with long hair and stained T-shirt ran in, made a very frantic and loud phone call about meeting another runner (I was later to learn this was Black Eyes). As he came out of the phone box, Dawg asked him if he had a nugget [pound coin]. He was sweating quite badly and hurriedly reached in his pocket, pulled out a handful of change, threw it at Dawg and ran off down the road to score. As we stood there, three drug runners in expensive clothing cycled past. They all had hoods and caps and the mobile phone hands-free kits. Dawg said these guys were the main runners for the Afghan dealers. Dawg now had his £10 for a rock then one young man who we'd seen on the bike earlier came cycling around us and nodded – he said he had 'fresh food' [drugs]. He sped off towards a nearest estate and Dawg and I followed quickly. We went into an alleyway and Dawg went in and stood by the stairs. Before he was able to do the deal, the guy who had left the phone box hurried in and handed the runner £10 and a rock was swapped. 'Happy customer' said the runner. Dawg asked to see the rocks first and reassured the runner that he wouldn't take them but wanted to check them. The runner started to get aggressive. Dawg hesitated to make the deal and said he wasn't sure, so the runner got even more frustrated and said 'fucking go elsewhere then' and told us to leave. Dawg refused and the runner got angry. In the process of this, he dropped some of his rocks on the floor and Dawg went to step around them but the runner then said 'don't even fucking think about it' (as he thought Dawg was going to rob him). I started to back away saying 'ok, man, let's cool it'. The runner then accused Dawg of trying to 'fuck with him' and asked him why did he phone him in the first place if he didn't want to deal – Dawg then said he didn't call and this made the runner even more angry [because not only was he wasting his time but he became suspicious] and he reached for his back pocket and half pulled out a knife saying 'I'll fucking slit you now' and half lurched towards Dawg. I backed off further but the runner wasn't interested in what I was doing or what I was saying. Dawg said 'I am not trying to rob you but I am not afraid of you.' Dawg didn't really retaliate but the runner kept threatening him with the knife.

(Field notes)

Most drug deals I observed were either crack rocks, heroin 'bags', or both – known as a 'one-on-one'. Typically, a one-on-one cost between £15 and £20 depending on the quality and size of the crack – the norm was £10 for 0.2 gram for a crack rock. Normally, each drug cost £10 to £15 but some dealers give discounts if purchasing crack and heroin together, while other dealers insisted that the quality of their product should not signify discounts and keep the price for a one-on-one at £20. Either way, these small denominations don't seem to last long:

> £10 would get you a £10 stone, which is about three pipes, very small ones – depends on your crack habit. There might be some people who can smoke a £20 rock in one pipe, depends on your money, what sort of money you got. When I had loads of money, I would smoke loads of crack or inject. But because the way things were in the end, I just got what I could get – sometimes I would get a £10 stone and £10 heroin [a one-on-one].
>
> (Pudge)

There are even a few dealers who sell a one-on-one for £30. These dealers claim their drugs are of the highest quality and only established, known buyers have access to these transactions. Most dealers, by principle, are strict with their charges and rarely permit underpayments. Some crack users estimate there to be as little as 10 per cent cocaine in crack, and indicate that crack is mixed with broken glass, rat poison, talcum powder and various amphetamines. How crack users access supply, however, appears to depend on their hierarchical position in the crack scene. This position seems to be determined by a number of different elements – in particular, the amount of money they can potentially generate and/ or the frequency at which they make transactions for crack (Chapter 5).

Conclusion

This chapter shows that, for a significant period of time, it has been difficult to measure the number of crack users in Rivertown. Furthermore, despite repeated reference to the number of crack users and the increasing problems they pose for treatment services (Chapter 2), local resources to deal with the problem do not seem to have materialised effectively. Some crack users in this book have some experience with these services but, for many, contact is for short periods (Chapter 6; Chapter 8). I begin the findings chapters with an analysis of pathways into crack use and crack careers.

Chapter 4

Becoming a crack cocaine user

Right, years ago, I can't remember how long ago, I was working making tarmacs – and I was earning myself £1,200 a month and I was working overtime. That's why I was getting so much money but I didn't have time to spend it. So what I done is I took a week off. I bought clothes. I was going out but there was still a lot of money left so I didn't know what was I going to do with it. Now, I've already tasted heroin. I've already tasted crack but I liked it so I thought 'right, I'll go and buy myself a little rock' so I bought a £50 rock. It was nice. I was working, yeah? So the rock was nice. Then I took another week off, then another week off, then another week off. Then my boss said to me: 'We don't want you any more. You're not even fucking coming in. You're sacked'. So what I'm trying to say is one minute I'm a working-class citizen and this is how the crack's taken over, do you know what I mean? Then the next thing I know I'm not working any more. Say like you took smoke [crack]. You won't be addicted to it but you'd like it. You would like it. You'd like the feeling. I think the first time when you take it, it's good for sex. You can go on and you can fuck for hours and you can chat; chatting, talk a lot of shit but you're rabbiting on 'Yeah man. This is good'. Then you take another one. Then you take another one, then another one and the next thing you know the tables have turned, and you'll be sitting here [points at me then at his seat] and someone else will be sitting there [points at my seat] asking you questions.

(Cuz)

Introduction

The principal aim of this chapter is to analyse how and why crack users start to use crack. For crack users that I met in this cohort, there tended to be no 'moment' when 'the crack life' became the chosen pathway. This research points to two main pathways into crack use (Brain *et al.*, 1998): through recreational/social/non-dependent drug-using pathways ('recreational' hereafter) and through already-established heroin/opiate pathways ('established' hereafter). Mediating these pathways into crack use are individual decisions (Booth Davies, 1997;

Haines *et al.*, 2009) made under various social-structural (Dunlap, 1992, 1995) and contextual pressures (Dunlap and Johnson, 1992; Parker *et al.*, 1998). These factors play a part in not only the decision to use crack but also subsequent decisions to continue to do so (Evans, 2002; Giddens, 1984) over the course of the crack career (Malchy *et al.*, 2008; Moore and Dietze, 2005). Both pathways have implications for identity construction (Bauman, 2007). This chapter therefore lends some understanding to the process of becoming a crack user (Becker, 1953).

Pathways into crack use

Crack users in this sample do not appear to be a homogeneous drug-using group and crack-using pathways do not always seem to be progressive. In Chapters 1 and 2 we saw how different people often moved swiftly between different levels of use for different reasons. Not everyone progressed to extreme stages of heavy crack use at the same rate. By the same token, there tends to be no moment as such when 'the crack life' becomes the chosen pathway. Many crack users reflect on crack's increased availability which seems to mirror recent shifts towards a consumer society (van Ree, 2002) – characterised by rising affluence, falling working hours, increased time for leisure pursuits, relationship and family pressures. Moreover, consumption is no longer seen to be exclusive but, instead, people find and express their identity in specific patterns of consumption (Abercrombie *et al.*, 1994). Indeed, one particular form of identity expression is through the use of drugs (Miles, 2000), in particular, at a time when drug use has become 'normalised' across various age groups in the UK (Parker *et al.*, 1998; Pearson, 2001). This research shows there are two main pathways into crack use: through recreational pathways and through established pathways. The following section on crack-using pathways accounts for these two different routes.

The recreational pathway

Many crack users who start using crack recreationally reflect that the decision to use crack helps to resolve various individual and social problems. Before trying crack, many feel they had underlying psychological/emotional problems; had experienced family breakdown and bereavement; felt hopeless, guilty and ashamed; had low self-esteem and low levels of confidence; and/or a tendency toward sensation seeking. Some also seem bored of life and are looking for some excitement (Blackman, 1995). For most in this study, it seems to be a complex combination of the above that influences their decision. For recreational users, the decision to use crack over other drugs seems to be that:

1   it is available and many try it in different social contexts – among friends, party and club scene (see Parker *et al.*, 1998; Ward, 2010);
2   the 'high' is appealing and attractive;
3   many are looking for a 'new buzz';

4   it is not instantly addictive and does not need to be consumed daily – unlike heroin;
5   it can be structured around responsibilities such as the working week/family commitments;
6   there is an attraction of the deviant lifestyle that comes with it – crack, status, sex, etc.

Interacting with the rationale to use crack are socio-structural and contextual factors which not only assist in the decision to use crack but also lay foundations for continued use. For example, when Madmax's father died when he was young, the experience of poverty was sharpened. He reflected that he used to 'suppress his feelings' with alcohol from a young age because of his 'rage'. Aged 16, he left school and was expected to help support the family – both emotionally and financially. He needed to find quick, profitable ways of supporting himself and his family. He and his friend quickly realised that there were significant amounts of money to be made in drug dealing since others in similar positions outside of mainstream education were also resorting to such measures. Initially, drug dealing started with heroin but soon moved into cocaine as it became available in the mid-1980s (see Chapter 2):

> It started when I was in secondary school, I had a friend who could get a lot of heroin. He said 'I can get this, we can make some money lads'. So we sat down, and he said 'this is cocaine we are talking about' and we were like 'what?' We were 16–17 and this was in 1985. We set up with a few customers – making £1,000 a night selling cocaine, no heroin, no crack. £60 a gram it was then. I saw the money turning over and I thought 'I am in this'. I wanted the quick money, I wanted an easy life. It was so quick, I liked that. Easy come, easy go.

By the early 1990s, and with the advent of the rave scene, he was operating as a cocaine and ecstasy dealer. He was attracted by the party lifestyle and started to use heavy amounts of cocaine. He said he ran into trouble with the police after 'getting sloppy' with too much 'cocaine in his system' and reconsidered his options after a short prison sentence. When he was released he was keen to get back into drug dealing since he had exhausted legitimate avenues '[a long] time ago'. It was only a matter of months later that his dealing networks introduced him to the 'new ting [thing]':

> Crack came on the scene, on the rave scene. Another friend had a cousin over from Jamaica, we used to flex [hang out], this was my first day of taking crack because we were selling powder at the time and popping 'E's and he said 'you have to stop selling the coke man, we have the new ting' and he brought me down to the toilet. So we are in this dark club, this dungeon … He said have you tried this? I said 'what the fuck' but his face said it all, he blew the

smoke at me – oh my god, the sweet aroma. [Pause] He looked at me and he couldn't talk properly. I hit this fucking thing [smoked it] and all I could hear was bells ringing in my head. I was like oh ... my ... god, it knocked my E for six, the crack rush then. I was like, 'that is what I wanted'. He said it is 'washed rock', same powder, just wash it up. [I] started to learn how to do it myself, then telling everyone that we had a new one on the market. 'Try it in a spliff but I know you'll be calling me back'. The Jamaicans tagged on to my networks. They [the customers] would come out and I was the hustleman, I already had the customers. I was smoking though, I was treating myself even though I was smoking. I was drinking £150 champagne – I thought I want some of that good life. I want some Dom Perignon and Clicquot and shit like that. I want to drink like the big boys. I was living it large.

(Madmax)

Pathways into crack use are also dependent on context and peer associations. For example, Rem had a good upbringing, her mother was a probation officer and a psychiatric nurse and father a social worker. Rem said she 'didn't blame anyone' but couldn't believe she could have been 'so stupid' to get involved with her boyfriend who 'got her into drugs'. Feeling lonely aged 27 and unmotivated by her job, she met a man who introduced her to heroin: one year later she said she was 'smoking crack'. Depressed because of the relationship, she said she attempted to go through detox with her boyfriend who 'promised' to go in when she came out. He did not and she said she 'ended up back on crack two days later'. The flat she had rented for 15 years, after her parents moved back to the US, was accumulating debt and was lost, along with her birth certificate and passport. Without ID, she reasoned that she couldn't claim jobseeker's allowance and couldn't find the 'motivation' to 'go to the US Embassy'.

The experiences of bereavement and family breakdown are also typical for these crack users. When Em's mother died, the family struggled to cope with the loss. Her father turned to alcohol and the family structure started to collapse. At the young age of 14, and finding relations difficult with her father, she started to spend long weekends in London with 'some friends'. As her weekend absences continued, her brother started to experiment with heroin and left the family home. This put further pressure on the family and exacerbated her father's anger and frustration, which increased his propensity to violence against family members. Em increasingly felt there was little to keep her at home. After further visits to London, Em was introduced to a man who was selling crack. The 'first few times' she used crack, she said it was unproblematic. However, because of poor family relations, weekend visits extended into week-long stopovers and, with this, crack use increased. It was not long before she was bingeing on crack for days. Soon after, she was persuaded that sexual favours would earn her larger amounts of crack. By the age of 16, she said she had become homeless and was living in crack houses: 'I had nowhere else to go and I used to sleep in them [crack houses], bath in them, eat in them and take my drugs in them,' she reflected.

Other factors cited for pathways into recreational crack use include exposure to drug use in families and/or pro-drug attitudes among family members. Ish reflected that, at the age of 10:

> I've been in the [bed]room when my brother smokes it [crack] when the smoke comes out and I just liked the smell. My mate got it out one day and I said 'my brother smokes this' and I just liked it and I got on it every day because I was puffing. Every bit of money my mum and dad were giving me I'd spend on crack so that was good.

Here, Lively T reflects on her progression through a range of drugs which, she felt, resulted with experimentation of crack:

> I think it was down to my childhood. My mum and dad used to smoke weed and things like that, and I realise that was what triggered it off. I thought it was okay to smoke, and then weed started onto something else, and it always escalates from one thing to another. I didn't care. I liked it. I liked what it [crack] did to me. I thought I was good.

Many crack users who start using crack recreationally tend to structure it around weekends. G reflected how there were 'some people that go to work and they survive at the weekend on a certain amount [of crack]'. He said: 'they'll either do it from Friday until Saturday, recuperate Sunday and go back to work on Monday, or that might be a scenario once a month.' There doesn't seem to be any linear pattern or timeframe to heavier crack use. BD's recreational crack use was sustained for a considerable amount of time, and it was only when he started to experience relationship problems that things started to change:

> I used crack successfully for fifteen years before anyone even realised that I had a problem. In that time I managed a bar and I lived in Spain. I kept my smoking to weekends, and at that time, you would never have known that I was a drug user. It's only in the last five years that it really got out of control. It took me that long to stop. Some people go from start smoking and six months later they're like crashed; some people are quite successful. I've met rabbis, doctors, police officers, nurses [who smoke crack].

(G)

Although no one in the sample was in this 'transition' phase of crack use at the time of fieldwork, a few recalled how, at this stage, they perceived crack use to be a 'reward' or 'treat'. MRS 'liked the buzz' when she first tried it but 'used to leave it': 'I could do it that way for a while,' she said. For some recreational users, there is an attraction to the crack lifestyle and what comes with it – the crack, the status, and the secrecy. For these reasons they felt it was important to keep their crack use hidden from their family and friend networks:

Some people go from bingeing to crashing straight to nothing to living in crack houses. But most people will start off bingeing – maybe once a month. Most people will start off very lightly smoking. They'll meet someone who smokes and they'll have a phone number, and they'll do the odd little smoke here and there. They'll phone someone up and that person will deliver to them but most people who deliver only work certain times of the night; like twelve o'clock at night until two in the morning, something like that. After that it's pretty hard to find someone to deliver. So what will happen is one day they'll smoke over and still have money left over and want to smoke some more but their man's off (the person they know – maybe one or two – is off) and that's when they come to south London then and, the first time, they'll probably buy something on the front line; might get something quicker but smaller, might get ripped off, yeah? After this has happened a couple of times – sometimes they get some, sometimes they get ripped off – they'll probably meet someone who says 'Yeah, but I know somewhere I can take you where you can get something' and that will be their first introduction to crack houses and they'll be taken there, they'll be introduced and whoever the hustler is might come in, 'I've got a geezer who's never been to Ends before, tell him they're 20 pound stones', and they'll be 10 pound stones obviously, or it will be buy one, get one free, and that's your first introduction. This is a good idea, I can come here and get my dick up these women. Apparently, there's a ready supply of cocaine. I've not got to be dangerous at home. This is alright. It saves me sitting in my house being all paranoid about my girlfriend coming home or anyone finding any evidence. So you might get into the pattern of smoking it at home but for the last bit you'll got to an End somewhere and have a bit of a laugh. Then you'll get to the stage where 'well, I might as well just go straight to the Ends. If I'm at an End I can buy half a sixteenth you know once I get to know them'. And that's when from when you start smoking crack you pretty much know that's when you're on the slippery slope. Because when you find one you soon find out where there's others and you'll meet people in there and people there are obviously going to entice you to spend. A lot of them that's their whole ambition is to entice you to spend so they can have a smoke because you're new to the game, aren't you? And the first time you play any game you don't know any of the rules and any foul that can be committed so it's quite easy for you to get taken advantage of is the best way to put it – half-ripped off. The thing is if you rip a man off £10 you rip a man off for £10 that's all you're going to get but if you can – a lot of the time it's all about – 'I'm your friend. I'll look after you. This is what I say. Follow me. Just sit there. I'll get this for you.' You're smoking your stone, you don't want to be running around. If someone's running back and forth to the dealer's for you and he might come to you and the price was £20, so make it £15 now, so you're still going to give him a smoke, you're still going to make a fiver on him and then, sooner or later, you're start buying yourself and start going to Ends yourself and, once you start doing that, then that's when you've got … it's like having twenty-four hours sex on tap. You're starting taking advantage. Then you start abusing. Then it'll start abusing you. That's pretty much the circle of it. Obviously people enter at different levels … but, sooner or later, you're going to end up probably in crash in some way. It's all going to go a bit pear-shaped because, even if you've got some money then you can just smoke whenever you want – there's no barrier. So the more money you've got the faster your life will come tumbling down because if you have no value to your money. You know if you're on three grand a week and you've got fifty grand in the bank, you're spending a hundred pounds here and a couple of hundred there it doesn't seem nothing but you can only maintain that for so long, because you know you can spend three grand a week and, even if you're earning three grand a week, you must have outgoings for a grand a week. That's how people live. … Some people, like I said, will crash very quickly – other people won't. It depends what else is going on. A lot of it will depend on who they have to hide it from. If they haven't got to hide it from anyone – if they're not in a relationship. If they're married it'll obviously take longer because they can't keep disappearing for [binges for] two, three or four days at a time. Some people who are smoking pipe are the exception because if you have the money you won't go out and spend a hundred pounds. If you've got like two grand you're out of two grand easily – or a grand – because you're so tired that you can't get any sleep. That can take a day or two days. These are big chunks out of a seven-day week out of someone's life. I think that makes it quite … I don't know. It's a very deceiving drug. Unlike heroin where you can have physical addictions and physical signs like track marks, foils you know – the physical state of someone where they can lose their appetite – the effects of crack are very, very short lived. You're high for a very short time and the comedowns are comparatively sharp – a very rapid comedown but for a comparatively short period. You know you can be awake for three days, have a good night's sleep, wake up the next day and be eighty per cent back to what you were before. If someone's using heroin they're stoned for eight or nine hour periods. If I'm smoking crack and I know you're coming around in an hour's time I can stop smoking, have a bath and when you come around to all intents and purposes be normal. You don't have that kind of rapid recovery from other drugs. Therefore it's very, very, easy to hide.

(BD)

Many reflected that the use of crack, at this stage, starts to provide some regular, but transient, stability, away from pressing life issues. A few said they use 'nicknames' to avoid being discovered and to avert blemishes to the core self identity: 'Another thing is that no one really knows people, so they stay anonymous so no one snitches on them, so people don't know where I am from and they only know me by nickname,' said Iverson. For some users, crack seems to remain secret not only because of the potential stigma attached to it but also because of the social shame it may bring on the individual if people are aware they are involved in that lifestyle.

An exploration of becoming a crack user follows a short examination into pathways into crack use for established users.

The established pathway

Those who are already heavily engaged in using drugs such as heroin represent those who start to use crack through established pathways. Many of these people said they had already experienced past abuses. They had, for example, grown up among families with drug or alcohol problems; suffered from learning or mental health issues; experienced difficulties in mainstream education and work, and/or relationship problems; been imprisoned; had been involved in or were involved in crime, prostitution and/or homelessness. As a consequence, most of this group are already socially stigmatised and excluded. This group seem to use crack to augment existing drug use practices. They seem to do this because:

1   the crack 'high' is appealing;
2   crack is perceived to add an additional 'buzz' to their current drug-using repertoire;
3   crack seems to complement already quite fatalistic attitudes they have towards their life.

However, most in this cohort have learnt that heavy/binge crack use has negative consequences which is why they tended to 'stabilise' themselves after crack sessions with strong alcohol, cannabis, heroin or prescription drugs. Those already involved in established drug use also make individual decisions to engage in crack use. However, the nature of this group's precarious socio-structural position also seems to contribute to their crack use. Crack users in this group say that the decision to use crack is made possible through the increased availability of the drug through existing heroin markets, and through drug user and homeless peer influences. Indeed, at the time of the fieldwork, crack and heroin were both equally prevalent and, during most observed transactions, one drug was not normally sold without the other as Philo illustrated:

[Then in the early 1990s] It was unusual for dealers to be selling both, whereas nowadays [2005] it's the norm. Dealers have adapted to the market, basically. I was a heroin addict and got into crack. I liked speedballs. I prefer powder coke and heroin, that's my favourite drug. I got into injecting crack when I couldn't get hold of any powder coke one time, and that got me more than anything had ever been able to get me before. And now I even got so into my crack I even detoxed off heroin on crack, you know, because I was paranoid … Back in the early nineties it was difficult to score crack and heroin from the same dealers, so usually sort of, you know, one person would be selling crack someone else would be selling heroin.

Interviewees felt that drug dealers in London quickly saw the potential lucrative business of crack cocaine and this, they felt, resulted in a shift from heroin use to heroin and crack use (Brain *et al.*, 1998; Harocopos *et al.*, 2003). Big T said he was introduced to crack through 'tasters' and 'freebies' from dealers: 'I remember when I started [using crack]. I was offered it free. You could buy heroin and get crack for free. Buy one, get one free! That's how cheap crack was.' Most crack and heroin users say they start to use crack after they have developed a tolerance for heroin. Crack, they say, adds an 'extra buzz' to their drug-using experience:

> Now whoever takes crack and heroin likes taking them together but a couple of years ago, it was just like with the heroin and then the crack or the crack and then the heroin – not together. That's why now. I don't know what it is now. People are going crazy. They're going crazy looking for the buzz. They're looking for the buzz. That's my word on it. The bus that never stops. It's always going. It never stops.
>
> (Cuz)

For a few, like Alwight, crack and heroin, or speedballing, seems to signify a deeper, more destructive form of drug use:

ALWIGHT: *I would describe crack as kind of sexual feeling – it is orgasmic. It is very powerful – you feel very powerful. It doesn't last very long. It is like an orgasm, an intense high but straight away you start coming down.*

DAN: *What about a speedball?*

ALWIGHT: *It's just something I ended up doing. It is more destructive – it is kind of like I have lost the plot. You can imagine, if you take a powerful opiate [heroin] which is a downer and a powerful upper [crack] the effects are hard to describe, you don't know whether you are coming or going basically. It is very intense.*

In another example, Shake said he was 20 when he first smoked heroin 'on the foil'. He first started injecting heroin as his tolerance for the drug increased. After using his arms for ten years he said he 'switched to bigger needles'. However, he was introduced to crack through a dealer and started smoking crack pipes to complement the heroin 'buzz'. As his tolerance grew once again, and through peer influences on the streets, he started to mix crack with heroin for injection:

SHAKE: *I booted heroin first and it escalated to the point where I started injecting [heroin]. Then I smoked crack on the foil but after a while I started injecting. So now I do both because it is better.*

DAN: *How long does that last [the crack]?*

SHAKE: *The crack lasts about 5–10 minutes. The heroin has no effect on how long the crack buzz lasts but the heroin kicks in at just the right moment to bring you down so you feel ok. A lot of people smoke crack and use heroin to come down to ease themselves.*

DAN: *Why do you speedball then? What is so special?*

SHAKE: *The person gets immune to using it so they use it intravenously. The effects are the same but my immune system has a higher tolerance. Injecting enters the body more quickly. I can only feel a buzz by injecting. Smoking a [crack] pipe won't give me any feeling.*

A few, however, are not bothered about what drugs they take. In essence, their aim is to be intoxicated regardless. Shake also said: 'There are a lot of people around here, not just people that use both like me, but crack only users. I am a multi-user – I use anything: heroin, crack, cannabis, alcohol – anything.' These crack users indicate that, having developed a reliance on crack, many see increases in drug spending. For example, Brummie (aged 28), who grew up in care, was 16 when he first started using heroin. By the age of 20, he was homeless and had started injecting heroin. Aged 21, he said was injecting crack and heroin. He said he was introduced to crack when he was 'hanging about homeless' and the people he was with were 'piping [crack]'. Although he had 'heard' of crack he hadn't tried it: 'Er ... I was cooking some brown and this geezer says "do you want a bit of white to put in?" I said "yeah ok". See what it was like and it was alright.' This had implications for his drug use expenditure:

DAN: *So how much money did you need for brown before crack came on the scene?*

BRUMMIE: *£50, or 2–3 bags.*

DAN: *So when you started speedballing, how much did you have to make a day?*

BRUMMIE: *£100 at least. Say Sunday, Monday, Tuesday, I don't get much money but after Wednesday, Thursday and Friday, it gets a bit easier.*

Similarly, Bradda moved from Portugal to the UK to try to stay clean from heroin in 1998. He was, however, quickly thrust back into drug-using contexts while staying with a group of homeless people in a squat. He was subsequently introduced to crack:

> I learnt with people that was already here and I went to fix, for a fix with them, to the same place and I saw them mixing the brown and the white and I asked them what's, what kind of buzz do you get? And they told me you get the buzz of the white and after, straight after you come down with the brown. And I said 'let me try', I try it and I say 'fucking buzz, fucking buzz'. That's why it's so fucking difficult to come out [recover from].
>
> (Bradda)

In these two short sections, it is evident that pathways into crack use seem to be mediated by individual decisions which are embedded in social conditions and shaped by complex socio-structural and contextual factors. The process of becoming a crack user, however, has consequences for crack user identities, the trajectory of crack careers and ways out (Chapter 8). In the next section, the process of how crack use and crack user identities evolve is examined.

Becoming a crack user: the implications for self identity

The process of becoming a crack user is not simply a process whereby the 'drug engulfs the drug user' but rather how crack users start to make sense of who they have become. Their decisions to use crack and subsequent decisions to continue seem to arise from interfaces with various social structures over time (Giddens, 1984). Indeed, there seems to be no linear pattern or timeframe from heavier binge crack use to continual crack use. For those who are introduced to crack through sex work, homelessness and other heavy drug use networks, crack use seems to augment their deviant and drug-using identities. For example, Pudge, who started using heroin before crack, was homeless when he first was introduced to crack through a drug dealer. It was not long before crack had also become part of his drug-using lifestyle:

> I think the day-to-day use of crack for me was that I would get up, get money and go and buy £20 bag of heroin and £20 rocks, use that and immediately after that get a fag and something to eat, then I would be out stealing money again and that would be it until 11pm at night from 10 in the morning – constant all day long. Chasing this and chasing that, chasing the crack.
>
> (Pudge)

A different identity transformation appeared to take place in those who progressed through recreational pathways. This cohort tended to keep their crack use secret from family and friends because of crack's illegal and deviant social image. Keeping it hidden seems to help them evade personal feelings of guilt and shame of their activities (Goffman, 1963), and, as a consequence, may have promoted early habits of self-denial – the fact that they use crack and the extent to which they use it. Some associate its use with a different identity:

BAZ: *[You start off] By smoking with normal people, you go to pub to drink like you get away from your missus or your surroundings. You know, maybe, it is a party, just a different social scene. In the beginning, it is like that.*

DAN: *It is quite settled, recreational.*

BAZ: *Sometimes you might live with your wife or girlfriend so you cover it over and go somewhere where she don't know and you can do that there [smoke crack in a crack house]. Maybe you have kids. Until you get deeper, you realise you are in the wrong place. This could be a crack house, a crack house is nothing, it is just a room, a space in time you can hang out, pay your rent in crack. No one is concerned about you, so you can forget about that. People go there 9–5 like a release, like people go to a pub. If you can work and sustain it that way, you are ok but in due course, all that is going to disappear because it will overwhelm you, you get bigger, you take more, the more you have, the more you spend, £1,000 will go in a second.*

When recreational crack users increase levels of crack use, this often leads to increased interactions with others in the crack scene (Chapter 5). Exposure to this space seems to put crack users at greater distance from conventional identities and they increasingly seem influenced by other deviant actors, their cultural practices and the environments of the crack scene (Chapter 5; Duff, 2007).

For example, Iverson started using crack recreationally when he was employed and had a family. In interview he said he spent nights away, increasingly obsessed with the status he had developed in a crack house. This excerpt shows how the deviant identity is confirmed by significant others who he perceives to be 'below him' in the crack scene hierarchy:

IVERSON: *The smoking gave me an ego, so I become the king and they become my subjects and I need them around for the drug to work for me because that is what the drug gives me, it brings out your personality, it brings it out more, if you have low self-esteem, the drug will reduce it to that, if you are confident, it will multiply it, if you have psychotic problems, then you think things are happening, so these kind of people I would control, 'sit down, there is nothing chasing you' and they would listen to me because the drug is coming from me even though I am not the dealer, I am the distributor, the link ... Like say we are smoking, in our house, we used to smoke from left to right and you come in and start blazing, you will get beaten for that. You shouldn't do that, you should ask first. Maybe someone else will to gain favour from me, 'don't do that, don't disrespect the man. The man is sharing out, wait your turn'. Then they are sucking up to you, trying to put out your pipe and everything even though it is not what you want but you get used to it.*

DAN: *So you develop a behaviour to respond to it.*

IVERSON: *Yes, you need it to make the drug work for you. You get praised, they [Low Life] say 'we have been worried about you' and you think these are your friends and they are using friendly words to them. Some people might give but you never get back, because none of them give you it back so you work on your instincts but they are never right in these situations because you're under a false sense of security.*

For reasons of new status and hierarchy, many former recreational users express narratives of enjoyment early in their recreational use; that is, it is both exciting as well as pleasurable, and gives them a sense of personal empowerment. For many, lengthy binge crack sessions at weekends are not problematic. First, it is not perceived as addiction because it is not used every day. Second, it is not reflecting the deviancy of their actions (Lemert, 1951). Some also say that because there are no signs of 'addiction', as they see it, it is easy to justify what they do and continue to use crack:

It's going to be harder with crack or rock addicts because remember as I said they are in denial already and they don't realise that they're just as bad as the heroin addict. They think they're one up. 'No, no, no I'm alright' because, well I'd say as much as ninety per cent of them wake up with no withdrawal symptoms or anything like that and they take that as a thing that they're better and they're not better. They have got a problem just like people who take brown. They have issues that need addressing. It's to get them to realise this and it's not going to be easy.

(G)

While many struggle to locate the precise reasons for increasing crack use, there appears to be another shift in levels of use when users start to perceive crack as a 'reward' or 'treat'. Here, the narratives also seem to shift, and perhaps as a means to deflect responsibility for their actions and escalating circumstances, they start to 'blame the drug' for life's mishaps. This is perhaps unsurprising because the hegemonic rhetoric of government and media on crack use – and other drug use – suggests that it is the drug that is responsible for the misery and destruction of the user (Booth Davies, 1997; Reinarman and Levine, 1997, 2004). Indeed, many crack users in this study start to ascribe similar beliefs. Recreational users reflect on their 'crack addiction' as if it is something that has invaded their bodies. 'It was gradual,' Shy H said. 'I'll tell you, about a year, it could have been. I can't say exactly. It gradually creeped up on me.' Lively T, who is a sex worker in recovery, also seems to suggest it (crack) 'crept' into her life:

LIVELY T: *Yeah. I did it [crack] once and I liked it that first time. I wouldn't say that got me addicted to it. It's just like you do it again. You start it on a weekend. You do it occasionally on a Saturday or a Sunday as a good thing and it just creeps up into your life more and more without you realising it.*

DAN: *Really?*

LIVELY T: *Every time you've got money the first thing you think about is that sweet feeling and what it did to you – was crack – until you buy more and that weekend becomes four days a week and then it becomes five days a week … And then you're fucked. You're so bad on it that you'll do anything for it.*

DAN: *And you didn't notice this happening?*

LIVELY T: *Yeah, but I didn't care.*

DAN: *You didn't notice that you were using more?*

LIVELY T: *Yeah, but I didn't care. I liked it. I liked what it did to me. I thought I was good. I used to brag about it.*

The description above about escalation of use appears to be placed on the drug, signifying a shift from personal responsibility to passive responsibility (Maruna, 2001). At this stage, some described how crack binge sessions blur, and as a consequence started to interfere with their conventional routines, affecting their commitment to family, work and housing and payment of bills. Here, Bruv reflects on the process of drifting into this lifestyle:

That was when I started to smoke in the early 90s. Then, I didn't know who to get it from. I used to travel all the way to [south London] to get it. There was a time when I stopped. I smoked in a spliff first, then freebased, then piped. The pipe is the most intense ... Before it was just me and a few people. They would come over, there would just be a few of us. We'd be up all night. I lost track of time and missed things in my life, work, appointments – especially with the council. Now I guess it just escalated because from then on ... well, last year was the worst. It was the roughest time I have had. I was committing crimes, I did three months in prison and I was homeless. I was expected to phone all these places. I was fucking homeless ... When I first used it, I could wait, you know, I could wait until 10 at night or something. I could go without it all day. Never. Now, as soon as I get it, I open it. It is out of control. I normally smoke about £150 a day and nothing else. I started to notice me using it more on my payday, it would be my treat. But I would still fill myself with food.

(Bruv)

Some reflected that increased 'rewards' or 'treats' are connected to coping with feeling unmotivated in work, pressure in relationships and family problems, coupled with the appeal of the crack binge. This reward mindset seems to become more prevalent, with users believing they deserved more 'treats' for having 'been good' without it for a few days. However, inevitably, some of these treat sessions develop into a cycle of repetitive heavy binges of varying lengths, with short rests in between. With one foot in the conventional world, where some seem to feel a little redundant and bored, it seems liberating and empowering to know that they have one foot in another world where they have higher status and a new identity. For example, when Iverson progressed from heavy binge weekends into occasional weekly treats, he started to steal from his employers:

IVERSON: *Some people used to gather round me because I was different, I was too honest for my own good. It was unusual for someone to say 'I will be there at four o'clock and I will have you two things [crack rocks]' and I would be there, I would come religiously. But other people didn't deliver [were unreliable] so that is how I got people, do you see, I have got you now. You are mine.*

DAN: *Only temporarily.*

IVERSON: *Well sometimes I would promise two [crack rocks], then give three because I want to be the big man and I have ten things [crack rocks], and I have given away seven. So then we have a competition to see who can stand the longest [smoke the most] so I can say, I can handle it more than you, I have more money than you. People come to you, you get their attention.*

DAN: *That is quite a responsibility.*

IVERSON: *You have to function on all sorts of levels, in the real world. You have to show face in there [crack scene], to the outside, to the workplace, put your mask on, take one off, put another on, take another off. But in the end you forget who you are.*

Sadly, during the fieldwork, Iverson dropped out of rehab; he found it diffi-cult to face up to the things he had done in the past (Chapter 8). Continuous binge weekends and weekday treats make some tired and unmotivated to maintain aspects of conventional lifestyles. They appear to yearn for the next crack session:

> Gradually, gradually, gradually my job got worse. I couldn't get up in the morning and I'd make excuses. I actually let the tyres down on the van because they had a puncture. I couldn't go to work and the man had to come around and sort them out, so I could have another hour's shut-eye.
>
> (JC)

An internal psychological battle seemed to develop whereby crack users asso-ciated the 'new identity' as the drug:

> I thought I had it under control, remember. I'm not noticing what it's doing. I think, 'Oh, all right, today I'm not going to smoke, and today I never really smoked'. You haven't got it under control then, have you? And that's how it creeps up on you. I'm telling you [talking to an imaginary crack pipe as her eyes light up] 'You're not going to stop smoking for too long. I want you to smoke me tomorrow. You've had one day's grace' so that's how it started to creep on.
>
> (Funky D)

In this way, some recreational users seem to divert responsibility for their actions on the drug (Sykes and Matza, 1957). This appears to mark an important period in becoming a crack user because it is during these cycles that crack users lose significant stability in their lives as a result of family disownment/break up, loss of work, eviction, arrest, conviction, imprisonment, presentation in rehab (Becker, 1963; Ray, 1964). This also seems to mark the discovery of the deviance of their crack use, and these processes and/or a combination of these processes, act as a catalyst to reorganise their self identities as a means of response to the social reac-tion around them (Lemert, 1951). In most cases, this results in increased crack use. Here, Def Jam recalls how her crack use increased after her children were taken into care. The action to protect her children may have been necessary, but note how the crime control agencies also play a role in the confirmation of the deviant and stigmatised identity through degradation ceremonies (Garfinkel, 1956):

> [After long binge periods of up to four days] I ended up losing my kids. Well when I say losing them they went into care because I was smoking one partic-ular morning and I wanted more money for drugs. He [ex-boyfriend] pulled a knife on me. I was fighting with him to try and get this knife off him but I was scared. He ended up getting caught but I did not stab him but the point is I went around there and it would not have happened if I hadn't gone there so the police came. The neighbours heard the commotion and the police came

and arrested me and I got done [convicted] for wounding and then while I was in the cells they took the kids because I was in there for four days on a four-day lie down. Then, in the end, I got back. I couldn't get the kids back well, to be honest with you, it wasn't that I couldn't get the kids back I was too busy smoking drugs and it just got worse and worse.

(Def Jam)

What she said she hated most was being portrayed in court as a 'dirty person' and how the authorities made the case 'look better for them'. In an effort to get her children back, she attempted rehab several times but dropped out on all three occasions within a few weeks, finding it difficult to face up to her past. She left one rehab prematurely when pregnant. She reflected that her experiences with social services had made it difficult for her to 'trust people'. She resented the way the authorities denied her access to her children despite her attempts to get clean. Without understanding the full implications of her actions, she said she signed a declaration that meant her daughter was put into care abroad. This only made things worse, and when she found out she had cancer, her life deteriorated further. Her mental health suffered and her crack use increased:

I just thought I was going to die. I was still smoking drugs and still putting my kids through loads. In the end I just wanted to die to tell you the truth. I used to go to train stations onto train lines and lie down and when the trains came I used to get scared and get up so it wasn't that I really wanted to die it's just that's how I felt. That there's no point because you're going around and around in a circle because I tried to come off it [crack] a few times and I had tried rehab.

As her crack use increased, over time she was arrested more frequently, which truncated her funding abilities from shoplifting and pushed her towards sex work to fund crack use:

DEF JAM: *What happened was I was on the run that's how that came about. The police wanted me. They wanted me for … I done it [sold sex to fund crack use] one time before that and then I stopped. Then when I started up full-time properly was when the police were looking for me and I didn't want to get caught. I was on the run for ages so I started doing prostitution.*

DAN: *That's why you couldn't go into shops – because it was too dangerous and you might have got caught?*

DEF JAM: *Yeah. I started doing the prostitution because you didn't have to sign on [at the social security office] and the police couldn't find me. They couldn't keep up with me.*

Experiencing these processes also prompts the interaction with significant others in and around them which also confirms the identity. In the context of this research, this was within the social space of the crack scene (Chapter 5). A further reaction to this identity shift seems to be the necessity to 'maintain face' among the wider community and others participating in the crack scene. This seems to augment the denial many have constructed around their crack use (Goffman, 1959, 1963). Most blame their fall from conventional life on the 'drug' so therefore most see these manoeuvres as necessary to avoid feelings of guilt and shame (Giddens, 1991) and as some attempt to retain self-respect (Bourgois, 1995). Some, like Cuz, employ ways of 'showing face' – that they are in control of their world – when really this appears to be self-denial of their position.

CUZ: *In a whole day I was up until God knows what time because I was staying in this like bins because I had nowhere to go. What I first left the rehab I stayed in a crack house and the crack house did my head in because every second the door was knocking, the door was knocking and people were in and out, in and out and I couldn't handle it. So I left there and I stayed in this it was like a basement in a block of flats where people put their rubbish in; like it was two rooms but the block of people didn't use the second room. They just used the first room. They just like opened the door and put their garbage there so what I done was I cleared that room and I used to lay where the door was and if anyone came in they'd have to push me so I'd wake up. So I felt safe. I found a quilt. Someone threw a quilt out in the second-hand shops and a pillow. I found it, wrapped it up, put it in a black bin bag and took it with me.*

DAN: *But then you had to look decent when you went out [to shoplift]?*

CUZ: *I did. I looked a lot smarter than I do now. Even my probation officer used to say that to me. I know it's weird because what I used to do was in the morning I used to go into the hospital every morning, have a strip wash. I used to wear a suit. When I came into this hostel I came in, in a suit and I used to go in and change my shirt every day and change my clothes every day. I used to nick seconds [second-hand clothes] because you can get some decent ...*

DAN: *Really?*

CUZ: *Not swap it. I used to just nick it. I used to take the shirt, throw the shirt – because like it's dirty now. I used to throw it away and put a nice ironed one on. It's alright. It's ironed. Have you ever been in a second-hand shop?*

DAN: *Yeah, yeah.*

CUZ: *It's alright. You can get some decent clothes from the second-hand shop nowadays – like really decent stuff and I used to just nick a suit or nick whatever I needed. I used to do this every day. That's why I used to look smart. Even my probation officer said to me 'Cuz, are you sure you're homeless?' When I walked into my spot worker [outreach homeless worker] she didn't believe that I was homeless. She's going to me 'Cuz, are you sure you're homeless?' I'm going 'yeah I am'. The reason why I need to do this is because of what I was up to – that I used to go out stealing because I needed to look smart to get my drugs, do you know what I mean?*

DAN: *Yeah, yeah.*

CUZ: *So that's why I had to look smart and when my spot worker found me – because I told her where I was – and she half-believed me. She came around about two/three o'clock in the morning and I was up smoking crack and she came up and she then realised that I am homeless and then she found me [a hostel] so I was on the street for three months because they didn't believe that I was homeless because I was smart because everyone's got an image of a person. If you're homeless then you're a tramp. Because I know a lot of people and I didn't want people to know that I'm on the street. I don't know – that's how I am – I was embarrassed.*

If this image isn't maintained, feelings of uselessness and shame are experienced and may be compounded by criminal convictions but also significant personal losses, through family and friend support frameworks; accommodation; erosion of self-esteem, self-worth, self-respect and dignity (Box, 1981). When Lively T started taking crack, she started robbing people. She felt quite guilty and ashamed of these actions because they contravened individual and social morals.

LIVELY T: *Yeah, whereas that thing before when you're robbing … you're robbing people and things like that and you're conscious. My conscience kicked in and started hurting me for what I was doing to people and how I would feel if it was done to me.*
DAN: *So did that hit you, when you were in the nick?*
LIVELY T: *Yeah.*

However, some seem to continue to attribute these experiences to the drug. They think it is drug that has led them down a more precarious pathway in which, as they see it, they are committing more serious offences, involving themselves in greater risk practices and neglecting themselves and others. When life's poor decisions are reflected upon (Giddens, 1991), this appears only to lead to increased crack use:

> When I lost my two boys I started to feel lonely and that's when I really became an addict because I thought: Fuck it. I'm living my life around crack because I couldn't give a shit. Nothing else. And I smoked around the clock. The next day – I was like a robot.
>
> (Funky D)

Crack users return to crack use when troubles resurface because it is – and has been for them – available and they appear to have constructed its use to resolve problems (Young, 1971). Yet, for recreational users at this stage, it seems to become part of the core of their identity. For example, while interviewing Scruff in a park, our discussion moved towards understanding the daily circumstances of crack use:

SCRUFF: *No. I wouldn't say that. It's just all part of their routine. It's all part of the …*

DAN: *… ritual?*

SCRUFF: *Yes ritual. That's a perfect word for it – ritual because that's what it is. It is a ritual. As I said to you the other day you'll find that people very often with a lot of users the quality of the actual drug they're using will become irrelevant to a lot of them. It doesn't matter. They don't give a shit. That's not the point. It's more the ritual.*

DAN: *Really? Ritual rather than the drug?*

SCRUFF: *Yes. Absolutely yes. As I was saying to this guy, 'don't buy it off of him. It's pure shit' which and I wasn't lying, it wasn't crack. I don't know what it fucking was but it wasn't crack and he said 'I don't give a fuck' because part of the ritual is going to a dealer, meeting the dealer, scoring, using.*

DAN: *Do you not see yourself taking part in this ritual?*

SCRUFF: *No. Why do you?*

DAN: *Do I?*

SCRUFF: *Do you see me?*

DAN: *No. It's not for me to say though.*

SCRUFF: *Why?*

DAN: *Because it isn't.*

SCRUFF: *It's a fake world anyway. So therefore why not? It's as much for you to create as it is for me to. You're part of it.*

DAN: *I'm just trying to make sense of it.*

SCRUFF: *Yeah but you are part of it. You are part of my thing. Do you understand? Therefore it is …*

DAN: *… it is for me to say?*

SCRUFF: *Absolutely. You are within that circle now.*

The shift in the structure of the identity also appears to have implications for the individual's ontology. Ontological goals (Giddens, 1991) also seem to shift from conventional means to discourses of social exchanges in the crack scene (Chapter 5; Preble and Casey, 1969). Scruff continues:

SCRUFF: *They're [crack users] in a fantasy world and this has become their life. This is their fantasy world [using crack and other drugs].*

DAN: *Fantasy world?*

SCRUFF: *Yeah. This has become their purpose. This is the main thing in their life so they're inventing a need to learn about it.*

DAN: *Experiment? Explore?*

SCRUFF: *Knowledge about it. The more you know about it – like it's a beneficial thing. You know how to mix the brown. You know how to get the best possible hit off the pipe. So fucking what? It's not something you need to know. It's not what anyone needs to know. If someone thinks they need to sober up might convince themselves that the best way to smoke will be on a glass pipe and the best way to do it is this way and that way and people crush it up into powder and other people say it has to be in a lump. It's just all in their head. Whatever you've created as a necessity to yourself. You're not happy until you've done that. That's what you've created for yourself and that becomes your objective and unless you achieve that objective each day then you're not happy and once they've achieved it your objective or one of your goals then you're happy now.*

So when shame and guilt are realised, they seem to become a core part of self identity, and these feelings are often internalised (Bourdieu, 1984). Consequently, for some this appears to start to confirm who they now are and, for some, crack has now become awkwardly entangled with different emotions:

A crack user can always find an excuse. I could always find an excuse to use. I don't know if I told you last time. If I was sad it was to make me happy, if I'm happy it's to celebrate; if I'm poor it's all I can do with my money; if I have money it's to celebrate that I've got some. I can always find a reason to use, you know?

(BD)

By the time I met them, many of the users had amassed criminal convictions, were homeless, and had exhausted significant family and friend networks: predominantly surviving only in the precarious world of the crack scene (Chapter 5). In that world, they are increasingly vulnerable to crime control strategies and hostile social policies (Chapter 6). Therefore, the risks of their actions are amplified (Rhodes *et al.*, 2007) and, taken together this seems to increase the chances of health neglect and involvement in risk behaviours (Farmer, 1997; Wilkinson, 2006). This also seems to be because of the cultural practices that they start to assimilate as a result of participation in the crack scene. However, because crack use, for most, has become such a central feature of their life, its use appears to supersede 'safe' decision-making. For example, 'experiencing the crack buzz' is given precedence over the potential risks and dangers of various crack-using techniques. In this conversation, which summarised some emerging findings from the study, Cuz and I discuss how these dangers might surface:

DAN: *Crack users have to burn the toxics off foil before smoking heroin.*
CUZ: *Yeah.*
DAN: *Or before smoking crack.*
CUZ: *Yeah.*
DAN: *If you burn the toxins in the foil cylinder in which you inhale the smoke you're doing a lot of damage to your neck ...*
CUZ: *... and your chest.*
DAN: *Because of the hot smoke, yeah?*
CUZ: *Yeah, plus you're holding it in.*
DAN: *So that does more damage?*

CUZ: *Yeah, but when you hold it in it's for the buzz. You're thinking it might give you a little extra more buzz. I don't know. When you see me smoking it I'm like this [simulates crack-smoking position] and then I blow it back through the tube and I'll always blow it back through the tube.*

DAN: *Why?*

CUZ: *To collect [excess crack] and then I've got something else to smoke. When that's finished on the foil then that tube − I'll open that tube up − and I've got a load of ... recycling.*

DAN: *Recycling? Blow back through tube. I've seen people do that − open up the tube and smoke it with another tube.*

CUZ: *Yeah.*

DAN: *And if they're desperate they'll do it again.*

CUZ: *Say like now I've got a couple of lines off the foil and I've smoked that. That foil − I'll make that foil into a tube, then open the other tube up and smoke that.*

DAN: *Yeah I've seen that. I don't know why I didn't record that before.*

Yet, such strategies to prolong use and to 'enjoy the buzz' appear to have potentially harmful consequences. Similar behaviours are noted among crack injectors. Indeed, some suggest that injecting crack by itself or with heroin destroyed their veins quicker than injecting heroin alone. While they attribute this to the crystallisation of crack in the veins thereby blocking them, observations indicate that others seem convinced that they had not injected the crack and, as with crack smokers, are attempting to get as much from the 'crack buzz' as possible. Therefore, a few crack users seem to increase the number of flushes they apply to the injecting area. This, combined with complications of finding veins, using the same area, and repeated attempts made for potentially harmful behaviour. On returning to Scruff:

He pulled down his trousers revealing the numerous scabs and bruises from injecting. He had one main abscess from months ago that had congealed into a huge scab − it was purple underneath. His legs were all swollen from the DVT and he had no socks on because his feet swell up. He had varicose veins where the blood couldn't get through. He said he knew he was making it worse by injecting in his leg. He started trying to find a vein in the knee area and crouched to force the veins to come up [to the surface of the skin]. It looked as if he had been there [injected there] earlier today or yesterday as the wound looked fresh. He withdrew it as he had no luck from the knee so he then pulled his trousers down further to the upper section of his left leg − he had to crouch again to force the veins to the surface. He put the needle in several times at a 40 degree (or so) angle then withdrew it − he had no luck. He searched around on the same leg for another spot. He then switched legs. This time he had better luck as within a few seconds of looking in the same sort of area he got a sort of slow influx of dark red blood. He drew it [the syringe] back to check [that he had the vein] then put his thumb on the needle and pressed the needle into his leg. He withdrew and injected several times. He left the needle there for about 10–15 seconds after and withdrew it and did his trousers up.

(Field notes)

Increasing involvement in health neglect and risk behaviours appears to be located within key turning points in crack careers and crack user identities. For example, my field notes recorded this event between Blood and Dawg in January 2005. Blood, unskilled in finding veins for injection, needed Dawg to inject him with heroin to bring him down from the crack high:

Blood had no clue how to inject but he had seen Dawg prepare the brown in a spoon.[1] The problem was that Blood managed to prepare it but 'skin popped' the needle [in the past] and didn't get the vein. As a result, he got half the feeling he should have and the skin pop left an abscess on his arm.

(Field notes)

On this occasion, Blood and Dawg were smoking crack pipes before Blood solicited Dawg's help. After a wander around the room, aimlessly picking things up and putting them back in the same place – as a result of smoking crack – Dawg felt he was ready to administer the heroin injection. The needle did not affect Blood in the first instance because blood came into the needle quite quickly after Dawg had poked around under the skin for a few seconds. However, Blood was still unsure that the vein had been found and said he had a bad feeling about it – Dawg took the needle out and put it back into the same vein again:

BLOOD: *Go down again, down.*
DAWG: *You off?*
BLOOD: *Yeah.*
DAWG: *I have to block it off there or it will go too far.*
BLOOD: *Ow, pull it back. Shit.*
DAWG: *It's in. I want to press down so it goes in.*
BLOOD: *Go on then … It's still hurting, Dawg, shit, nah man.*
DAWG: *It's in.*
BLOOD: *It's still hurting – I don't trust that thing.*

It is useful to consider this moment against Blood's crack-using career. When I had first met Blood five months previously, he was smoking crack and heroin yet periodic homeless spells since had put him in more vulnerable and unpredictable drug-using circumstances. As a consequence, he seemed to hold less care for himself because these unstable experiences laid the foundations for him to experiment with injecting. When Dawg had not been able to help in such situations, Blood had either unsuccessfully tried it himself or enlisted the help of other street drug users: not always with much success. My field notes record Blood reflecting on his first injecting experience:

> I asked him what would happen if Dawg couldn't inject him and he said he would get someone else to inject him. I knew he had some rough experiences on the streets – I knew that he had had a dirty hit in a squat and been hospitalised. That particular time, I think he shared a spoon with someone. When I asked him about whether he had contracted anything from sharing paraphernalia, he said he had had immunisation from all hepatitis diseases.
>
> (Field notes)

Greater involvement in risky drug-taking practices also seems to be associated with disintegrating physical and mental health, depression, heightened feelings of hopelessness and fatalism about the future. Indeed, truncated pathways appear to correlate with the use of more crack and other drugs – which invariably point to increasingly risky practices:

> I have already been there with the crutch – cast on my leg for ten months, I have been out shoplifting with the cast on my leg so I can't run away because needs/must. Needs/must. But I have done silly shit before ... I have shared spoons and needles and got hep C. I can't afford to get HIV but I am lucky to be alive.
>
> (Shake)

Rock bottom? Tattoo and Irish

When Blood wasn't with Dawg, he spent increasing time with homeless crack users. On this occasion, I meet two of them (Tattoo and Irish) when going to meet Blood on the streets. This narrative seems to highlight feelings of hopelessness and fatalistic attitudes to the self:

This is Tattoo and Irish

> Blood came out of the phone box and excitedly shouted 'Dan'. He was jumping up and down next to Irish, a homeless crack user. Since Blood had said there would be another, I asked of his whereabouts; he then came limping out of the underground station – this was Tattoo. I had seen them both approaching people for money outside other underground stations in the area. Tattoo was dressed in tracksuit bottoms, what looked to be a leather coat and jumper. He had tattoos all over his face and body. His left leg was badly swollen – as I was to see later – and he relied on one crutch which seemed to act as his leg. He limped towards me and acknowledged me. Irish, on the other hand, was more talkative – telling me how he had been injecting for 17

years and that he was unlike anyone else because, in that time, he was still able to find veins for injection.

There then followed some fuss over what should happen next because they were all excited about scoring. Blood disappeared into the phone box to make a call to the local Rivertown dealers. Irish sent Tattoo on his way in advance as it would take him twice as long to get to the squat – even though we had to meet the dealer or runner to score. For some reason, Tattoo didn't go to the pedestrian crossing and limped across the road while the traffic aggressively honked at him. Irish, Blood and I left to make the exchange outside a pizza place.

After a 20 minute walk, I felt we were lucky to only be waiting a matter of minutes – perhaps because there were two exchanges to be made? Both Irish and Blood wanted to do crack deals. A teenage figure on a moped flew past us and tooted his horn. Blood leapt to his feet and started following him down the road. Irish left promptly to meet the dealer and I was instructed to hold Irish's huge bag, full of dirty clothes. The runner parked behind some houses but was still in full view of everyone walking past. He didn't even check around or anything as he removed the tightly-wrapped packages of white and brown from of his mouth. He first dealt with Blood, since he was the first to race off without anyone else. Irish then did an exchange. Blood got a one-on-one and Irish got a two-on-one to share with Tattoo. I acknowledged the runner but he just nodded to me as we all left together.

As we walked, Irish revisited our earlier conversation about his injecting practices. Some people, he said, created problems for themselves by injecting in the same site over and over again and that was how they damaged their veins so quickly. He told me that he tended to inject one area, move on to a different site, and come back to that place sometime later so as not to totally wreck the vein.

The hospital squat

We arrived at a hospital and there were some people at the entrance of the fire exit – which is where most drug users went in. Blood told me not to look at them as we walked straight past. He had obviously been in this situation before. We reached the fire door and Blood stuck his fingers through and unhinged the lock. When I last came here, Blood assured me that no one really knew of the place – apart from drug users – and that we wouldn't be seen. To get to 'the hospital squat', as some call it, you follow an alleyway, past some windows and another fire exit – which could be seen from the hospital – and take a door left down some stairs (Figure 4.1). As we walked down the stairs, I started to see the paraphernalia. Each step became dirtier as I descended. There were crack pipes, foil, tourniquets, tissues, syringes, needle caps and cardboard boxes. It was very poorly lit. There was some light coming from a gap – where the car park was. There were people walking past at various intervals.

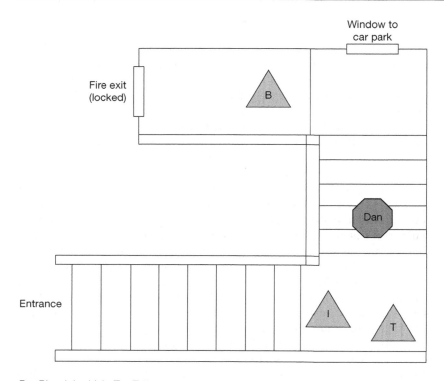

B = Blood; I = Irish; T = Tattoo

Figure 4.1 Hospital squat

There was only one place where we could not be seen, which was half way down on the second set of stairs. It was difficult to be seen through the car park gap, or the windows where hospital staff were walking past or even at the bottom of the stairs where staff were working on the bins around. At the bottom of the second set of stairs was a small space which was piled up with rubbish and paraphernalia. There was also a door at the bottom. Nevertheless, people still walked past.

As they all started to settle on this second set of stairs, Tattoo took his coat off and a rotten smell seemed to emerge. It wasn't a body odour smell. I could only think it was the leg, which Irish had said was rotten from gangrene.

Irish preparing the injection

While Tattoo continued to take off his jacket, Irish started to get two bits of cardboard together and set them up on the first set of stairs which directly faced the windows up ahead where staff were passing. Irish set up two bits of cardboard on the steps. To the left of us, blood stains marked the walls where someone had flushed blood from their syringe up against the wall. Irish started to work quickly and set up two needles, one for Tattoo and one for himself. Blood had retreated to the second set of stairs to smoke crack and heroin.

Tattoo started rummaging through some small plastic bags for things which Irish needed. It reminded me of a doctor operating and requesting certain tools to complete his work as Irish would say 'Tattoo, water' or 'Tattoo, needle'. Irish got out the bottom of an old soda can end – it had bits of citric stuck to it. He poured in the heroin and added 100ml of water. He mixed it together and used the reverse end of the syringe to crush the two substances together. He then ordered Tattoo round again and asked for a light. Tattoo fumbled around in his coat pocket with one hand and pulled out a lighter. Irish lit the patch and started to heat the mixture over it. He was making a speedball to share with Tattoo from two white and one brown, yet he only added one white and one brown. He must have kept the other white to himself without telling Tattoo. As the substance turned a light brown colour, he unwrapped the white and dropped it in. He then crushed the white with the brown. He added a filter and drew the substance up into a large syringe but not through the needle into Tattoo's large syringe. He injected half into his own needle and left the rest in Tattoo's syringe.

Irish started taking his trousers down to try to inject his legs. He then tried to go inside the left leg. He tried in the same sort of area several times but had no luck. There wasn't much blood but I could see the air building up in the syringe. He kept shaking and flicking the syringe to get the air out – he even squirted some over my shoulder by accident. After three or four attempts in both areas on each leg, he then decided to go in the arms. He seemed to be distracted as he took his shirt off in the cold, and tried to inject in the stomach. He tensed his stomach and leaned forward but no vein appeared. He breathed in again and tried but then said it had to be the arms. He had a few marks on his arms but nothing severe. Eventually, after about 20 minutes, he found a capillary under his left arm. There were several small marks where he had been in the same area before. To his luck, I guess, he only needed to put the syringe in on the second occasion before he managed to get a dark red colour into the syringe. After injecting two thirds of it, and flushing slightly he finished it off.

Tattoo injecting

While Irish dressed himself, Tattoo spread his coat on the floor just behind where Irish had injected. He was still in vision of the windows at the top. Blood was still going about his business on the stairs and was fussing over finding a lighter with which to smoke a pipe. Tattoo sat on his coat and, while showing visible pain, started to take down his trousers. He rolled down the left leg of the trousers to reveal the DVT and gangrene in his left leg. The whole left leg was twice the size of the right. From the calf downwards, the leg was wrapped in bandages. His leg was also bleeding through the bandages. He suddenly spoke with a very deep voice, talking about how he had developed gangrene and DVT. Apparently he had jumped over a fence in a squat and cut the back of his knee near the tendons. He had neglected the wound and it had got progressively worse. Although he eventually checked himself into hospital, he lost patience for a resolution and was not given anything to detox from crack and heroin. He was told to lie still in hospital for six weeks, but because he was withdrawing from the drugs found it difficult. The wound got larger, and he lost patience and checked himself out.

I moved closer to his knee and the rotten smell became stronger. On the left leg, under the knee was an open flesh wound. He was also injecting in the groin on that side and had developed DVT in the same leg. He already had the syringe ready which Irish had prepared for him. He injected in what looked like an abscess on the upper part of his right leg. Within a matter of seconds, he had the flow of the blood in the syringe – and this was in his 'good' leg which also didn't look too healthy. As he removed the needle with the same hand which held a smouldering cigarette, blood dripped out of the wound. He mopped a tissue around the area. After a few minutes, Tattoo leaned over to his right hand side and his eyes started to close. Meanwhile, Irish had started to get restless and chatty. They managed to get themselves together and packed some of the recyclable equipment away. As we left, three other drug users came down the stairs – likely to do similar things. Thankfully, we were leaving.

(Field notes)

Conclusion

This chapter has discussed pathways into crack use and how crack users become a crack user. Mediating pathways into crack use are individual decisions (Booth Davies, 1997; Haines *et al.*, 2009) made against socio-structural and contextual influences (Dunlap and Johnson, 1992; Dunlap, 1995). Therefore the process of becoming is one through micro-social interactions with various social institutions that generate meaning over time (Giddens, 1984) – in the context of socio-economic strain or despair (Agar, 2003; Dunlap and Johnson, 1992; Dunlap, 1995). Together, these seem to play a part in the decision to use crack and subsequent decisions to continue to do so (Evans, 2002; Giddens, 1984). The chapter shows that, for many, using crack appears to become a natural/situated/normative response to dealing with socio-structural problems (Dunlap, 1992; Singer, 2001; Young, 1971). Importantly, however, it seems that denial becomes a central feature of crack users (Goffman, 1963; Maruna, 2001) which serves to deflect feelings of shame and guilt (Giddens, 1991) and individual responsibility for actions (Sykes and Matza, 1957). Many start to see themselves as powerless victims, blame the 'drug' for life's mishaps (Maruna, 2001) and develop increasingly fatalistic attitudes (Chapter 7) manifested through damaging cultural practices and risk behaviours (Farmer, 1997; Wilkinson, 2006). Importantly, this seems to amplify individual feelings of shame, and has consequences for how they interact in the crack scene (Chapter 5). The next chapter is devoted to the function of this particular sphere.

The social organisation of the crack scene

The drug will disgrace you and put you in situations which you would not normally be in, you blot out things you would not normally blot out. You could say something jokingly and it would be received completely differently. Your money can't save you in those situations. You are far from reality, you don't know what is going on. Most people are making decisions for you, because it is a place [crack scene] of takers, some people are takers, and somebody is being took. If you are new, you will get took.

(Iverson)

The crack scene is kind of weird it's like a whole different culture. If you are not in it, you can't really see it. Say like an area like Rivertown, if you are a user, you become known as a user with all the other users – it's like a club and it opens doors. Somebody will introduce you maybe or just by your appearance – your clothes are shabby, you might smell a bit, you look severely underweight, you look like a addict – sometimes it's enough – you hear stuff word of mouth. You might meet a mate who is using crack and he'd tell you about a place or he'd bring you and once you have been there once and you are with someone who vouches for ya – you can go again on your own.

(Alwight)

Introduction

Continued crack use for many appears to result in increased interactions with significant others in the crack scene (Matza, 1969) – a space which offers meaning and identity to crack users (Zinberg, 1984; Fitzgerald, 2009). The crack scene, its players and their interactions are shaped by the political economy (top down) of crime control agencies, social policies and the configuration of welfare services (Agar, 2003; Bourgois, 1995; Chapter 8). It is, however, also influenced by its own cultural norms (bottom up) (DeCorte, 2001; Fitzgerald, 2009) and its environments (Duff, 2009; Schwandt, 2001). These two elements appear to operate in tandem (Duff, 2007; Rhodes, 2002) to determine how the local crack market operates and how crack users access supply (Chapter 3). This chapter first shows how this happens and suggests that access to crack hinges on hierarchical position in the crack scene.

Second, this chapter shows how participation in the crack scene also shapes individual identities (Dovey *et al.*, 2001) and collective cultural practices (Singer, 2001; Young, 1971). To some extent, this is done through the social exchanges around the use of crack and other drugs (Preble and Casey, 1969), but also the use of these drugs within crack scene environments (Duff, 2007). These 'environments' – public settings, temporary accommodation and crack houses – also seem to influence crack user identities (Duff, 2009; Fitzgerald, 2009), as well as amplify experiences of individual shame, anxiety and insecurity (Rhodes *et al.*, 2007). Therefore the architecture of the crack scene appears to influence crack careers (Malchy *et al.*, 2008; Moore and Dietze, 2005), offer life meaning (Maruna, 2001; Preble and Casey, 1969) and provide ontological security (Giddens, 1990, 1991; Lasch, 1985).

Crack-using clusters: High Society and Low Life

At different times in their crack career, crack users appear to hold different hierarchical positions in the crack scene. This seems to be attributed to the level of money they generate for their crack use, which in turn affects the benefits they receive and priority they are given from crack dealers. In general, there appear to be four clusters of crack users in this study (see Table 5.1). Crack users do not necessarily remain in these clusters because as crack careers evolve, abilities to fund crack use can shift along with frequency and mode of use, as I showed in Chapter 2.

Professional, organised alliances seem to be pairs/small groups of crack users ('High Society') who are able to generate large sums of money. Their crack smoking seems to be generally high and their visibility in the crack scene low due to their stealth and expertise.

> You could get the odd person who had a good job in there [the crack house] but I'm talking about the smart people who go out and make their money and buy clothes and shoes as well as drugs and they don't let themselves go, like they're bathing and that.
>
> (Em)

These users may have their own private smoking venues, are often welcomed in exclusive crack houses or are blessed with personal crack deliveries to their homes – either way, their dealings appear less visible. Because of their ability to generate large sums of money, they are given priority by crack dealers. For example, BD said:

> You have what you call 'your day smokers' and 'your night smokers' and what will tend to happen will be they'll form a bond-like relationship: so

Table 5.1 Clusters of crack users

Crack scene ranking		Crack-using cluster	Crack consumption	Mode of crack use	Principal form of funding	Public visibility	Crack dealer priority	Crack-using environments
High Society	High	Professional, organised alliances	High	Smoking	Credit card fraud, burglary, shoplifting, sex work, clipping, theft, social security cheques, stable employment	Low	High	Crack houses, private flats, own homes
	High	Individual entrepreneurs	High	Smoking	Credit card fraud, burglary, shoplifting, sex work, clipping, social security cheques, stable employment	Low	High	Crack houses, private flats, own homes
Low Life	Medium/low	Ad-hoc, disorganised alliances	Context dependent	Smoking/injecting	Social security cheques, shoplifting, theft, sex work	Medium/high	Context dependent but generally medium/low	Improvised settings: crack houses, temporary accommodation, public settings – parks, car parks, alleyways, derelict sites, etc.
	Low	'Crack heads' or 'ponces'	Context dependent but generally low	Smoking but predominantly injecting	Social security cheques, sex work, sex-for-crack exchanges, begging, 'poncing'	High	Low	Improvised settings: crack houses, temporary accommodation, public settings (as above).

you're a prostitute, I'm a credit card. You nick the card but you can't work during the day – there's not a lot of business down the road during the day, so me in the day [when I did it] and we'll smoke together and you do the punters and we'll smoke together. Do you understand what I'm saying here? It's making that twenty-four hour cycle and that's really how it goes. You tend to find a lot of smokers. So if I'm a shoplifter or a thief I tend to have my favourite girl and my favourite geezer – he might be a burglar. So you might be my mate but I know he's a burglar or you do cars. You do them at night. I do the shops during the daytime and we'll be smoking partners – not exclusively. It's not like we're married but if you're there and I'm there I'll make sure that you've got a smoke and then if I'm there at night, obviously I can't shoplift at night because there's no shops open, you're burgling or a car thief then you make sure I smoke.

These clusters also tend to be wary of including others in their established networks/agreements. In another example, Sneaks reflected on how he established a closed crack-smoking group made up of high-earning crack users. He had firstly bartered out his flat to a crack dealer, received a daily allowance of crack and was subsequently permitted to establish an exclusive crack-smoking group in the crack house. The group was distinguished by those who could generate large amounts of money; those who could 'control' the drug when smoking; and those who sustain a 'good vibe' when smoking crack [good conversations]. The 'inner circle', as he called it, was separated from the 'madness of the living room' where the crack dealer stayed. Here, he reflects on how crack users were selected to be part of this alliance:

SNEAKS: *Oh yeah. He was in the inner circle. That was without doubt. He was in mate.*
DAN: *It sounds it.*
SNEAKS: *Four hundred pounds he used to give me over the course of the night but I used to lend up to about a hundred pounds' worth. I used to go to sleep and wake up when I saw the smoke. I had so much smoke [crack] that I didn't even have to get my quota* [daily allowance from the dealer for the barter of the premises] *– sometimes for a day/two days. That's how much smoke I had but remember that I've got other friends. The inner circle made money. My friend who was a shoplifter, he was also the burglar, the car thief. The next man was a car thief, the next man used to come and sell trainers to the house; he got the chequebooks and cards. These are money people.*
DAN: *So to get into the inner circle you had to reach a certain level of … ?*
SNEAKS: *No. I had to like you. If I didn't like you it didn't matter how much you brought I didn't want you in my room because there's got to be a vibe. There has to be a vibe for you to smoke. There has to be a vibe that you could put down your drink and not worry about it. You could put down your smoke and everyone watched everyone but no-one's going to touch it because that man's in the inner circle. They're all powerful. If you've got your smoke you ain't going to trouble him. The money people*

in the circle we don't need to nick other people's stuff because we've got our stuff.

DAN: *Were they friends?*

SNEAKS: *Some of them became good friends but see you couldn't have too many people in the inner circle anyway because it was only one bedroom and you couldn't all get in the bedroom anyway.*

DAN: *How would someone get in the inner circle?*

SNEAKS: *Well you'd be taken on whether I liked you. You'd be taken on whether my friend – the girl – could get on with you because she's a girl and you're going to want to make advances to her and she's not interested in that. She's just interested in her smoke. If she wants to go with a bloke she'll go with a bloke. It don't have to be because he's got crack, you know. So we had to have certain rules in the inner circle; that everyone got on with everyone and basically everyone gives a fuck about Sneaks because if you fucked up Sneaks that he lost his flat then you lot wouldn't have this cosy little room that you could come in and smoke, sit down comfortably and you haven't got to be frightened that somebody is going to draw a knife. You knew that if certain people got barred it's because they had a tendency to become aggressive and draw knives.*

DAN: *On their buzz, yeah?*

SNEAKS: *On their buzz. Threaten people, they'd argue with everything you say like the day before or the week before. So it was important that you had to have harmony. I had to feel safe. I couldn't smoke with people – when I'm buzzing – that are like schizophrenic; like they could do anything dangerous, like they could hurt my friends because if you hurt my friends you're taking away that harmony.*

Crucial to participation in professional, organised alliances is a common goal to share the crack-taking space. Similarly, individual entrepreneurs ('High Society'), who are also high earners, appear to have a similar status in the crack scene. They appear as skilful and diverse in their criminality or, perhaps, are employed and spend large sums of money on crack. As a result, crack dealers prioritise them and their exchanges and, in some cases, give them credit in advance. A former crack dealer turned user, Baz said:

> I would maintain the high order by giving people top ups for spending extra amounts. I might say put a little tenner on top, encourage them to come back, get the customers, so when they do have money they are not going to go to this house or that house because Baz gives little top ups. They will get more from me and they have the peace of mind knowing that no one is going to bother them.
>
> (Baz)

Similarly, Em reflects on her actions as a sex worker/clipper:

> I'd make my money and then I'd just go and sit in a crack house for the day until the night-time again … I used to get a lot of credit from dealers – a lot

– because they knew how much money I used to earn. Nine times out ten I could go out there and smoke my first six £10 stones for nothing because I used to get credit from so many different dealers.

(Em)

In another example, early in his crack career, Iverson's monetary reliability and punctuality ensured he got credit from the dealer – up to £100 in advance because he said he was a 'sure bet'. This gave him a certain 'status' he said. He described himself as the 'king', who 'fed the mouths' of those who 'couldn't graft' in the crack house. During this period, he reconciled:

If you have no money, you have no status. Money rules. You could be king today and slave tomorrow. Like I was the king so if I had money people wanted me, but when I had no money, people would leave me. It is a selfish thing. So it motivates you to get back the status. Like money is drugs and drugs is like money, it's a currency. Money is status. I am king because I have two stones say, it is the middle of the night, and you need it so I am king because I can sell it to you for £30, you need it. Or I could go out and buy a £10 stone and divide it into quarters and you would come in and you can't complain because it is our house. That is what you get … If you are the king, people are watching out for you 'don't touch that, it belongs to him' but you have paid for it anyway because by giving them you are buying them and they are depending on that. They will do anything because they know they will get a smoke. It is exactly the same in society because if you have nothing in society, you have nobody … They will do anything for you [Low Life], you have the money. Girls, suck my dick. And the men as well, suck my dick. That is how it goes.

(Iverson)

At the time of interview and during the fieldwork period, these clusters of crack users were in a minority in the sample, although some were able to reflect on these times past. The majority of crack users in this study seem to have either never reached or spiralled down from this stage of crack use and were poorly equipped to earn large amounts of money for crack. Instead, these clusters – 'Low Life' as some called them – seemed to rely predominantly on petty crime, begging and fortnightly social security cheques. Some, as we have seen, have severe physical and mental health problems as a result of risky drug-using practices and are more likely to be injectors (Chapter 4). While many of this group complain about crack's poor quality, most seem more concerned with doing the deal and smoking/injecting (Preble and Casey, 1969) because it seems to go some way to balancing their ontological framework (Chapter 4; Giddens, 1991; Lasch, 1985). They may be easily spotted by shop staff when attempting to shoplift, or turned down when offering sexual services. Others are banned from certain areas because they are wanted by the police/crack dealers or have outstanding debts with other crack users in other areas.

Those in recovery from crack use consider these populations to be at the 'lower end' of the crack scene – 'Low Life', 'ponces' or 'crack heads'. Perhaps they have this view because they have taken steps to come out of this scene and see themselves as 'better people'. The public visibility of Low Life appears high but the priority given to them by crack dealers is low.

> It is like a seller's market, drugs. They don't need to advertise it, especially with people like myself – I am addicted to it, I have to see them – they don't need to call for me, I need to call for them. I can phone them up and it can take them an hour to come and meet me if they choose so and I will stand there like a tramp waiting because I am desperate and I need it. That's the situation you are in, they're in control. When it comes to class A drugs that is how it is … the point really is if I have money for one pipe, if I haven't then I will try and squeeze two or three but generally it's one.
>
> (Pudge)

> Most of the people who deal with the pure cocaine and crack don't want to deal with the street junkies, you know the ponces, for small little bits of money because they'll get you caught. The majority of them are out shoplifting and what have you. If they're in a cell and they're clucking the police know that they'll give up a name – most of them do – so sensible people don't really want to deal with them. I mean I wouldn't if I was dealing any sort of weight [in drugs] – if it was my business. If I was doing it on a commercial scale I wouldn't want anything to do with street people. I mean they are the lower end of the market.
>
> (Silver)

In general, Low Life seem to have limited gains from their situation, often resort to street deals in alleyways, outside hostels, among street markets, in parks and car parks and street corners. These deals, made in public, often result in crack users locating nearby makeshift environments to use their drugs. This could be more private places like crack houses, but also include public settings such as alleyways, parks, car parks, derelict sites, phone booths, etc. They may use crack houses but are often deterred by dealers because of the attention they may bring to their operations.

These crack users frequently reflect that the environmental conditions where they use crack are often unfavourable and that this does not aid the 'crack buzz' (Zinberg, 1984). Because they appear to be lower down the crack scene hierarchy – and struggle to make decent money for crack – they feel they get the poorest-quality crack. In addition, as other high-earning crack users see it, the fact that these clusters are unable to do a 'day's work' and resort to activities such as begging seems to put them at the bottom of the social ladder in the crack scene. In the absence of reliable and regular means to muster funds for drugs, many 'Low Life' therefore combine their funds and/or paraphernalia to obtain drugs through the 'moral economy' (Bourgois and Schonberg, 2009). In this scenario, Tall Guy and Bail have an ad-hoc agreement to share their social security cheques between them for crack and heroin. Bradda, however, lingers around them, keen to involve himself in the deal by recommending a good dealer and, by doing so, hoping to share some of the drugs. Eventually, he persuades Tall Guy to give him the money and call his dealer:

Tall Guy went to the post office to cash his social security benefit. He used my phone to call the dealer. Bradda and Bail were in close pursuit. It seemed like all three were now in on the deal as they followed Tall Guy around. Tall Guy asked for a two-on-two. It seemed common etiquette to use the stereotypical language of the dealers. 'Can I see you, bruv?' or when he phoned another dealer 'can I see you, blud?' – something between black or Jamaican talk. I think this may be like adhering to the codes of dealers – to gain the respect of talking in their language. Maybe the dealer will arrive sooner? Maybe they will be prioritised when the dealer gets a load of calls at once? The problem was that the use of code appeared to make no difference at all – we still had to wait. I recalled from other street deals, some waiting times [for dealers/runners] exceeded one hour. A few calls were made and we were told to meet back at the hostel. When I returned from a walk to the shop with Bail, Bradda had been feeding Tall Guy's paranoia and they both started accusing me of being a policeman. There then followed a small spate of arguments between Bradda and Tall Guy because the dealer had not arrived. Tall Guy made another call to his dealer but after several nowhere conversations, the dealer finally admitted that he only had heroin. Tall Guy tried another two dealers but they were not available, so Bradda suggested that he make a call to his dealer. For £35, they would get the two-on-two but their requests appeared to be low down on the priority list. We waited a further half an hour – Bradda kept calling him up 'where are you, bro?' Tall Guy was getting annoyed because he was starting to withdraw from crack and heroin, and had already missed his appointment at the drug service to pick up his prescription. Perhaps he would have struggled to make his appointment anyway as he wanted to collect his social security late to avoid certain people. He seemed to think it would be ok if he turned up in the afternoon but would he have been able to if he had £160 in his pocket and was about to use crack and heroin? We sat there – the situation intensified and Bail said to Tall Guy, 'get your money back and we'll go elsewhere'.

(Field notes)

Because the deal is of minimal value, there seems to be little interest from dealers – and even their runners. As a consequence, their spending power appears minimal and their crack scene rank appears lower. Indeed, 'Low Life' may face lengthy waiting times for dealers:

I cycled past Scruff on the Bridge at 12am on a cold Saturday night. He was begging and had managed to get together £20. Silencer was also waiting with him, smoking a dog end. I sat down and gave my midnight snack – pastries – to him. I asked if he remembered my face as I had seen him outside the tube station with Black Eyes and Jack the Lad. We started talking and at first I think he was a bit cautious. Indeed, he confessed he had heard I was a copper, but he said he'd wait to see for himself. They invited me to walk with them to score. As we were walking, I started talking about the area and people, types of drug practices. We walked down past the bridge and the tube station, and walked to the college where I had once seen Cuz score openly during the day. It was getting on for 1am and Scruff and Silencer said they had few options to call dealers at this time of night. The dealer, called 'Alfie', apparently drove a bus during the day and dealt crack at night. Scruff made the call from his mobile and was told to wait for 15 minutes at the 'usual place'. We then walked back on to the high street and down past some derelict garages. We reached the bus shelter and started waiting – every time Scruff thought he saw the car pull in to the road opposite, he got up from his spot in the bus shelter, often disappearing for a few minutes at a time leaving Silencer and I talking. Silencer was trying to be patient but was sweating by the withdrawal from crack and heroin. We had been waiting about an hour and it was close to 2am. I was contemplating leaving when Scruff saw a BMW pull over in the road. I then cycled off to let them do the deal and Scruff then came back over the road to where Silencer and I were – they offered me a smoke but I declined. We then walked up the road towards the tube station and took a left into some deserted estate car parks. We sat down next to a garage – I left my bike and Scruff sat with his back to where people would normally walk past. He then picked up a Red Bull can, dented it slightly and took the lid off and pierced six holes in centre of the dented can. Silencer was to have the first pipe. He was very impatient as he didn't even put much ash on – he took only three puffs of his cigarette and sprinkled what ash he could on the dented can while Scruff broke up the crack. Silencer immediately put the pipe to his lips, hovered the lighter over the crack and inhaled. Very soon after he left to inject. Scruff said he was shy and didn't want to do it in front of anyone. Then Scruff had his first crack pipe. He seemed to dip his lighter towards and away from the crack as he burnt it. He smoked a few pipes and then debated with himself whether he was going to inject crack. He tore off the end of a beer can and put the crack in the centre, added some water and then started to crush up the crack into a cloudy mush. He used the end of the syringe to do this. He already had a filter on the can – I didn't see where it came from. He then drew up the substance into a syringe and pulled up his left leg scattered with huge abscesses, scars and scabs – he admitted that his legs were a complete mess but had well defined calf muscles. The skin was in really poor condition and it was bruised and broken underneath where he had missed veins when injecting. He first tried to find a vein in his leg, and pressing the needle in, poked around gently. Suddenly, blood rushed in but he didn't move his hand close to the needle end to push the crack in – he hadn't found the vein but he kept moving the needle in and out, but not taking it all the way out (perhaps some fixation). After about two minutes, he gave up and excused himself as he said he needed to use an upper area of his leg. He got up from the dark corner of the garage and moved towards the dim light, dropped his trousers and kneeled. He held the needle in his right hand and pierced the skin on his upper left leg. Again, he dug around in the same area, withdrawing the needle slowly and putting it back in to try and find a vein. By now the syringe was dark red with blood. He was kneeling for about four minutes. I kept looking over my shoulder as we were right in the middle of a car park. He then gave up and did his trousers up. He came back to the former spot, sat down, pulled up his trousers on his other leg and tried in his calf muscle. I didn't see exactly what he did but he seemed to find the vein quickly. About 20 seconds after injection, he said his jaw felt numb and that it was 'good shit'. It was now about 3am.

(Field notes)

These two groups of users – High Society and Low Life – may not necessarily remain static either because, from time to time, crack users might get a 'touch', which often results in a heavy crack binge. For example, a month or so later, Scruff said he had received £5,000 from his aunt and decided to live the 'high life' for a while. Whether this was the case, I will never know, but he did end up indulging in hotels, casinos, sex and, of course, crack. However, it was not long before the old lifestyle beckoned:

When I met Scruff at the hotel, I didn't recognise him. He had had a haircut, shave and had bought new clothes – the problem was he still smelt quite bad and was wobbling all over the place in the hotel lobby. He looked slightly healthier but thinner and he had some scabs behind his ear. We went to the fourth floor and as I walked into the £80-a-night room there was a very young looking girl on the bed, sitting there smiling. She introduced herself as Pix. As I walked in the room, it smelt of body odour and there were used syringes, ash and crack pipes on the side desk. Pix felt awkward and was quiet. Scruff kept talking to me and when she spoke he interrupted. Pix said she was 24, had been using crack and heroin since she was 14, had been selling her body since she was 16 and had been raped by a gang of dealers last year and as a result had a child which her mum cared for ... her family, she said, had cast her away. Scruff was hot and took his jumper off to reveal his thin body. I could see his bones and the blue veins running down the front of his stomach. I then saw a syringe needle on the floor which had broken off – I pointed it out and Pix warned me not to touch it yet picked it up with her bare hands. When Scruff started talking how he had spent £1,500 the other day, she started crying. He didn't seem to notice. Scruff decided that he wanted to score some crack and although he owed one dealer £100, he still phoned and asked to meet him outside to score a one-on-one. I wasn't sure what he was planning because he didn't seem to have any money whatsoever – it had all gone on hotels, casinos and sex workers. Still he made the call and went to go and meet the dealer. When he left, Pix started talking about her drug use. She showed me her arms where she had injected. There were no marks on the main section of the arm but where the arm bent there were some abscesses, but she injected in her groin … She firstly lifted up her T-shirt to reveal how thin she was and then undid her belt and pulled her trousers down – she had two scabs almost symmetrical to each other on the groin where she had been injecting. They were a yellow colour. Scruff returned and sat down quickly – he immediately started to unpack the small wrapper of crack while Pix faced the television and looked disinterested. He reached for his glass pipe and stuffed a bit of gauze in the top of it. He managed to get 2–3 lumps of a £10 rock on to the gauze and flicked the lighter underneath it to melt it into the gauze. Immediately after, Scruff started to 'act digi' and his face started moving around in jerky motions.

(Field notes)

Less than two weeks later Scruff was hospitalised with severe vein problems. Soon after, he checked himself out and returned to begging on the street. All the money he had was gone. In most cases, it seems a 'touch' only temporarily alleviates low status. Equally, when crack user networks are disrupted (Chapter 6), there are implications for where and with whom crack users deal and use. In this example, Dawg and Blood, who often relied on Bones' access to 'high-quality' crack through some Afghan dealers, had to make alternative arrangements with dealers they didn't know in the same housing block when Bones got arrested:

When we reached the bottom of Dawg's block of flats, the runner came down and coughed up two small packages out of his mouth. Blood complained about the size and was told that was all that was available as they were 'reloading'. The rock looked very small, even by £10 standards. The runner shrugged his shoulders and Blood quickly accepted the deal. They both looked around and the deal was done in the hallway of the tower block – all because Blood couldn't wait and the Afghans couldn't be used.

(Field notes)

Consequently, as Dawg saw it, this meant greater risks to his 'safe haven', as Blood was to learn a few days later:

We arrived at Dawg's at about 11am and telephoned the dealer [in the block below]. We went down to reception area of the block and a runner came down dressed in sports trousers and a vest – he beckoned us through near to the lifts. Blood wanted two one-on-ones – one for him and one for Dawg. The runner didn't even look at me but apparently said not to meet with another person there – me or anyone. Nothing much was said between them to start with and the rocks looked a lot bigger than the ones Blood got a few days earlier. As the runner went back in the lift he said to Blood 'only come here when I tell you to' and Blood replied 'I have a mate here so I come here when I want' and then laughed slightly. The lift was closing on the runner as this was said and he then came out and said 'What's that, blud? Do you think it's funny? Are you fucking laughing at me?' He grabbed Blood and pushed him into the other empty lift and put his hand on his trouser pocket to insinuate he had a knife. The runner banged Blood's head against the lift then Blood started nodding, saying he understood. After this, Blood said he wouldn't deal with him again – then two hours later was saying he was going to phone them to score again.

(Field notes)

These crack-user hierarchies also seem to have implications for the day-to-day experience of using crack in the crack scene. For the professional, organised groups and entrepreneurs, life seems relatively comfortable as access to quality crack is plentiful and high funding capabilities yield benefits. Nevertheless, as I have shown in Chapter 4, this can quite quickly change. However, for the Low Life – the ad-hoc, disorganised groups, 'ponces', or 'crack heads' – daily existence seems to be particularly volatile as the next section highlights.

The day-to-day experience of using crack in the crack scene

For the lower end of the crack-using population the day-to-day goal of using crack appears to be jeopardised by the pressured interactions of the crack scene. In particular, paranoia, mistrust, violence and victimisation seem to be high among this group (Anderson, 1990; Bourgois, 1995). In many respects, such interactions seem to be part and parcel of the fabric of crack scene culture and, as a consequence, also become part of the social and cultural framework of individuals who navigate this space (Chapter 7; Friedman *et al.*, 1998). These unpredictable and often violent micro-interactions, however, are further shaped by social control mechanisms (Chapter 6) and crack-using environments (Duff, 2007). For now, attention is devoted to the latter with special consideration for the impact on the individual.

Crack scene environments

Thus far, I have established that those at the lower end of the crack scene seem to be more vulnerable to volatile social interactions (Bourgois, 1995; Dunlap, 1995). In addition, this group seem to express dissatisfaction with regard to crack-taking experiences. Crack scene environments therefore also affect these individuals; in particular, how such environments foster feelings of individual insecurity, shame and anxiety (Chapter 7), and how this, in turn, impacts on individual identities (Duff, 2009). Crack scene environments are public settings, temporary accommodation and crack houses, and these locations seem to influence the interactions, practices and identities of crack scene players (Bourgois, 1995; Parkin and Coomber, 2009). Attention is first given to public settings, before an examination of temporary accommodation and crack houses is presented.

Public settings

While the crack users in this sample make an effort to find secure crack-using spaces, quite often, such environments are either unavailable or unknown to them. These crack users tend not to hold rank and are often left to locate improvised settings to use crack. Many seek out public settings, and while there is some attempt to minimise risk of public visibility – so to avoid detection and affirmation of deviant activities – some seem to have become de-sensitised to using crack in public settings. This appears to occur in the crack-taking moment and, over time, seems to confirm the normalcy of their practices. For some, being exposed to the public gaze does not necessarily seem to stimulate individual feelings of shame and anxiety. An example of this is highlighted through one such public crack-using experience with Cuz and Gums:

> The hostel's policy was 'no drugs or alcohol on site'. Although many took the risk, there was also the danger of being interrupted or pestered for drugs by other hostel residents. Similarly, the 'Safer Rivertown Policies' had also put more police on the streets and there was a genuine paranoia that police intrusion was imminent (Chapter 6). So when Cuz and Gums scored crack and heroin nearby the hostel, there were few options for a crack-smoking venue. On a cold and windy day, they settled behind some shrub-like bushes in a small public garden and tried to smoke crack. I crouched with them behind the semi-naked bushes. I thought we must have looked pretty stupid trying to hide because we were in complete view of some people eating their lunch, someone waiting in a car across the road and a few young people smoking cannabis on a bench nearby. While both Gums and Cuz seemed to have locked out the rest of their social surroundings, I seemed more conscious of our visibility. As we attempted to get comfortable, I switched on the tape recorder:

GUMS: [Attempting to place crack in gauze on crack pipe] *Yeah. It's a bit slow – it doesn't fly off if you see what I mean. Put the card next to it. Hold the card next to it and I'll push it on. Go on.*

CUZ: [Crack falls off] *Oh for fuck's sake man!*

DAN: *They aren't taking drugs as well are they?*

CUZ: *Yeah. They're smoking cannabis.*

GUMS: *What I mean is you've got my back behind me? You can see behind me?*

DAN: [I move to shield their activities from the wind – not from the members of public] *Yeah, yeah. That's what I mean, yeah.*

GUMS: *You don't have to worry if anyone comes, if someone runs over.*

CUZ: [As he is about to smoke his pipe] *Right I'll see you the other side if the wind fucking don't get it before.*

GUMS: *That's what I was going to say. Melt it with your hand.*

CUZ: [Wind blows strongly] *Oh you slag, you bastard it's gone* [crack is blown off the pipe]. *Hold that one as well.*

GUMS: *I've got it* [the crack rock]. *Melt it quickly with your hand* [into the gauze to secure it].

CUZ: *Fucking wind! It ain't going to let me do this, is it?*

DAN: *Do you want me to come around there?* [to improve the shelter from the wind].

GUMS: *No you're alright where you are.*

CUZ: *What's the lighter like? It only just took – just this fucking minute. I've got it stuck on my hand now. It don't want me to do this for some fucked up reason.*

DAN: *Ok?*

CUZ: *Let me get all that. I got a little bit of it. Oh mate! Look it's stuck on there* [too far down the gauze].

GUMS: *Yeah I know.*

CUZ: *What a fucking shame, eh? Wasting lots of money and I can't even get a decent pipe.*

The frustration of losing a 'smoke' seems to override the potential shame of being 'in view' of other members of the public. In another episode I witnessed, in a drug deal, Tooth had scored some crack and heroin and was eager to find a location to smoke. Having recently been released from prison, and without access to Cuddles' flat, he resorted to looking for an estate stairway to smoke. We walked on to an estate that he said was 'notorious' for drugs. My field notes record the order of events:

We tried a few doors but they were locked. As we tried other doors, council workers loading up the rubbish looked at us but Tooth didn't even look at them and we just tried to maintain a normal conversation. We finally had a bit of luck when someone came out of the estate block and we had access to the building. We went up the stairs to the first floor. He reflected on how warm it was because he used to sleep here. Some residents even used to give him food from time to time. We walked up to the top floor to check no one was in the corridor, although I have to say it would be pretty obvious what he would be doing should someone pass. He opened up his foil and placed both the crack and heroin in the middle. He heated it and mixed it together; it formed a light brown colour and ran quicker [than when heroin only was smoked on the foil]. The foil was very thin, and had burnt holes in some places. His hands and fingers also looked burnt. He said that he had burnt holes in the foil before and the drug solution had dripped on his leg, burnt through the skin and left scars. We started to hear a woman walk up the stairs, he quickly folded up the foil and put in his pocket and we continued our conversation. While Tooth seemed to show some discomfort at the interruption it seemed like it was a normal occurrence. The woman said nothing and I apologised for blocking the stairs. It took him about 10 minutes to finish it as he kept talking in between.

(Field notes)

For these crack users, using crack in public settings does not appear to raise levels of shame and anxiety in the crack-taking moment. This study shows that, to some degree, some crack users de-sensitise themselves in these moments perhaps in an effort to normalise their practices. Some are used to making use of improvised public settings to use crack and, as a consequence, seem to have adapted to the potential for public exposure. As Rose (1993) and Butler (1990) note, social identities are produced and reproduced through the repetition of performative acts in public. In the context of this study, some crack users' activities in public settings therefore seem to authenticate crack taking which serves to weaken the social identities of the 'crack head' (Nelson, 1999; Chapter 7). Therefore, the more normal they consider their practices, the more they may convince themselves that there is nothing inherently wrong about what they do.

Temporary accommodation

Thus far, various environments in the crack scene support tense social interactions and have implications for the crack-using experience and individual identities. This was also the case for crack users in different forms of temporary accommodation. Here, crack users are concentrated in a geographical space and are bound by restrictive rules. In addition, many have come to know each other in that same space. At the same time, many of those in temporary accommodation have to wait years for move-on accommodation and one quite normal way to pass time, as they see it, is to take crack and other drugs. Consequently, many in these locations not only engage in crack use but are also vulnerable to other drug and risk practices (Briggs et al., 2009). These specific social pressures seem to have an impact on individuals because the day-to-day social interactions in these environments also assist in identity construction and have a negative impact on crack career trajectories. Moreover, as with public settings, they also have negative implications for the crack-using experience.

This seemed to be evident when I went with Shake for him to score crack and heroin from a dealer in a local hostel. Having left the bus, we crossed the road to a hostel where I waited outside while he went inside. The dim street lighting hinted that dusk was approaching. A few minutes later, Shake came back and said we had to wait. 'Clucking' badly from withdrawal from crack and heroin, the sun was setting over his chances of a 'daylight fix'. We went into the hostel a second time, passed a man on the stairs who acknowledged us, and went down to a basement room which was lit only by the fading light from a small window in the corner:

> Shake put his drugs and paraphernalia on a flat door in the centre and went for a piss in the enclosed area. I started looking around at the paraphernalia on the floor. Some syringes had needles, others hadn't. There were tissues with blood stains on, empty citric packets, a few plastic crack pipes and another couple of extra strong beer cans. Shake maintained that he alone used the room but when I saw the needles he used, I remembered seeing different sizes in the room. Maybe he was convinced it was his spot?
>
> (Field notes)

Feeling nervous but trying not to show it, I directed the light to the spot where he had started to rummage through his paraphernalia. He began to 'cook up' the crack. This process did not involve heating the crack but just mixing it with citric and injectable water. He was clumsy in tearing out the filter. At first, he tore one that was too small and found it difficult to draw the crack substance into the syringe. Showing mild frustration he cut out a second filter. I got the impression the process was hurried because he 'wanted it':

> He stood up and quickly undid his trousers and dropped them slightly so the veins were free on the groin ... He then put the needle to the area of the vein. I kept looking at the door to see if there was a shadow overlooking the light but there was only the noise of the police cars outside.
>
> (Field notes)

I angled my torch so he could see whether he had found the vein. He injected. In his hurry, however, he forgot to prepare a swab to prevent the blood from leaking from the vein and frantically leant forward to rummage in his bag while the needle and syringe hung from his groin. He complained and said that 'it shouldn't be done like this in these circumstances', and blamed the crack for his impulsiveness:

> His legs started to bend and in the dark I could see him staring at the floor. He started to dribble and his legs started shaking slightly. He started talking as he was shaking and saying the environment was 'all wrong'. He said he wasn't enjoying the buzz and I wasn't sure whether it was because I was there or because some form of paranoia was kicking in.
>
> (Field notes)

It was at this moment that he stooped again and started to prepare the heroin injection. Motivated to 'put it right', as he said, he started heating the heroin. Further frustration came when the metal spoon he had got from a drug service heated too quickly and burnt his fingers. I felt that someone was going to walk in but maybe it was because as Shake had said when we entered that 'anyone could come in, and anything could happen'. It didn't seem to help the situation when I pointed out evidence of other people's needles and crack pipes on the floor. Once he had injected the heroin he put all the equipment away and with relief said: 'They [the police] can't do anything now, they're not going to approach me with a needle'. I was sure that the constant police sirens outside did not help the process because he started to accuse me of being a policeman. As in this example, crack-using environments seem to perpetuate insecurity, individual feelings of anxiety and risk practices (Rhodes *et al.*, 2007).

Such environments, however, also have implications for crack careers; in particular, movements between modes of crack use and involvement in risk behaviours (Briggs *et al.*, 2009). In this example, the danger of ad-hoc drug-using alliances is evident in the hostel setting:

Ish was desperate to score crack and heroin but did not have sufficient funds. He frantically knocked on each hostel resident's door in an effort to persuade them to share their drugs with him. The only person who would, however, was Tooth. Without much discussion, they pooled their resources to claim a one-on-one. It was only after they had done this that they faced a dilemma; Tooth injected drugs and Ish didn't (any more). For some reason, Ish realised this after the drugs had been mixed and cooked up together in one spoon. To make matters worse, Ish didn't have any injecting equipment. He wrapped the tourniquet around his arm and tried to inject into his hand with Tooth's used needle. The prospect of this made him anxious; he was sweating vigorously but this was his 'only' option he reasoned. Reluctantly, he injected himself. Ish was already worried that he would return to injecting crack and heroin on a daily basis while staying in the hostel. However, this moment was not in isolation because he had recently tried the 'groin injection'. The experience, however, did not go according to plan:

ISH: *I don't know. They think going in the groin you get a better rush – a better buzz – but you don't. It's all just the same.*

CUZ: *They just want it in there. They just want a vein and they get so frustrated because there's no veins and they think 'Oh yeah. There's the main vein there' you're talking five years and then it's dead. So they've got five years on one side, then another five years on the other.*

ISH: *I'll tell you what. My mate went in there once and he hit my artery and that's why I would never go near my groin.*

DAN: *You watched it?*

ISH: *He put it in me.*

DAN: *Serious?*

ISH: *He got me. He was going to get me but he hit my artery. That's why I'm so scared of putting needles in my neck because of the artery. I'm too young. I don't want to die. I'm waiting for detox. I'm going from detox to rehab but I'm waiting to get myself off all this.*

In this example, the environment acts as a facilitator to the behaviours and has the potential to alter crack careers through the involvement in risk behaviours in temporary accommodation. In addition, because crack use is so frequently interrupted in these social settings – or crack users suspect there is that potential – there are few narratives of satisfaction. When crack-taking moments are disturbed or things fail to go 'according to plan', the completion of the day's goals appears to be hindered and this appears to amplify feelings of personal insecurity among crack users. Similarly, while crack users seem to stave off ontological insecurity by completing these processes (Lasch, 1985), it is further complicated by the necessity to establish 'adequate' conditions in which to undertake the process: the crack 'buzz' is not enjoyed if the environment is 'not right'. However, it is evident thus far that very few environments offer this social stability – especially for those who seem to occupy the lower end of the crack scene – the Low Life. A similar form of anxiety and paranoia amplification also takes place in the context of the crack house.

Crack houses

Crack users not only make use of public settings and temporary accommodation to use crack, but also crack houses. Interpretations of the 'crack house' often stem from subjective experiences associated with particular moments in the crack-using career.

> A crack house is whatever people decide is a crack house. That's the whole thing about the drug; there is no 'haves' and 'have nots'. It's all about people's perceptions and people's illusions. There are no 'haves' and 'have nots' and rules.
>
> (Scruff)

> I mean, there are generally places that would fit my understanding of what the term [crack house] evokes for me, you know, which is a sort of crack-dedicated, crack-smoking den or crack, you know, crack-smoking den. But, you know, there certainly are places like that, but I think the label refers to more than that. And I think that users would refer to a crack house to mean one of the really chaotic places where people are primarily doing crack, but doing other things as well. So the squat locations where everything goes, anyone known can come and go, things like that.
>
> (Philo)

Although, there is some ambiguity over the term 'crack house', crack users generally agree it is a place where crack is either used or dealt – or both (Inciardi, 1995).

> It can be a flat or squat or anything, yeah. A place where you can go and smoke your drugs, that is a crack house. Or you can go in, buy, score your

crack and smoke it. You don't have to smoke it there but it is up to you. There are other places which just deal through the door. Most crack houses have about 15–20 people. I know, I had one myself. It was on the local estate here about 18 months to two years ago. Because I was using drugs, I had a couple of people approach me and ask me if they could use my premises, Jamaicans yeah? They would pay me in drugs and that was how it started. People started coming quick and before I know it people are smoking there 24 hours a day, prostitutes in there doing services, complete madhouse. It was my dad's flat. He doesn't smoke, he is a boozer. He wasn't bothered as long as he got some. A lot of these crack houses they are only open for three or four months. There is so much activity going on that the police catch on, but as soon as one closes down, another opens up. It all got out of hand within a couple of weeks. People were smoking in the kitchen, bedroom, girls in the toilets giving services for money or crack.

(Shake)

You find a crack house that you like because crack houses are different. You've got crack houses where you just smoke white. You've got crack houses where they do white and brown. You've got crack houses where they do white and brown and they let people fix. You've got crack houses that are mainly men. Bradley uses the one which is just for women. You've got crack houses where – some of them are nice, some of them are grotty. Some of them are nice like this when they start out. Some of them are squats.

(BD)

This ambiguity of definition seems convenient because most crack users in this sample disassociate themselves from the crack house because it symbolises stigma and shame (Parkin and Coomber, 2009) – for the same reasons, crack users refute association with the term 'crack head' (Chapter 7). UK literature suggests that crack houses are where crack users develop a sense of belonging, and, because of this, they prefer to use crack in crack houses (Burgess, 2003; GLADA, 2004; Webster *et al.*, 2001). In this study, however, very few crack users confess that the crack house plays a significant role in their day-to-day lives. The few that do link it to the upkeep of a social status across the hierarchy of the crack scene:

DAN: *Do you feel attached to the crack house?*

IVERSON: *Oh yeah, yeah, yeah, because that is the only place you feel safe. It is the only place you can carry out your madness and it is the place you get used to. You get money, you head straight there because I need to show them, I am still functioning, to show people that you are alive, your courage, so you can think 'yeah, I am rich today and today I am telling the truth' because they expect you to be lying.*

Crack houses are generally considered to be paranoid and dangerous environments, and many reflect that taking crack in these locations is not enjoyable.

Many have either experienced or witnessed harassment, intimidation, violence and victimisation between other crack users and/or crack dealers:

SNEAKS: *Yeah and basically said 'He [the dealer] can't go nowhere. He's locked off. He's working for us. He's fucked. He's staying here. We'll let you go when we want you to go'. He's locked up there for he don't know how long for. So what he went and did was started to nick the money and nicking the smoke or saying that he didn't understand sterling from Jamaican dollars and this or that [when he received deliveries of crack]. Then he used to have his crack girlfriend. He'd be in the front room but then he would have two or three girlfriends. No girls that come in the house and you let them have crack and they have to pay you back. He'd give them crack and they'd have to get around him to pay him back in sexual favours. He started giving away crack and sending money from Western Union to Jamaica. So he was taking the piss for about three months. So this is about nine months back that they asked me to run it.*

DAN: *Long time for a house.*

SNEAKS: *Yeah. They were running it for a long time. A couple of brothers and cousins. They were the main men – the bosses above him. One of them he [the dealer in the house] ripped off about two grand and he came in. It was madness. I was in bed sleeping. There was only me there. His crack girlfriend was in hospital the day before. He went up to the hospital with her because she had an asthma attack so we took her up the hospital and she stayed there overnight. The geezer came in and kicked down the door and said 'where's the money? Where's my money from last night's work?' It was about three hundred pounds short. 'Oh well that's got nothing to do with me. You take that up with so-and-so.' 'Where's my money?' the guy said. It's a panic now. It's not enough money and he's brought out some stones, and brought out some other stones and the geezer's realised that he's not just selling East End stones he's selling Arabic stones as well so it kicked off. He got held down in the front room. He got his nose cut right across here with a knife – right across there [shows me]. You know like Kermit the Frog's nose? Mouth and that's how his nose opens. Now he's in shock now and I got cut 'Sneaks, where's the key, where's the key, where's the key?' I don't know where the key is. He's scared now. He wants to get out 'I don't know where the key is. I don't know where the key is'. He panics. Can't get out so he's jumped out the bedroom window. We're on the first floor. He's run off. I've got a couple of cuts on my head. I've looked in the mirror and said to myself, 'that ain't too bad. You'll live'. So I've gone to – he's my mate now because we've got friendly now – I've gone to the dealer 'let's have a look' and when he's let go, his nose has just fallen over and I ran in the bathroom and got flannel, soap, towels. 'Hold it over your nose like that'. We've got a phone in the house, phoned the ambulance. 'What's happened?' 'Yeah there's been an assault. A geezer with the house has been cut with a knife, I've been cut with a knife, need an ambulance.' So that's the call that I made but now if there's an assault over the phone the police come automatically. Well the ambulance came and the police came and I said 'no. I can get out of this now' and we're taken off to hospital and I still can't get out of it. He's got to give some story about how he's fucked about with some crack girlfriend's ... the geezer who uses crack has fucked about with his girlfriend and the boyfriend's come and chopped him up yeah? Then the police have come to me 'is that what's happened?' and I'm like 'yeah that's what's happened'. This was after about nine months. He's still in hospital. I'm back at the house by about three o'clock that afternoon and I found some stones on the floor so I thought 'this is me mate. I'm taking this for my injuries' so I took about four so I'm in the bedroom smoking indoors getting nervous, people coming to buy stones and the dealers came with the girl who was in the hospital with the asthma attack. They contacted her. She got let out that morning but, when they were knocking, I didn't know who it was so I wasn't letting no-one in. What I worked out was that they came back with her and she knocked on the door 'Sneaks, Sneaks, it's me' and I've let her in because it's her and two of them have bundled in behind and they're like 'Oh Sneaks, Sneaks let's have a look. Someone did that to you. It's mad. Well we can't have any more selling here. It's getting too mad. It's getting too dangerous' – fucking crazy.*

For this type of reason, very few crack users in this study considered these environments to hold safe sanctuary away from other pressures in the crack scene. Indeed, many crack houses are small flats; some housing as many as twenty crack users. These small spatial dimensions only seem to amplify interactions and increase risk through disputes, violence and victimisation (Inciardi, 1995; Williams, 1990). Users recognised the potential risks of using crack in these environments because they felt everyone was only concerned with getting as much crack as possible:

> I don't like all the mix-up. There's a lot of mix-up in there [crack houses]. There's a lot of arguments in there. You can just go to a crack house and you can hear the noise as you're coming up to it. There's people arguing 'No, that's mine. That's my cigarette.' That atmosphere is a total nightmare. You'll find everyone's your best friend in these places, especially if somebody walks in who's got money. They're bang on that person and it's just total madness.
>
> (Halle)

> Yeah I have and that's another thing why I don't like sitting in crack houses – people are injecting and you don't know what they've got. I'm clean. I haven't got anything and neither has my husband but I still wouldn't sit in a crack house because you don't know what's in the seats, if needles are lying about and that.
>
> (Mary)

The level of enjoyment crack users associate with using crack in crack houses seems to correlate with different points in the crack career and their ability to deal with situational pressures. Former recreational crack users acknowledge that when they used the drug at weekends – when they considered it to be 'unproblematic', and when the deviancy of their actions in various environments did not mirror aspects of a 'spoilt' identity (Chapter 7) – they tended to disassociate themselves from the 'crack heads' in 'crack houses'. Here, Funky D, who was in recovery at the time of the fieldwork, reflects on using crack in 'private flats', which was, of course, different to using crack in a 'crack house'. Note how she only starts to acknowledge that she used 'crack houses' when she had 'no choice' when really her crack use had started to increase dramatically:

FUNKY D: I started to smoke with my sister [in 1995].
DAN: What? In her flat?
FUNKY D: In her flat yeah – which I knew was safe. Nobody would come knocking at her door any minute. She smoked so I felt kind of safe there.
DAN: Comfortable?
FUNKY D: Comfortable and, as I went along, I found I did a lot of smoking with an African guy in South London. Remember these areas are between us but nobody knew about this man. Do you understand? It's not like everyone knew Charlie. He lives at number 30. Everyone goes in there, running their own smoke and runs off again so I felt quite safe there and then I did a lot of my smoking there. I'd go and make my money, score around the corner from there and I'm comfortable. I feel like I'm in a shell. I feel like I was in a shell.

Charlie's 'comfortable environment', however, was not always available. This prompted her to think otherwise, she said: 'Where am I going to go? I'm not going to a crack house. I'd think and I'd remember, Ray. Yeah. Down to Ray's.' Ray was a safe bet because she was not disturbed and it was important for Funky D to have a calm smoking atmosphere. However, Ray was not always around, and towards the end of the 1990s, Funky D had to negotiate different spaces in the crack scene. She didn't want family or friends to know about her activities and didn't want to smoke in 'crack houses' but said she had, on occasions 'no choice'. It was in these situations in which she missed the safety and security of Charlie's or Ray's residence. As she lost her entrepreneurial capabilities for funding crack through careless mistakes when shoplifting after long binges, she said she started using different 'smoking partners' in different premises. She said *they* started to take advantage of her even though she said she 'played by the rules':

Playing tricks on you because it's the way. That's why it's so important to get your lick because if you don't and if you get put off your track you'll fucking lose it. It's happened to me because this guy that I used to smoke with he started playing with my mind big-time. Really, really big-time. He played with my mind big-time. I was going out and grafting all the money because that's what I did anyway. When I was smoking reefs I'd go out, make my money and come back and I was very kind when I was smoking. I'd throw you a couple of rocks and if I needed something I'd call and go and get us some more and I didn't ask 'put five down, put ten down, put twenty down'. I'm not like that. If I've got it 'here are you can have yours' and, not only that, I respected that I'm in your house as well because, at the end of the day, I'm in your house smoking. I can't be blazing in front of you and not offer you something. Do you get me? But he played on this. He really played on this and, when the drugs finished, he would treat me like shit. He'd watch and see that it's coming to the last one and I'd give him a bit – it might be my last pipe or my last stone – and he'd start 'Oh have you finished? Have you finished Funky D?' I'm like 'hang on a minute. Let me just get my ... ' and that's why it's so important and, what he was doing was, if I didn't get that last bit properly he knew that he'd disturbed me and he knew that I'd have to go out and get more because I didn't just enjoy my last one and that was my last one and this is how that man would play with my mind so you know what that kept making me do? Run out around the clock.

(Funky D)

Convinced she would not return, however, Funky D continued smoking there 'on and off for about two years'. While she said she continued to have a 'few little brushes in crack houses' increasingly she sought 'private smokes'. Still, crack smoking in these flats was not associated with 'crack houses':

It's just me and maybe just the person and we're having our smoke, we're smoking our pipe and we're having a chat – we've got the telly on. That's what I call private ... but that's the things that go on in crack houses and I think those are the things why its so violent in crack houses because you get people 'fucking up your buzz' they call it. They 'fuck up your buzz' and a person will just fuck up your buzz because they want to be spiteful. They might be sitting there and they ain't got a rock and they ask you 'give us a pipe. Give us a pipe, Mark' and Mark goes 'I ain't got none. I've just come in off the road and I just bought a twenty so I can't do it. I can't give you a pipe'. You know what I'd do? I'd wait for you to set up that bottle and you'd have a lick. 'Can I finish that?' and it's all psychological but, had I given you some of my crack me and you would have been the best of mates. You might have respected my lick. Do you get me?

Reasoning that smoking at Charlie's or Ray's was 'private' because it was only a few people, Funky D said it was this which contributed to people 'going in and out' of crack houses because they had not 'got it [the buzz] right'. For this group (High Society), their perception of what they do in crack houses is different from those who use crack 'problematically' (Low Life). The latter group's limited spending powers, perceived low social status in the crack scene, extreme focus on using crack, and vulnerability to manipulation and victimisation all seem to have more severe implications in the crack house; particularly for women as G indicates:

G: Yeah. That's where I'm coming from. I've always called it 'washed rocks'. I take a hit and can't move for about three quarters of an hour and that was down to the quality of what we used to be able to get back in those days and you used to be able to wash it ourselves. Back in those days you couldn't go out on the road like you could today and go and buy something that's already washed and it's called crack and I think the reason that it's called crack and why there's a difference between crack and washed rocks is that crack it's the way it's prepared. If you've got something and you don't know how it's prepared nine times out of ten it's not going to be good and that's one of the main differences in quality of crack in those days to like what's going on today. Like today's crack houses are filled with prostitutes. Prostitutes run the crack houses. They're what – when I say run the crack houses – they're what give the dealers their profit. Ninety per cent of the men that hang out in crack houses are dopefiends, ponces who like this thing, can't maintain their habit, are tired of going to prison and effectively are scared to put themselves on offer to earn a pound note so what they do is terrorise the girls so, if you think of that scenario, how could one possibly enjoy a drug in that ...
[PAUSE]

DAN: ... environment.

G: ... in that environment and that is the danger of what's going on now in crack houses or why you'll see some people shooting up on steps or in phone boxes. A typical scenario: a girl will go out, she'll do a punter and she thinks that Tom or Harry might be at the crack house she'll try and avoid it but that'll be difficult if she knows the dealer's there. Oh she'll go there and try and get something and try and hide it in her bra or wherever and it's that sort of mad scenario there that's terrible or girls bringing back punters, yeah? This is where you need to be careful now. You're doing the research on this sort of thing yeah and you end up back in the crack house and you're not supervised by someone who's predominant in that area it'll be dangerous for you; given that I've just said to you that ninety per cent of the people are men. Let's talk about the men. Ninety per cent of the men that go to crack houses nowadays are just people that are addicted to crack mentally, you know it's a mental addiction, and they can't afford it so they'll do anything so I'm saying you're liable to be stripped of even this – they can sell that – they want anything. These are the main differences to back in the day to what's going on today. That's what I told you. What I said to you amounts to that. I didn't use those exact words but you think about what I've said, yeah? Crack houses have got ninety per cent of the men. The men in there who can't afford to buy anything apart from when they get their giro or some little madness might happen on the road. It's the women that go out and do punters that keep crack houses running and give the dealers their money. It's the women. It's like these men that are there are just there to terrorise the girls. That's why it's classed as the lowest of the low.

This does not necessarily affect the way in which all individuals and groups interact in crack houses. Some, such as Funky D, recognised that exposure to different types of 'crack house' seemed to affect how they behave in other venues as well across the crack scene. Similarly:

> I think it depends on who is around, who you hang around with that smokes. If you go around people that act differently, you will behave like them and that is a fact. I used to be around people that would smoke in spliffs. Me I'm terrible, I can't handle it. I think people are after me 'you're going to nick my pipe'. I get paranoid. I never used to be like that but that's what happens when you mix with people that do that. That's what having people around does – you pick up their habits.
>
> (Bruv)

Some seem to develop situational coping mechanisms – similar to those who use crack in public settings – that lock out the potential volatility of interactions in the crack house. They say they do this to experience the 'crack buzz':

SHY H: *Yeah. I mean I never liked it even when I was in the crack houses I was like 'what am I doing here?' and I knew what was going down. I knew everyone was trying to take advantage and stuff but I'd go because I wanted the drug.*

DAN: *When you used in the crack houses were you having a bad buzz in the house?*

SHY H: *It depends. When I'm on it I can just cut out. That's why it took me (why it went on for such a long time) and I could just cut out wherever I was. I was fine and never got carried away. It was only when I …*

DAN: *… came down?*

SHY H: *Yeah came down and when it ran out that's when it really hit home.*

The long-term implications of 'zoning out' may serve to isolate the individual from the crack scene and mainstream society. Moreover, the realisation that crack supply has diminished creates deep depression and personal anxiety that is exacerbated by the social pressures from others in the crack house. Some panic and get volatile. Some look at ways to trick others out of crack/money. Others, as discussed, respond by mobilising a way of 'zoning out' the pressured interactions which enables them to experience/enjoy the 'crack buzz'. It was evident earlier in the chapter that tailoring this ability to lock out the world may help them in similar contexts when using crack in public or other environments. So for the Low Life, while crack houses are risky places to go, they seem to be places where many end up going. In crack houses populated by Low Life, users report strewn syringes, needles and crack pipes, and blood stains which seem to act as symbolisms of stigma reflecting directly on to the core identity of the crack user. Being in these environments, with these people, among these symbols of stigma, may affect the crack-using experience and heighten feelings of risk and anxiety:

ISH: *It's a squat. They use it as a crack house. They've got into there and they've opened it up as a crack house for themselves so really it's no-one's. Anyone who's there shares it.*

DAN: *Anyone's and everyone's. So I could just walk in there?*

ISH: *Yeah. We could go now.*

DAN: *Ok, but there's basically there are no rules?*

ISH: *No rules. In this crack house you can smoke and you can inject in front of each other.*

DAN: *Ok what about the state of the property? I'm just thinking this place must be a fucking tip* [dirty].

ISH: *It is, it is. You've got needles and bottles everywhere – needles everywhere. They don't clear up. As I said, I went in there once, yeah. When I first went in there I didn't like it because there were needles all over the place and a lot of them didn't have lids on them. They could have stabbed into me and I don't know if any of those people have got AIDS. I haven't exactly asked them. As soon as I went in there I had two pipes and I walked out. The lady went 'where are you going?' and I said 'well, I can't sit in here.'*

DAN: *Right. So it's not the type of environment that you can relax in.*

ISH: *Even the way that I was injecting at the time ...*

DAN: *Were you?*

ISH: *Yeah, but I was using my own. I wasn't using no-one else's but, as I said, I was smoking crack and I was banging up but I couldn't get a vein and I was smoking. If I could get a vein I could bang it up. At the end of the day if I put it in the works – the syringe – and I can't get a vein it's wasted. It's gone down the drain and I've lost my drugs and it stresses me out and I go mad.*

In many narratives and observations of crack taking, diminishment of crack seems to be a stressful experience, but in crack houses, this pressure seems to be greater. No one, it seems, wants to be the one without crack in the crack house – especially in front of others (Williams, 1990). Otherwise, they might look redundant – they might look like that person who cannot work for themselves, who has to 'beg' and 'ponce' from others for more crack or a loan for crack. In short, this may confirm that they are one of the Low Life:

IVERSON: *Smoking induces psychotic behaviour, so like when I smoke, my eyes go straight to the floor looking for the white bits and they are staring at the floor, I think it is to do with the drug but the crack heads, the ones lower down in the hierarchy, are the ones that get played upon. Tricked and so on. Try and distract you to get your crack – there will be violence if someone reaches into my space. There is a code of ethics and people know you should not do that, it is unheard of, if you do that in someone's crack house, you would get done for it, you would get beaten because there needs to be order. Like say we are smoking, in our house, we used to smoke from left to right and you come in and start blazing, you will get beaten for that. You shouldn't do that, you should ask first. Maybe someone else will to gain favour from me, 'don't do that, don't disrespect the man. The man is sharing out, wait your turn'. Then they [Low Life] are sucking up to you, trying to put out your pipe and everything even though it is not what you want but you get used to it.*

The atmospheres in places such as public settings, temporary accommodation and crack houses seem to affect the individuals and their identities in these spaces. Some became paranoid and anxious; and this is manifested in the way in which they experienced the 'buzz' and adopted behaviours to which they have been exposed:

CRADLE: *Yeah because what I noticed as well was that I never used to get paranoid until one day this guy came around and it was like his paranoia rubbed off on me because he used to keep going 'ssh!' and, after he left, that rubbed off on me and I started doing all that madness.*

DAN: *Really?*

CRADLE: *If I was smoking crack I couldn't have no noise – nothing. That's why I stopped going smoking with people – no noise. No noise at all.*

However, these examples indicate that the environmental circumstances are rarely suitable and therefore individual anxieties and insecurities appear only to be amplified in such arenas (Rhodes *et al.*, 2007). Instead this appears to drive many crack users to increasingly solitary conditions, paranoid that others are either 'out to get them'; are out to steal what little piece of the world they have; or disturb the very moment of the day in which they have risked everything. As Shy H succinctly summarised from her experiences in the crack house; it drives many to feel increasingly mistrustful and isolated:

It's a very antisocial drug [crack] as well. Very anti-social. There's nothing good about it. It's, like I said, half the people [in the crack house] are all 'ssh. Don't want to talk'. Then the other half are talking. Talking to themselves, talking at people and it's like you can't have a friendship because all you're doing is watching how much they're taking and are they getting more than you? Anyone will backstab anyone just to get some more. So it's like that drug just takes all morals. Friendship, everything just goes out the window. You can start and you're fine with someone then, once you start smoking, towards the end it's like 'you've had more than me' 'No. You've had more than me' and that's what it's like and all you're doing is plotting a scam to get some of the other one. It's not a sociable drug.

(Shy H)

This sense of severe personal isolation poses a significant problem for crack users, and seems to have a bearing on how they perceive themselves in the crack scene (Chapter 7) and how they make changes to their lives (Chapter 8).

Conclusion

This chapter highlights how certain benefits seem to be available for high-earning crack users (High Society) which, in turn, affects their access to crack supply. The interactions among this group are generally different from those that take place among the lower end of the crack scene (Low Life) – who seem to experience higher chances of violence, victimisation and manipulation. However, as crack careers deteriorate (Chapter 4; Malchy et al., 2008; Moore and Dietze 2005), so too, it seems, do hierarchical positions. Equally, at the same time, the importance of maintaining the crack-using experience seems to intensify because it means much more for the individual to maintain it (Giddens, 1990, 1991; Lasch, 1985). Here, many crack users further deny their position (Chapter 7) and attempt to make the most of their crack 'buzz' for which they have 'worked' all day (Preble and Casey, 1969). Any disturbance or threat of intrusion appears only to heighten feelings of insecurity (Rhodes et al., 2007).

Some, like Cuz and Gums, may develop a normative, emotional barrier when using crack which may deflect feelings of shame and difference (Maruna, 2001), while others don't seem able to develop such a framework and are far more vulnerable (Shake), as their crack-using experiences – as they construct them – seem directly affected by socio-structural (Bourdieu, 1984) and environmental conditions (Duff, 2007). Therefore crack user identity construction also takes place in the cultural milieu of the crack scene (DeCorte, 2001; Dovey et al., 2001; Fitzgerald, 2009; Rhodes et al., 2007) and its environments (Duff, 2009; Fitzgerald, 2009; Schwandt, 2001; Zinberg, 1984) through reciprocal, interactional processes (Duff, 2007; Giddens, 1984; Rhodes, 2002). Indeed, these environments have a strong influence on crack user identities (Duff, 2009; Fitzgerald, 2009), because they may amplify individual levels of shame, anxiety and insecurity (Rhodes et al., 2007). For the Low Life, these social experiences in these environments seem to become embedded in their everyday practices (Friedman et al., 1998; Bourdieu, 1984) and this is important because it has implications for how crack-using experiences are lived in relation to environment (Giddens, 1984). The crack scene and its interactions are further shaped by social control mechanisms (Chapter 6).

Crack use and social control

Once in a prison system, to look for an easy way out is to look for treatment, but all it is is an easy way out of jail – they then staple cut their months and then they fuck it off [half their prison sentence and then don't turn up for treatment] – they are out of jail, it hasn't solved the problems; it has moved the problem on to somewhere else but the problem comes back on to society which is the main thing. It turns up in crime, prostitution, mental illness and they [the government] haven't solved the problem. It seems like the government like to have x amount of people who are incapable of working. It puts people in jail and it creates work for the Home Office or Prison Service – people get paid a wage from someone else's misery.

(Easy E)

Introduction

Forms of social control arise because of the various problems crack users are perceived to present to local communities and to themselves (Chapter 2). Social policies and law enforcement drives are implemented in an attempt to improve the 'quality of life' for the wider community (Duff, 2009; O'Malley, 2008) while drug treatment approaches are designed to divert crack users away from their drug use and criminal activities (Chapter 2). However, the execution of the former seems to have negative consequences for crack users and the organisation of the crack scene (Chapter 5). It is such policies that appear to thrust crack users into improvised crack-using environments (Chapter 7; Rhodes et al., 2007), which has some bearing on crack users' well-being and day-to-day drug-using practices (Becker, 1963; Bourdieu, 1984; Rhodes, 2002). The design of the drug treatment approaches, to some extent, also contributes to processes of social exclusion among crack users (Bourgois, 2003). Attention is firstly devoted to how this takes place through aggressive social policies, law enforcement drives and through the agencies designed to 'help' – drug support services.

Aggressive social policies

Crack users' social interactions in the crack scene seem to be exacerbated by hard-line social policies on drug users. In this study, two main policies appear to contribute to the significant displacement of crack users: the central government-driven Anti-Social Behaviour Act (2003); and local authority-driven Crack House Closure Protocols (2003). They derive from strategic justifications to target and resolve High Crack Areas (HCAs). Rivertown was thought to be one such area of concern and was identified by the government as an HCA in 2002. With the advent of the Anti-Social Behaviour Act (2003), many visible deviant and criminal activities, such as begging, loitering, drug using or dealing, were targeted and the police and authorities increasingly sought ASBOs on populations such as crack users (Matthews *et al.*, 2007). Some crack users indicate that this increases the pressure on them to offend in other ways. Funky D indicated that street drug users generally did little harm, in particular those who 'begged' – although it was seen as 'immoral' and 'anti-social' by the authorities (Safer Rivertown Partnership, 2004a) and others in the crack scene (Chapter 5):

> I look at it that begging, you're not doing any harm. If you don't want to give him nothing then you walk away. They don't say to you 'fuck off you tight cunt'. They say 'Be lucky'… So there's no harm, a man sitting there who doesn't want to go out stealing. So really they should leave him alone. Why are they arresting him?
>
> (Funky D)

Moreover, the way in which some Rivertown authorities go about seeking punitive sanctions against such groups also appears to use underhand threats of withdrawing funding from drug support services unless they cooperate with 'evidence gathering' on problem populations. In this interview excerpt, the manager of St Peter's Drop-In reflects on the awkward position in which the agency was placed unless they supplied evidence against the 'dangerous street drinkers' – who also happened to be crack users:

MANAGER: *He [councillor] convened these multi-agency meetings which were quite effective and we had the police, Connections Central, us, and a few other agencies if they turned up or wardens occasionally to try and address individuals who were being seen regularly. But then the monitoring that went on in those meetings gradually became a kind of tick-list of loads of people getting ASBOs. So then we weren't contributing figures to the meetings but were contributing kind of information about people's support needs.*

DAN: *Were you told that you were contributing information towards an ASBO?*

MANAGER: *Well, we were asked to and we said we wouldn't because what they wanted was evidence of people being seen on the street at a certain time with a can of beer and we weren't prepared to give that but they did ask us to.*

DAN: *Of course.*

MANAGER: *Well, no 'Of course' at all. They thought 'Well we're funding you … come on' [laughs] 'Give us the information'. They wanted us to serve the ABCs as well.*

DAN: *For them?*

MANAGER: *Yeah, so they wanted us to serve them to the drinkers and we again said that's not our role. We are the carrot in this equation and not the stick! You've got the police and the wardens so what do you need us to be nasty for? We are meant to be the nice guys! So we had quite a few run-ins with them over this and we really did have to face them down at times because they were implying that they would get our funding if we didn't cooperate and we had to actually just bite the bullet and say 'Get on with it!' … sometimes there are places that you don't actually want to go and from our point of view we were really keen to work with that group but we didn't want to work with them under absolutely ANY circumstances – it just didn't seem useful. So the data that was used to get the ASBOs after that initial tussle was just gathered by the wardens, the PCSOs and the police. It was logged on their system so if they were seen with a can of beer and every month the policeman who co-ordinated it would log up all the incidences so if you hit five I think in a monthly period you would initially be up for an ABC and then they'd serve the ABC on you and if you continued to hit that five mark they then worked towards an ASBO.*

Many of these 'street drinkers' such as Dawn, Babe, Shake and Clouds are also crack users. The chances are extremely high that they would log five cautions because, aside from a few using Connections Central nearby to collect prescriptions, they rely on strong alcohol to reduce the effects of crack. They are also local to the area, and having spent much of their time there – even if they were dispersed for unpredictable periods – saw it as their space. Although reluctantly, the agencies from which these populations receive support are also, to some degree, involved in their exclusion. By early 2005, St Peter's Drop-In had withdrawn all provision for street drinkers – which allowed them to drink safely on the premises – because they had been awarded a continuous funding stream from statutory agencies to deliver provision for DTTO clients. This meant their support for those who routinely came in on a voluntary basis disappeared. Instead, the former client group started to congregate outside the service on the streets. However, their new visibility appeared to be exactly what the authorities were looking for. While outside one day with the 'street drinkers', some community wardens became concerned they were causing problems for the community by sitting on the steps, quietly drinking alcohol:

The Red Coats [community wardens who inform the police if there are problems on the streets] came along – because it was a 'wet day' [the day when one could drink in St Peter's Drop-In]. The Coats were trying to encourage people to move on from drinking on the steps outside which had been the norm for a long time but recently they had always been asked to 'move on'.

Not that we were causing a problem and, although people were glancing at us as they walked past, our presence seemed largely harmless (I thought). When three people refused to leave under instruction from the Coats, they started to radio someone. Next minute, the director of St Peter's Drop-In comes out and tells us all to 'move on and to stop drinking outside' – wow, even the service director was telling us to 'move on'.

(Field notes)

Some weeks later, Dawn and Clouds were served ASBOs and started to appear more frequently in the north of Rivertown, outside the hostel where I met Cuz. The authorities in the local ward, nevertheless, hailed the scheme a success even though both women had disengaged from their local drug service (Aitkin *et al.*, 2002).

Law enforcement drives

Such populations are not only targeted for being 'problematic' on the streets but are also targeted in various drug-using locations. In this study, this policy approach is part of the Anti-Social Behaviour Act (2003), which led to local crack house protocols. Rivertown's Crack House Protocol (2003) was designed to be a joint agreement between the police, the local authority, various housing departments, registered social landlords (RSLs) and voluntary agencies. The rationale was to enhance existing legal procedures, give more power to the police, and speed up the process of closing crack houses. Under the protocol, when drug raids took place, the police were to exchange information with the council to help housing departments take legal action to close down crack houses and to provide support to 'vulnerable tenants' who had 'lost control' of their properties – either to other drug users or drug dealers. While the implementation of the protocol saw an increase in the number of crack house closures in Rivertown, it was difficult to conclude that the overall number of crack houses in Rivertown had decreased (Webster *et al.*, 2001). No evaluation of its impact was undertaken. Moreover, many crack users said that other crack houses became available as others were closed down (Burgess, 2003).

Nevertheless, central government research was quick to celebrate its success. In 2003/04 there had been 'over 100 crack houses raided … over 50 arrests … and over 55 referrals [to treatment]' (Bovaird, 2004: 4). However, it was difficult to discern whether all the properties were 'crack houses' or, indeed, how well those who were referred did in treatment, even if they were referred and managed to turn up. The issue received further examination the following year after another batch of crack house closures, although there was still ambiguity in what the police considered to be a 'crack house'. Local police data showed that, from April 2004 to June 2005, there were 105 referrals to the Rivertown Crack House Protocol; however, after initial investigation, 53 were not considered to be 'crack houses'. Local research found significant gaps in the protocol and its strategy. Bailie (2003) found there was a lack of a police/local authority communication strategy on drugs; lack of police/community consultation on the drugs issue; insufficient involvement of partner agencies in police operations; and a lack of planning to follow through and prevent displacement from police operations.

Crack users feel that more intensive help should be systematically offered to those tenants affected by the closure of such properties. One housing officer said that after crack house evictions, drug users are not referred to drug support services: 'People do get evicted from a crack house or put in prison and are not helped. It is probably when they need most help.' Moreover, when crack houses are closed, another seems to open in the nearby area – even in the same street: 'This one that got raided the other day, they've started up two blocks away again. They were over at 19 first – that got raided – then they went over to 29 – that got raided – now they're at 39' [Lady Di]. It isn't long before 'word on the street' indicates where other potential places to use crack become available: 'My flat was opened up and within two days the word was around. People then know it as a crack house and people start coming round' [Bruv]. It is in these conditions that the social networks of the crack scene tend to thrive:

> Like my sister. She lived in the house but she was clean. She had a kid. She kept everything under control to a certain extent. At the beginning this is how it all starts. Sent her to school, everything's fine, people come around, smoke, then more people find out you're smoking and more people come around, knocking early hours of the morning, and things just escalate and you never used to want to smoke at two o'clock in the morning, but someone's knocked at the door with a smoke so you let them in. That person tells another person that they've come around so another person comes around the next day. So she ... would become a prostitute with that kid in the house and everything.
>
> (Fam)

> It's about immediate needs, getting those needs met one way or another, and that sort of situation spirals that other people involved also jump at an opportunity and the whole thing sort of gets out of hand. No one's really controlling the situation, or necessarily setting it up as clearly as I've described it. It evolves. The same around a lot of squats, I mean ... the place I talked about, at the moment the two guys who are using that place are trying to stop anybody else going in there and not taking anyone else there, but I suspect after a relatively short period of time will compromise that principle and in no time at all it will become a really chaotic [drug] using den and, at the moment, the reason E said to me he didn't want to take anyone new back there it's because you get too many people coming and going, it will get closed, the neighbours will call the police, you know, etc.
>
> (Philo)

The combination of the Anti-social Behaviour Act and Rivertown's Crack House Protocol appeared to have direct implications for off-street drug-using environments as well as on-street, public drug-using settings (O'Malley, 2008) and this appears to impede crack-using practices, making them more pressured and risky (Rhodes, 2002). Scruff identified this shift:

SCRUFF: *Any places that I know of that are outdoors that are outside where people go to use or, over the last few years, where people have gone to use there's been a real clamp-down. A real surge in closing all these places off, cancelling that, shutting them up and locking them up, whether they've been sheds or corners of parks or whatever. The council have been locking them up or ripping up parks or whatever, making them no longer accessible and there's less and less places for people to go and use which isn't going to stop them using. It's just forcing them more into the open and that is what's happening and you notice more and more paraphernalia and stuff being more open – more visible.*

DAN: *And I suppose today is a classic example* [after Scruff injected in a park and was seen by park workers and a young family].

SCRUFF: *There you go then. There's less private places for them to go so they're having to take bigger risks if you like.*

These pressures, coupled with the mistrustful alliances into which crack users are often drawn in these unpredictable environments (Chapter 5), appear to have significant consequences for the ways in which crack users interact. Because those spaces are increasingly monitored and prohibited, an 'amplification' process appears to take place which affects crack user well-being (Singer, 2003) and the crack-using experience (Becker, 1963). It may be that the paranoia surrounding the illegality of their actions (Chapter 4; Reinarman and Levine, 1997); the pressured social interactions (Chapter 5); the fear and anxiety of being unable to 'experience' the buzz (Giddens, 1991) interplays with a broader paranoia about the potential for intrusion from the police or disturbance from other crack users.

> One time when I had my flat I'd done a bit of shoplifting and I went home. I sold the stuff, went home and sold all the stuff, got some crack and I got paranoid thinking the police were coming so I was out the window, looking out the window ssh ssh ssh and I had this bird with me and I was like 'shut up! Just shut up' and she was just sitting there.
>
> (Gums)

> It's just like everyone's sitting there [in the crack house] and smoking crack and you don't know if anything's going to kick off with trouble or if it's going to get raided by the old bill [police] or anything can happen.
>
> (Bombshell)

Indeed, such a self-reflexive awareness of illegal actions against the potential for intrusion also seems to affect the behaviour of those using crack, and, to some extent, seems to influence the environments in which crack is used:

FUNKY D: *You get paranoid and, when I first started taking my pipe in '95, I got paranoid then. Not to the stage that I was like 'there's people at the window'. I'd peep out of the window, don't get me wrong, but I was alright but as it went along – as my drug use got more – and I think as it started to get out of control and the types of drugs that I was smoking I think I got more paranoid because I'm telling you I had some drugs that were fucking shit. In 2004, when I stopped doing it, they were shit. I don't know if they were rat poison or what and they just made me feel ... 'oh my God I can't even smoke it.' I'd run out, literally run out, leave it there, run out, go back to get something different because I couldn't smoke that because I felt so fucked up – and then I'd never forget I remember this guy who had just got some drugs and he said it had just come from Jamaica and it sent me really, really paranoid. Now I don't get really paranoid. I'll get the 'odd look out the window' but I'm alright but my paranoid like we were talking the other day I'm paranoid because I know what I'm doing is wrong and I'm a criminal and I'm sitting here smoking an illegal drug and I know it's wrong. I'll be looking out the window. I'm not one of those people who say 'Oh look there's a white thing in the tree.' I'm not that kind of paranoid. 'There's a mad people out there. There's all those white things in the tree.' I'm not that kind of paranoid. I'm paranoid about outside and getting found out that and I'm a criminal. I might have a case. I'm that kind of paranoid. There's different types of paranoia.*

DAN: *I think that's all tied in with the whole climate of paranoia around this drug; not just taking it but fucking dealing it, to be around it, everything, people that know about it. It's a climate of paranoia.*

Thus macro structural pressures seem to have implications for attitudes to the self and the individual framework of the crack user and this seems to be manifested through unpredictable behaviours, day-to-day discourses around crack and risky cultural practices (Bourdieu, 1984). In many respects, an accumulation of these experiences may foster personal barriers between the individual and conventional society which may augment already embedded perceptions that mainstream society cares little for their existence; that the agencies designed to 'help' don't seem to be able to offer sufficient resolution; and that the complex individual problems they have amassed seem impossible to resolve (Chapter 2). This may, therefore, complement feelings of distance and shame and, as a consequence, many become more fatalistic and appear to lose faith in a way out (Chapter 8). Unfortunately, some agencies designed to 'help' crack users are also, to some degree, involved in their exclusion.

Drug support services

The way in which some drug support services are structured seems to contribute to the social exclusion and continued transiency of some crack users (Bourgois, 2003; Bourgois and Schonberg, 2009; Leibow, 1993). Rivertown deals with a substantial number of problematic drug users (Chapter 3) and there are limited places for rehabilitation (Chapter 8). Therefore, strategic decisions need to be made about who is most capable of making changes – who can be most responsible for themselves (Petersen, 1997; Rimke, 2000). However, for crack users this philosophy seems to do more detriment than good. The initial problem seems to be that access to drug treatment is more available through the criminal justice system, rather than for someone walking into a drug service with the intention of making changes to their lifestyle.

The locus of drug treatment is driven through the criminal justice system (Chapter 2). On arrest, drug tests are mandatory and arrest referral workers offer drug users treatment options in custody suites. For many crack users like Cuz, however, this only angers them because it does not reflect their genuine motivation to pursue lifestyle changes. They feel resentful that their advances for change are dismissed and that service engagement can only take place on the terms of the State. This disparity is reflected in waiting times for access to drug support services. For example, criminal justice clients receive assessments and prescriptions – if necessary – on average within three days from Connections North and Central. However, those accessing Connections North from the community – i.e. walking in off the street wanting to access drug support services – wait up to three weeks for a full assessment. This is more difficult for crack users than heroin users because they are the most unreliable in attending appointments (Fox et al., 2005; Weaver et al., 2007).

Prison-based drug programmes rely on CARAT workers referring on to community drug services. However, although some say they 'get clean' through these channels, on returning to the community, many are not directed to the right agency. While efforts are made by some agencies to prepare crack users for release, there is little they can do about those who receive short sentences – which crack users predominantly do (Reuter and Stevens, 2008) – because workers do not get sufficient time to get into prison to make assessments. In addition, on release, many crack users fail to turn up for their appointment with community drug services (Weaver et al., 2007). These problems have been endemic in Rivertown in the five years preceding this research (Fox et al., 2005).

The sheer volume of drug users in the area seems to have signalled significant changes to the configuration of drug support across Rivertown. This seems to be linked to the need to improve performance figures for those engaging with drug support services and entering treatment. Local policymakers adapted the process so that more commitment was required on part of the drug user. Instead of clear-cut yes/no decisions over funding for day programmes or rehab, drug users instead need to 'prove' they can engage and show their motivation to get clean:

Before DATs, you'd go in, see a guy on remand, do the assessment, bring the assessment back, discuss the findings, a decision would be made for that person, and it would be a yes-or-no answer: you can go to rehab or you can't. But now it's not like that. It might be 'yes', it might be 'no, you can't go to rehab, but when you get released you can make contact with drug services, engage with their service, show us you've got some motivation, and then they will bring you back to our attention and we'll look at getting you into a more structured treatment environment'.

(Manager – Substance Misuse Team)

For someone using heroin only, this process seems to be easier than for those using crack – or who have crack use as part of their drug-using repertoire. Heroin users seem to be less of a gamble for policymakers because they don't have such a poor reputation for dropping out of services (Chapter 2). Furthermore, it ensures that funding based on 'drug users reached' is not lost by a service if their client drops out of treatment. With commitment from the drug user, however, much more seems possible. Unfortunately for this belief, crack users with such commitment in this sample are in the minority (Chapter 8). While for some, the priority to attend a drug service is low given poor referral links and lack of stable housing, others are simply not aware of support. Despite the introduction of the statutory-funded Crack Service in Rivertown in 2002, many in the sample have little or no knowledge of it (Chapter 2). My field notes recorded a visit to Crack Service with Cuz and Babe. The staff probably presumed I was also a drug user because I was with them. Having heard about Crack Service through Cuz a few days earlier, Babe realised it was local to where she lived:

[I] came back to Crack Service at about 3pm, walked in and gave my name as 'D'. I had my hood up and walked in with Cuz and Babe. There was some sort of training going on and in front of us were a crowd of people [workers] clutching mugs of coffee – they were taking a break from the training (think it was for auricular acupuncture). I said little and stood there. One of the crowd of staff immediately said as we walked past, 'you can have someone stick fresh needles in your ear in there, if you want' – this was directed at Babe and her response was negative. She hadn't even heard of Crack Service and she only lived around the corner. We sat down while the crowd of about 7–8 workers stared at us. After five minutes of standing there, one 'new girl' walked up to me and said 'you're new here' but after a brief chat then went back into the room where the training was going on. Cuz started to make us tea and toast – he himself had not been in there for two months. The crowd of workers then dispersed and there was one guy at the reception. We sat there and the [reception] guy made no attempt to make conversation with us. An ex-user came in who was now working as a builder – he talked more to us but sort of kept his distance a bit. He had just finished work and came in for a cup of tea – he came in with a nice new bike but said nothing to the [reception] guy... I looked on the wall and there were two notices saying the office would be closed for three days for 'staff training'. I then saw the opening times of the service – from 1.30pm to 4.30pm. Cuz and Babe decided to go outside for a cigarette; it was approaching 4.30pm and the training was still going on. The ex-user came outside for a small chat. Then promptly on 4.30pm, the [reception] man walked outside and said 'hey, guys, it's 4.30pm and we're closing'. In a sort of defensive tone, Cuz said 'where else can I go?' The guy said St Peter's Drop-In [but they were closed for the day as well] and another place for alcoholics... Cuz then asked him if he had a list [of other services] but he said 'no'.

(Field notes)

While this not only highlighted Babe's initial negative experience with Crack Service, it also illustrated some of the approaches of staff towards those who managed to access the services during the three-hour drop-in period in the after-noon. While a few users I met reflected on good experiences with Crack Service, these tended to be related to when the service had offered a more flexible opera-tion, and counselling at any time during the day. Shy H, for example, reflected how she was one of the first clients of the service in 2002. She was positive about the support and efficiency of the service:

What's good about them was that you could actually go back and say 'I've used' [crack/drugs] and they would still deal with you and that's, as I said, what's so good about Crack Service. Their whole philosophy is that you can tell them that you've used and they're fine with it. They're not like 'oh get off our programme or stop using'.

In particular, it was the 'hour available for counselling' that helped her. However, she then revealed: 'They've changed all the staff because I went in there recently and it's very different. To me maybe it's not as good as it was. I think they've gone downhill a bit.'

The Crack Service outreach worker indicated that the drop-in times were reduced because of 'funding restrictions'. At the end of 2002, crack users could access the service seven hours a day, five days a week, yet by 2004 it had been reduced to three hours a day. In the same period, the immediate availability of counsellors five days a week was reduced to twice weekly by appointment only.

Crack Service's principle provisions are counselling by appointment, detox teas, massage, acupuncture, advice and harm reduction, but crack users perceive this to be inadequate and outdated (Chapter 2). Those that were aware of Crack Service appear to have learnt quite quickly that, as a site to resolve crack use, it had little to offer them. Even Crack Service workers admitted in interviews to me that the provision is inadequate for crack users. However, arguing the case for additional provision was difficult, partly because the harm reduction agenda generated little appeal with the local authority:

We have to keep on their back [local authority], we have to keep demanding these things. We are trying to have this open at the weekend. But it's a slow process and we need to keep pushing these things. Syringes have been a nightmare; they didn't want to give us syringes. And then the syringes weren't enough, people needed spoons. And then there were other issues and then the virus [HCV] was spreading everywhere, so then we had to educate them. And they wanted us to collect evidence of this, but these things take time. I mean, if you think four years ago, crack services did not exist at all because they didn't know what to do with crack users, and the people who gave out methadone felt it wasn't needed, and all these populations of drug users were getting no services at all. And their lives were getting messier and messier, much worse than opiate users.

(Crack Service outreach worker)

As a former crack user, he had some insight into the needs of crack users. Here, he reflects on trying to establish harm reduction provision for crack users which, he had hoped, would increase awareness of Crack Service. Despite his efforts, he was discouraged because it was not 'legal' and would generate 'bad press':

When I started to do outreach I immediately felt the need that I needed something to give them, as I noticed that crack users didn't particularly want to talk to me. I had nothing to offer them. Very little to offer them, so I felt the need to make some health packs. Some condoms, some paraphernalia, and if not the pipe itself, at least the mesh. So they don't need to use the ash from the cigarette, that's meant to be bad. Some health bits and pieces. So I phoned [the Drug Co-ordinator] and I phoned all the people involved in the needle exchange and it wasn't legal. They said, if you want to do this, it's your responsibility for this to go down the service and you could have terrible press. So I left it.

(Crack Service outreach worker)

Without support from senior providers, promotion of Crack Service and its provision remained limited. Conversely, the voluntary-funded Cross Street Harm Reduction employed ex-drug users to operate a harm reduction outreach service at the social security office, at various temporary accommodation centres and in drug-using hotspots. With some degree of success, crack users commented positively on their efforts but generally agreed that their intervention was not enough. This good work seldom translated into further investment. Despite funding increases from central government to solve Rivertown's crack problem – because it was considered an HCA – areas of provision were reduced – predominantly counselling and outreach. During the fieldwork period, the stability of Cross Street Harm Reduction looked increasingly uncertain in light of reduced funding. They had also lost key staff who had driven the harm reduction agenda.

The uncertainty of the provision and the loss of key services did not appear to help access to crack users. Without proactive strategic intervention, accessing the population became limited. The allocation of £4.8m for drug treatment in Rivertown in 2004/05 was supposed to fund the crack/stimulant services in providing both open and available provision. Yet it was difficult to see how this translated into frontline support for crack users. As I write in 2011, Crack Service still retains the same drop-in times (1.30pm to 4.30pm), still operates appointment-only systems and is now only open four days a week. In Rivertown, access to most other drug support services are also restricted to normal 9–5 office hours and none of the drug services are open in the evening or at weekends.

Even if crack users are aware of Crack Service, the configuration of the service did not appear to be congruent to crack users' lifestyles. Many needed to negotiate appointment systems and rigid opening times. Unfortunately, from the observations I made of Crack Service, honoured appointments appeared to be quite rare. On another occasion:

> From 10am to about 12pm, no one came into the service for any type of appointment. Why didn't they just have a drop-in all day, instead of limiting their time to appointments in the morning? The staff weren't doing anything apart from smoking cigarettes and using the internet.
>
> (Field notes)

Nevertheless, most drug support services in Rivertown, including the two prescribing services (Connections Central and North), operated 'appointment-only' systems. The 'stimulant service', which operated from these two services, was designed to offer one-to-one counselling to cocaine and crack users. However, it consisted of one stimulant worker working between two services. She was available for one afternoon a week from 1pm to 4pm. Such counselling services would have been beneficial if crack users were able to keep appointments. Instead, the offer of this provision tends to set crack users up for failure:

DAN: [Going through research findings] *Barriers to engaging in services: even crack users with the best intentions of quitting have little time to approach services.*

CUZ: *Yeah because all they're thinking about is to get their other fix – their next fix. They haven't got time to go to a service and sit down there and chat to them, like [name] he's not on any methadone. He's made so many appointments but he's never been ...*

DAN: *... to follow them up?*

CUZ: *Follow them up because the first thing he's gonna do when he wakes up in the morning is to go and beg – to make that little bit of change to get his first fix of the day and their appointments are always in the mornings so he can never make it.*

Crack users generally operate outside these conventional time frameworks so appointments don't appear as landmarks in their daily routine. Those who try to engage with Connections Central or Connections North are given 'appointment cards' by the stimulant worker. The 'stimulant worker', who operated between Connections Central and Connections North, revealed that her three-hour weekly counselling services had 'ten open cases, five in Connections Central and five in Connections North'. The cases mainly consisted of cocaine snorters and amphetamine users. None in Connections Central were crack users and only two in Connections North were crack users. The worker thought the appointment system operated well for her clients but she had often had 'no shows' – most tellingly, this was the group of drug users that could keep appointments.

The concept of appointment systems seems therefore only to complement already fragile levels of self-esteem among crack users. BD, for example, said crack users 'looked for excuses' to use crack and that something like a 'missed appointment' would only serve to complement a notion of trying, but failing, thereby increasing feelings of shame and helplessness. Additionally, as with referral links from prison, some referral processes between different agencies are also unclear, and have implications for engagement. Several drug agency workers linked this to the need to retain as many clients as they could, because if numbers dropped, funding for the service could be jeopardised:

> Because of the organisation ... there is a rivalry. If they give you these people to work with, then next year when we come up for funding renewal, we are passing on our clients, then we don't get the funding and the agency goes down. So somehow, we all have to show something ... which I think we can do because everyone is important in their own sort of way.
>
> (Manager, Rivertown Referrals)

While some staff are aware of the limitations of their services, as a solution some tended to refer crack users to other services in different boroughs around London. This had implications for their involvement in any kind of support provision local to them, and contributed to their transiency. A conversation with the manager of Connections North highlighted their role in this process. When there is little other alternative than to refer crack users to Crack Service, the manager implies that 'there was always that service across the other side of London':

MANAGER: *With stimulant users it's different. It is usually when they come to you, it is very much, not that opiate users or alcohol users don't come to us in crisis, because they do, but with stimulant users it is 'I need something and I need something now'. And then you asking them to wait a week is just not good enough. You've lost them. It depends what we've got available to offer them and I don't think that this service is particularly geared at the moment to working with stimulant users. There are other places in Rivertown where we would direct people to go.*

DAN: *Yes, I agree with you. They do live fast lifestyles. The window of opportunity is much smaller than it would be for another drug user. Where might you direct someone who was a stimulant user?*

MANAGER: *If we are full up on Wednesdays and they can't wait until Wednesday,* [we would] *probably* [refer them] *to Crack Service.*

DAN: *And that is a crack-specific service.*

MANAGER: *Yes.*

DAN: *Ok. But they are only open three hours a day.*

MANAGER: *I know.*

[AWKWARD PAUSE]

DAN: *No, it's ok, I'm just trying to work things out in my head.*

MANAGER: *Well, there are places like* [service], *which is 24 hours* [where they can go].

DAN: *That's in north London, isn't it* [and Rivertown is in south London]?

MANAGER: *It's residential. It's in* [name] *and it's London-wide.*

This referral process may be complicated by a number of other service appointments which crack users may have elsewhere. Consequently, many travel in and out of the borough in an effort to attend different appointments. Moreover, most crack users know that drug support services have waiting lists and can't be accessed immediately or during periodic moments of motivation (Dorn and South, 1985). This seems to deter them from engaging or continuing to engage. If they manage to engage, they are asked to quantify a drug that they say they use sporadically and many find it difficult to locate its role in their current lifestyle. They also need to undertake a series of assessments which examine 'how risky' they are and whether they are the 'type of drug user' appropriate for the service. After this, they may be sent to another service that has 'specific' treatments for their drug use:

> If I walk in there [drug support services]. For me to walk in somewhere – being a user – that's something hard for me and afterwards they're going to say to me 'oh you're not a crack user. You're a heroin user. Can you please go to another place' so they're passing you around. They're really passing the buck, aren't they really? So they should deal with both of them.
>
> (Cuz)

One drugs worker from St Peter's Drop-In felt strongly that crack users were not provided with needs-led care packages, and instead were made to fit with what services could offer:

> Sometimes you have to make the service fit the person, not the other way round, and this sometimes goes against the requirements of the funders – sometimes a drug user has to be turned away because they live in the wrong borough, or had the wrong type of drug problem. Basically, some services are too specific in what they can help with, and this is usually specified by the funder. For a service to provide several services, they may have to be funded by several different funders, which creates a monitoring and reporting nightmare.

Some complain that they are categorised as one particular 'type of drug user', and are told to see another service. Indeed, service configuration in Rivertown seems more appropriate for opiate drug users rather than crack users or poly-drug users (Chapter 2). Equally, some crack users said they had to adhere to certain conditions to gain support, and therefore fabricated aspects of their crack use and life circumstances. This has implications for denial of their crack use (Sykes and Matza, 1957). So after seeking support and help from the right agency, within rigid time frameworks and appointment systems, some have to comply with a number of conditions before they are able to fully access services. However, some conditions of engagement also appear to be mysteriously linked to housing in Rivertown:

DAN: *Which services do you see?*
ISH: *Just Connections North*
DAN: *But what do they do for you though?*
ISH: *They give me methadone.*
CUZ: *Yeah but that's through the hostel though because you're in the hostel –
        Connections North.*
ISH: *What – the methadone?*
CUZ: *No – the Connections North. You have to see them because you're in the hostel.
        That's the conditions. Once you're in the hostel you have to go on medication.*
DAN: *Even if you don't want methadone?*
CUZ: *No. As Bottle said – he don't want methadone does he but they're telling him if
        he wants to stay here he has to go and get a script.*
DAN: *Fucking hell! So what if someone hasn't even tried methadone before?*
CUZ: *No but they're giving him. Everyone in there takes it, except them three drinkers
        and they've taken it in the past.*
DAN: *So basically if you own up and say 'I use heroin. I stay here'. 'Right get yourself
        some methadone'. What if I don't want it?*
CUZ: *You're out.*
ISH: *You're out – back on the streets.*
DAN: *So do many people lie?*
CUZ: *They'll know anyway if you're on it or not.*
DAN: *That's wrong.*
CUZ: *That lady – do you remember that Molly – who I said hello to? She's the drug
        worker.*
ISH: *If she finds out she'll throw them out.*

Even if crack users do not need/use methadone, they may have to just to get housing and drug support. Such conditions and exclusions only seemed to add to their frustration and undermined hopefulness about change; especially given that some may have to lie to get a stabilising drug that is unlikely to benefit them. When continually faced with such barriers and conditions, some rationalise that their efforts are pointless (Dorn and South, 1985; Fletcher *et al.*, 2009), and return to crack use (Evans, 2002). Indeed, reflecting on his experiences with another service in another borough, Cuz was told that he needed to prove that he could remain drug free for seven days. He felt this was unrealistic and dropped out from the service:

> I went there and she said to me that I've got to come for a week – for seven days – and every day I come I've got to take nothing so they expected me to get up in the morning, go there clucking [withdrawing from crack and heroin].
>
> (Cuz)

Once crack users develop negative perceptions of services, word usually spreads quickly across the crack scene resulting in credibility problems for local drug support services and the treatment system in general. These negative views also seem to be augmented by face-to-face experiences with drug support service staff (Bourgois, 2003). Unfortunately, there seem to be immense social and cultural differences between some professional workers and crack users, and their day-to-day personal treatment seems inconsistent (Leibow, 1993); while some workers tend to be empathetic, others are careless in how they interact with them. This disparity may damage overall relationships between services and crack users, and contribute to distance and feelings of shame. For example, while waiting for Bail in the hostel one morning:

> I arrived a little early to the hostel – the guy on reception had to go upstairs to get Bail because I was early. I was left talking to the staff. One particular woman, who I had known for some time in the hostel, started talking to me about what I was doing. She already knew because I had told her a number of times but for some reason couldn't remember – she said that it took someone with a 'special personality' to be able to do what she does for the hostel. To be honest, I had heard a lot of bad rumours about her … many crack users from the hostel found her hostile and unapproachable. This was confirmed some minutes later when a chap started banging at the door with a can of extra-strong alcohol in his hand. Her tone changed. 'You can't bring that in here – get out. You know the rules, no drinking. Get out,' she shouted. Her tone changed again as she resumed our conversation 'sorry about that' (like it was some inconvenience to me).
>
> (Field notes)

Crack users feel frustrated by workers who show a lack of empathy and understanding of their circumstances, and even more so when they are instead stigmatised for their activities through their treatment by professionals (Chapter 2). At times, this general attitude seems to be aggravated by the medical treatment rhetoric, suggesting that 'the drug user has the problem', that the 'drug user is responsible for their actions', and that their 'drug use is a lifestyle choice'

(Petersen, 1997; Rimke, 2000; Young, 2002). This philosophy was reflected in my discussion with some drug workers. In this excerpt from an interview with the manager of Connections North, the topic had moved on to using drugs like crack and heroin on top of methadone prescriptions:

DAN: *So what about the issue of using on top of a methadone script?*

MANAGER: *We work with them. We usually ask them if they have enough methadone if they are using on top. But we don't discharge anybody for using on top of their scripts. Ever.*

DAN: *I didn't think that. I was just curious. Because we are coming into some of the myths now. People have told me that using [drugs] on top [of their methadone] increases their ... that they will need more methadone.*

MANAGER: *[very quietly] Yes. So we put the methadone up.*

DAN: *Does that just continue and continue?*

MANAGER: *No, because it will get to a point where they would stop using [crack and heroin] on top. Or maybe they just don't want to be in treatment. People that we see are generally adults. They can choose whether they want to use or not. And we don't have any judgements on that. I mean, if you want to go out and use heroin and you are fine with that, then you are making an adult lifestyle decision. I can respect they are making that decision. But if you are not ready to come in and try to sort that out, it doesn't matter how much methadone we give you or alternative therapies, you are not gonna stop using. But we will work with people that ...*

In some cases, staff appear to apply moral judgements to life choices but crack users didn't generally welcome this kind of treatment. Many had already made significant life reflections and knew what they were doing was not something they wanted to do (Chapter 4). In addition, much of the drug worker rhetoric did not seem to easily penetrate the protective film of attribution many had developed over the years that placed the 'drug as the instigator of their problems' (Booth Davies, 1997; Sykes and Matza, 1957). Therefore, despite any well meaning, and because users may struggle to recognise that they are responsible for their actions having been in denial for some years (Goffman, 1963), they often feel angry and humiliated at this treatment:

> Yeah. With me I like to – when it comes to my drug habit – I like to speak to somebody who knows what they're talking about not by a book because I think they're humiliating me. What the fuck do they know if they haven't been through it? They've got to go through it. They've got to see what this shit does to you, for you to sit there the other side of the table and to try to preach to me [is wrong]. That's the way that I look at it.
>
> (Cuz)

Additionally, some feel that service professionals in drug support services in Rivertown have trouble understanding the nature of crack use. Silver explained:

The workers there [in Crack Service] didn't seem to really know too much about it [crack use]. More of their information was based on heroin and alcohol abuse; a little bit about cocaine – 'just say no' do you know what I mean? Not quite good enough. You need to get to the root of the problem.

This is perhaps unsurprising given the absence of effective national and local strategies to deal with crack use (Chapter 2; Chapter 3). Such a lack of understanding appears to deter crack users from discussing their experiences, especially given some struggle to trust people and may use selective stories about themselves when engaging with services.

Conclusion

This chapter shows that crack scene dynamics also seem to be shaped through the political economy of crime control agencies and aggressive social policies designed to eradicate problematic/visible street drug users (Aitkin et al., 2002; Hall and Hubbard, 1998; Jayne et al., 2006; Seddon, 2008; Sparks et al., 2001; Van Swaaningen, 2005; Waterson, 1997). Efforts to deal with these structural forces can result in an amplification of personal insecurity and anxiety through attempts at risk reduction (Duff, 2007, 2009; Rhodes, 2002; Rhodes et al., 2007). In addition, for some, cultural practices seem to be internalised and reproduced (Bourdieu, 1984) resulting in paranoia, manipulation, risk and sex behaviours, violence and victimisation (Chapter 2; Chapter 7; Fitzgerald, 2009). Sadly, it seems that the agencies designed to help crack users are also, to some extent, involved in the political economy of their socio-structural position (Aitkin et al., 2002; Bourgois, 2003). With a life increasingly restricted to the crack scene, crack users attempt to find ways to deploy themselves in an effort to retain some respect and manage the self, as explored in Chapter 7.

The management of self and others

I know a few people who will take crack and just crack cocaine and they have a drink or some marijuana to come down. What makes you laugh about these people is they say 'I hate scagheads', people who use heroin, and they hate scagheads. I will always say 'what the fuck are you talking about, you cunt? You're taking crack and you're saying you don't like heroin users. It's the same fucking thing.' To me, as I've said to you, it's even worse. At least I don't run around all hours of the morning and, how can I explain it? Crack people will steal anything.

(Cuz)

If you're on crack and heroin you've got a bad habit, and the crack makes you lose all your morals. With heroin it's different. You do have a bit of respect for yourself and other people but with crack that all goes out the window. You don't give a shit about anyone or anything. You've got no morals about yourself. You just don't care. Crack is more dangerous than heroin.

(Bombshell)

Introduction

With increasing interaction in the crack scene (Chapter 5) and exposure to political economic processes that exacerbate personal circumstances (Chapter 6), crack user narratives indicate a need to sustain an image of themselves which does not reflect the true nature of their position (Goffman, 1963). Many seem to seek to display an image that counters their perceived socio-structural position in wider society (Bauman, 2004; Goffman, 1959) and across the crack scene (Bourgois and Schonberg, 2009). For example, many do not want to appear as 'crack heads'. Such a person, as they see it, symbolises stigma (Pearson, 2001; Simmonds and Coomber, 2009) and a loss of all morals. Affirmation of this attribute may have direct individual consequences for their identity and social position in the crack scene (Chapter 5; Matza, 1969). Instead, most suggest there is someone else who is 'worse off than they are' (Neale et al., 2006). Most commonly, crack users in this study directed this gradation toward 'junkies' who inject/use heroin, and the 'crack heads' and 'ponces', i.e. the Low Life.

This seems to help them deflect responsibility for their actions (Sykes and Matza, 1957), and instead attribute (Booth Davies, 1997) stigma to other cultural practices (such as injecting), particular actions (violence, sex and risk behaviours), certain peer associations (sharing paraphernalia, 'unclean' or 'diseased' crack-using associates) and/or particular crack-using environments (in particular crack houses). Crack users consider these features of the crack scene to harbour stigma that may potentially reinforce individual and social feelings of shame (Maruna, 2001; Parker and Aggleton, 2003). Conceding to these practices, with these drugs, in these environments, may reveal aspects of a 'spoilt' identity (Simmonds and Coomber, 2009) and this could have implications for individual self-esteem and self-worth (Maruna, 2001), which is probably why crack users find it difficult accept responsibility for their actions (Sykes and Matza, 1957). This chapter takes a closer look at these areas and how the self is managed in relation to others who occupy the crack scene.

The management of the self in the crack scene

Most crack users make special attempts to counter their socio-structural position (Goffman, 1959) by attempting to be responsible citizens, living normal lives (Bauman, 2007) – or as normal as possible under the circumstances (Bourgois and Schonberg, 2009). The success they have in doing so appears to be countered by the fact that many seem to develop 'spoilt' identities (Simmonds and Coomber, 2009) and fragmented life biographies (Bauman, 2004) over their crack careers (Chapter 4). Consequently, many find it difficult to locate a sense of themselves (Maruna, 2001). They rely, it seems, on a social image of themselves to confirm who they are (Cooley, 1964).

It is the management of this social image that seems to determine social hierarchical order in the crack scene (Chapter 5). This same image is used, where possible, to counter the 'crack head' image. Nevertheless, for both High Society and Low Life groups it seems to become integral to deploy the self in a way that can counter both the image which society holds and that which other crack users may hold. The need to 'show many faces' (Goffman, 1963) under pressured social and structural conditions becomes too difficult and many lose the ability to sustain these 'faces'. In this excerpt, Iverson reflects on how this produces major tensions on self identity:

> Stories of life, white lies, not even that, pink lies, totally disfigured, totally disfigured from reality. Amazing stories, like I am arguing with my own life. Sometimes like when I do it, when I tell somebody something, I actually believe it happened, like a job or a house, and I would believe it, I am taking more credit [to fund crack use] and until it hits you. Like I might say, 'my social security is coming tomorrow' and you spent it yesterday. So you wait for two weeks, go missing for two weeks, go to another area, you get money and show your face again.
>
> (Iverson)

Consequently, hierarchical status may be jeopardised when: a) some are associated with certain activities that attract significant stigma and receive further labels (Becker, 1953; Young, 1971); b) there is the potential for victimisation (Bourgois, 1995). In these instances, the 'self' seems to be exposed as increasingly 'spoilt' (Simmonds and Coomber, 2009). There may be temporary surges back up the hierarchical ladder (Chapter 5) but, in the main, this was the norm for most crack users in this sample. The result is they often develop increasingly fatalistic life outlooks as aspects of their mental and physical capacities diminish, and practical problems exacerbate (Farmer, 1997). These individual degenerative processes are aided through social interactional processes of 'othering' (Young, 2007). Othering takes place through social interactions and is a sphere of power relationships in which participant/s defines both him/herself/themselves and the 'other'; one is perceived in social terms as more powerful, the other as inferior. In the context of crack users, 'othering' appears to have direct implications for attitudes to the self; the more the self is perceived to be different or 'the other', the more it affects who they are and how they treat themselves.

'Othering' of the other

While many crack users attempt to live as responsible citizens and maintain social and intimate relations with each other, the volatile and mistrustful nature of social interactions in the crack scene makes this difficult (Chapter 5). Thus, a conflict seems to arise between their individual quest to counter their position (Bauman, 2004) and their pursuit of intimacy and trusting social relations (Bourgois and Schonberg, 2009; Giddens, 1991). This tension seemed particularly evident throughout the time I spent with Cuz during the fieldwork.

The vulnerability of Black Eyes

Although he seemed to have a poor reputation among other hostel residents, the stories of Black Eyes were almost like folklore. After experiencing a torrid background of sexual and physical abuse, homelessness, drug and alcohol use, and schizophrenia, Black Eyes had no other alternative but to await local authority housing while in temporary accommodation. He was, however, always socialising with fellow hostel dwellers, hassling them for money, drugs, and paraphernalia. He was also constantly victimised, bullied and harassed. Many other hostel dwellers seemed to laugh behind his back, relishing in the stories about him. He was, for most, known among the other hostel dwellers as 'the crazy one'.

Cuz, who also stayed in the same hostel, was the main projector of these stories. According to Cuz, Black Eyes' 'favourite activity' was smoking crack and masturbating and this, Cuz said, made him a 'freak' in the eyes of most. Cuz's other revelation was that he often searched other people's bins for used needles when he was withdrawing from drugs. This seemed to trigger resentment and stigmatisation among others in the hostel. They also didn't like the fact that 'mental health issues' and 'disabilities' entitled him to around £200 a fortnight in social security benefits. Most were envious of this income, and this seemed to make him more vulnerable to further bullying and manipulation. When he was first beaten up outside the social security office for his social security cheque, Cuz told me he had an 'opportunity' and offered to 'protect' him. Yet, although Cuz said he 'protected' and 'looked out' for him, the type of 'protection' he offered him involved selling him bogus crack and looking after his money:

> I met Cuz at 11am and we walked to the café to talk – he had apparently got fucked off [annoyed] with Black Eyes and decided to rip him off [take advantage of him]. Black Eyes gave him £200 to buy crack and Cuz made out that he got busted in a police raid as he was about to buy it – the police confiscated the money and he was left penniless. What he said he did was spend £150 on crack and £50 on clothes and toiletries. Black Eyes was fuming but believed the story – in fact, the whole hostel believed the story.
>
> (Field notes)

Any Black Eyes-related proceeds seemed to be directed to Cuz's 'smoking crack fund'. In an interview in November, Cuz described Black Eyes as a 'mug who sold his butt for crack'. Yet the manipulation and abuse of Black Eyes didn't seem to desist as his reputation for vulnerability spread. Others also took advantage of him, yet still he lent them money. Indeed, many had significant debts to Black Eyes. Three weeks later, Black Eyes violently retaliated when someone wouldn't repay their debt. A week later, however, he had left the hostel – the receptionist informed me he had 'disengaged'. Perhaps, with this, went his forms of social support such as social security, disability allowance, mental health medication and methadone prescription, and also engagement with drug support services. He was not the only one – the hostel where I spent much of my time over the nine months had a high turnover of residents. Nevertheless, this may indicate how othering results in increased stigmatisation and vulnerability. Such treatment, however, was not exclusive to Cuz's fellow hostel dwellers as I was to learn some weeks later.

The mistreatment of Babe

While waiting outside the DTTO office for his keyworker, Cuz met Babe – someone to whom he was immediately attracted. This seemed clear in their body language, the manner of their quick departure together and my exclusion from 'tagging along' with them after leaving the cafe:

> Cuz and I were left with Babe – a 36-year-old crack user who had just recovered from heroin addiction a few months ago. She was on a methadone and DF118 script. Her eyes were slightly sunken into her face and her cheeks were slim and tightly hugged her jawbone. Still she made a big effort [to maintain

her appearance]. She wore make up and new clothes but her teeth looked as if they were about to fall out: the gums were showing on the bottom. We talked in the café as people left after lunch. Cuz was making enquiries about her and apparently, according to others in the crack scene, she had AIDS. Tony came in while she was outside and told Cuz to double up on condoms for precaution. Cuz even made me call my workplace to find out about whether AIDS could be contracted through oral sex, as that is what he said he wanted from her. He left with £100 in his pocket at 3.30pm.

(Field notes)

When I called Cuz three days later he was contradicting himself by saying that she was 'just a fling' – probably because showing affection defied the masculine image he was trying to project. However, as we walked around that day, he seemed to show some affection for her in the words he chose but quickly played them down. He asked me if I thought she was 'pretty'. The next day:

I walked up to meet them – they looked very happy together. They said they were trying to help each other out [getting off drugs] by being there for each other. I got the impression Babe was more keen on Cuz than he was on her. But judging by what he said yesterday, Cuz seems to care for her even if he was trying to deny it to himself.

(Field notes)

Yet he had openly discussed his sexual motives with me before he went off with her the week before. In a conversation between them the same evening, he said:

CUZ: *The first conversation that me and Babe had – and we didn't even know each other – was about sex.*
BABE: *And we spoke about everything that was to do about sex.*
CUZ: *To find two people like that is rare.*
BABE: *And I felt that I'd known him for years and I could open up for him.*
CUZ: *We stayed together. When I first met her I said to her 'come on. Let's go and have a pipe' when we were in the café.*
BABE: *And what did I say to you?*
CUZ: *And she said to me 'what do you want?' She thought I wanted her to give me a blow job.*
BABE: *Yeah. That's because what men normally want. We had a pipe and he put a big fucking thing on there and I was waiting for him to turn around and say 'give us a shine' because that's what most people do.*
CUZ: *No. I wanted to get to know her.*

He said they had unprotected sex and 'stayed over at her place'. The next day they went to the local magistrate court; walking and laughing together, reminiscent of a couple walking out of a cinema. In the excitement of his new relationship and binge crack sessions, Cuz's absences from the hostel were noted by staff. The debts started to amass and they served him an eviction notice. Cuz was angry when he showed the letter to me: 'you have 14 days to clear your belongings and leave' it read. He owed £133 yet other hostel dwellers owed over £1,000. His anger resulted in further crack binges for some days. He also said he would 'burn down the hostel'. We sat down with the hostel manager a week later and Cuz managed to reach some agreement to pay it back. He was given a further 28-day period to 'display good behaviour' otherwise he would be evicted.

Nevertheless, as his relationship blossomed with Babe, he spent less time at the hostel. Consequently, our contact drifted. When I did see him, he confessed that he was still angry with the hostel and was using crack 'day in, day out' with Babe. This seemed to conflict with earlier intentions to 'get off drugs together'. When he did appear at the hostel, he appeared to unload this anger on to others around him. In his frustration of being hassled for drugs one day in the hostel, he had battered someone. Relations soured further when his 'old friend' Tooth failed to pay back a £20 crack rock. With no favours to call on in the hostel and poor staff relations, there was little to motivate Cuz to return to his accommodation.

One week later, my contact from Cuz drifted once again. Despite repeated phone calls, hostel visits and asking around, I couldn't locate him. He was evicted from the hostel some weeks later. Several of his 'associates' said they didn't know where he was but suggested he was 'head over heels in love'. Surely he wouldn't want other people saying this about him because it contradicted his street-wise image. This unstable period – characterised by heavy crack binges and one-man shoplifting operations in Hamleys – all seemed to have cascaded from the hostel letter threatening him with eviction and was augmented by his crack-smoking sessions with Babe. By now, however, he said he was also wanted by the police yet was still prepared to risk collecting money from the social security office. It was not until a week later that we were reunited and his relationship with Babe seemed to have become closer:

> Somewhere along the road Shake had bumped into Cuz and Babe and had told them I was up the road. I cycled further down. When I first saw him he looked as if he had lost a lot of weight – his torso was very thin. We walked to the bank. Babe wanted to withdraw money as her disability [allowance] had been paid into her bank account. Again, I was curious about this as they looked highly suspicious while withdrawing the £200. She had the pin code on her hand and kept looking around while Cuz typed it in – for some reason, he was doing it instead of her? Cuz was fiddling with the £200 and pocketed some of it when she wasn't looking.

> (Field notes)

Cuz said he was happy to share her disability allowance, which was spent on crack. It was not until a month later that we were reunited again yet he didn't appear to be overly excited to see me. Perhaps because I was starting to see a more intimate side to him that he didn't want to show? He explained how he had moved into Babe's flat and took a lion's share in her benefit allowance for his crack use. He said he had managed to persuade her to put him on the tenancy agreement so that if they split up the council would immediately re-house him. He laughed and called her a 'stupid fucking mug'. This was more like the Cuz I had known – the same one who exploited Black Eyes.

Othering in action

Later that month, I started to notice how Cuz spoke to some people about their drug use practices – as if he were looking down on them. In these notes, taken from a visit to an improvised crack-smoking location in a car park, Cuz seems to talk down to another crack user as he starts to smoke heroin:

> We walked to the top and turned left where the cinema was – there was a huge multi-storey car park above the cinema. I chained my bike up and we walked behind to the concrete stairs. There was an immediate smell of piss and shit. We walked up the very steep stairs to level 1. Tooth went to the lifts. One had an 'out of order' sign on yet Tooth pulled back the doors and inside was his sleeping bag and some second-hand clothes. It was his 'secret' place as he said. Before he started a relationship with Mary, Tooth slept here. Tooth closed the door and we went up another floor, there were even fewer cars. We then walked across the car park to the other end, towards the stairs. As we approached, we started to see empty syringe packets. We got to the far side of the car park and Cuz said this is where he used to sleep. I walked closer to the walls and could see sprays of blood where syringes had been emptied. The floors were also bloodstained, but it wasn't as noticeable. The place stank of piss. Near the railing was a little ledge where some had thrown away their syringes, pipes and foil. It felt like a very dirty place. We walked down a level and there was, what looked to be, an old-looking man who turned out to be aged just 27. The man was shorter than me, had a full beard, bags under his eyes and blood stains on his cheeks. He had a full head of hair but looked in his 40s. His hands and nails were black. Cuz said he had been on the streets for six years. The man had just finished speedballing and was packing his equipment away. He was quite shy but responded to me when Cuz said he met me in prison. He was hungry so I agreed to buy him a cheap burger from McDonald's. Tooth seemed wary of him and told me to be careful with anything I might have visible as the man would steal it.
>
> We then went to McDonald's. I bought the burger for the man and said I would meet Tooth in an hour while he went off to score. By the time we returned to the car park, Tooth was with Mary. He had already returned and had an impatient look. Cuz walked up to him and gave him the foil. Mary looked out of the window to check no one was coming and Cuz went for a piss. I crouched down to talk to Tooth. He took very little care in preparing

the foil, I didn't even see him heat the bottom to burn away the toxins. He made a very short foil pipe and started to chase the brown down the foil. He chased it around in a circle, rather than up and down. Cuz came over and stood over him. He seemed to be proud not to be doing the same thing [smoking heroin – even though he smokes heroin]. To make himself feel that he didn't want it, he started to speak out loud about how it was a 'shit drug' and that he didn't want anything to do with it.

(Field notes)

In addition, Cuz had a tendency to try and show me that he could maintain conventional social relations (Bourgois and Schonberg, 2009) but had disdain for other behaviours linked with crack scene stigmas, such as sex-for-crack exchanges – even though he often boasted about his sexual conquests with Babe. This may have been linked to my role as researcher/friend, which had implications for what he told me. In this excerpt, Cuz again seems to be directly involved in these interactional processes of othering. These field notes record a short social exchange with a damaged young woman who had recently been released from prison:

As we arrived in town, Cuz pulled up a young woman who he recognised – she had just been released from Holloway prison that day. She must have been around early 20s, had slicked-back hair into a pony tail, a few yellow teeth and fairly new clothes – she looked unwell. She was drinking a can of extra strong lager when Cuz asked her what she was doing. 'Rock' she said and smiled to show the few yellow teeth she had. She asked Cuz if he 'wanted a shine [blow job] for two quid'. 'Dirty bitch' he sneered. She then asked me if I wanted 'some pussy?' I politely declined and after that she seemed to lose interest in the conversation. Her attention switched to the arrival of police officers across the street and she then kissed us both on the cheek and left.

(Field notes)

He later called her a 'desperate crack head'. Crack users, like this young woman, seem to find it difficult to counter their social position in the crack scene (Bauman, 2007) which is why many seem to want to attempt to avoid the label of 'crack head' – because it may have direct implications for social standing, individual identities and attitudes to the self (Maruna, 2001).

The stigma of the 'crack head' and their social acts

A crack head? Well you [points at me] would call everyone who uses crack a 'crack head', but society would say that but then in the crack world, you will see the crack heads, they are more visible. The crack heads act mad on the road or differently – they are not controlled. Apart from the glazed eyes, a crack head is someone unkempt, drooling at the mouth, no shoes. They are mad, acting insane but they stand out like sore thumbs. A crack head will

also beg off you so you say 'here you go, get out of my face', but next time
they will forget they asked you already and one day it will resort to violence
because they keep doing it and get it off someone else. It [crack] makes you
greedy, see I wouldn't do that because of my pride and I would want to show
that I have got more than you have got so a crack head would rather beg than
help himself. I don't want to be seen as a crack head so I will make sure I try
and walk straight and calm but often the eyes give it away so I end up being
conscious about it which makes it worse.

(Iverson)

Here, an awareness of the potential to be seen as a crack head seems to lead to
further individual signs that the symbolisms of the 'crack head' are apparent. In
this study, no crack user wants to be perceived as a 'crack head'; someone who
has abandoned all social morals or the 'lowest of the low living among the low'
and someone who has forgone all important aspects of their life in favour of crack.
For these reasons, such a label carries significant amounts of stigma – not only
from wider society (Box, 1981; Bourgois, 2002) but also from those in the crack
scene (Simmonds and Coomber, 2009):

Well, a crack head will be someone who's living, breathing, smoking crack
rather than putting food in their belly. Literally let it all go to pieces, in dirty
clothes. From when they wake up until they go to sleep – all they do is
make money to smoke crack, smoke crack and make money to smoke crack.
Perhaps in a really small tiny, tiny, vicious, vicious circle. They've never got
any cigarettes. Never got nothing. They just want to hit their money. They
won't do no shopping, won't do no laundry, won't pay no fags. They won't
do nothing. That's really what you call a crack head.

(BD)

So with some people, their sense of morality – their sense of right and wrong,
their dignity, their self-respect – all that goes out the window. These are
people [crack heads] who don't care if they're homeless and living on the
streets.

(Sneaks)

Such people seem to be the target for others in the crack scene – crack dealers
as well as other crack users – because their role, as some see it, is to make others
feel better about themselves. Silver certainly looked down on people like this and
said he used to entertain himself by 'messing with their heads':

That's why I say I used to rip off a bit of a bit of a rizla and put it on the floor
and if I could get my hands on a packet of sugar I'd drop that on the floor
and they'd [crack heads] be going [imitates searching on the ground]... or
crush up a bit of polo. I'd wind them up. When you get a rock it's only so big.

They've smoked so much of it. It was there when they opened it. The pipe's been there on the table all the time they've been smoking. How are bits going to be over on the floor? I mean I've seen people searching on the floor fucking continually looking while they're smoking. [Sarcastically] 'What? Did you think you'd dropped a bit that big and it's bounced ten foot away and grown in size on its fucking way?'

(Silver)

Importantly, descriptions of a 'crack head' are made in the context of the 'other'; someone who the individual hasn't been, is not, or will not be. Crack users seem to label others 'crack head' because they seem to think there is always someone else 'worse off than they are'. Essentially, this seems to strengthen a self-denial of their own position and may protect the self from the stigmatising consequences of the label (Goffman, 1959). To avoid this label, many crack users attempt to sustain a positive image of themselves in the crack scene (Goffman, 1963) – one that dwells in the perception of the other (Cooley, 1964). This seems to be particularly successful for the entrepreneurs and the organised crack-using groups (High Society) – or those who had held such status, such as Iverson:

Once you have an identity, a presence, you have to maintain it if you want your status, so all the beggars and ponces will come up to you and say 'ah man, you always give me a smoke' and you say 'alright, now go' and he is your friend again. But if you don't maintain it they can change, but they don't remember until you give it to them. They are genuinely gone.

Those who can successfully maintain these identities do not seem to be considered 'crack heads', as crack users see it, because they still function in the mainstream sphere in some capacity or are able to covertly manage their crack use so it does not interfere with life responsibilities and personal well-being. The way in which these groups and individuals seem to respond to their deviancy (Lemert, 1967) is to show others in the crack scene how much crack they can use or how much of a successful crack user they are. Very often, an investment in this identity results in increased crack use (Chapter 4).

Until you get deeper, you realise you are in the wrong place. This could be a crack house, a crack house is nothing, it is just a room, a space in time you can hang out, pay your rent in crack. No one is concerned about you, so you can forget about that. People go there 9–5 like a release, like people go to a pub. If you can work and sustain it that way, you are ok but in due course, all that is going to disappear because it will overwhelm you, you get bigger, you take more, the more you have, the more you spend, £1,000 will go in a second.

(Baz)

The implications of the 'crack head' label seem greater for those lower down the chain in the crack scene. As the narrative of Black Eyes indicated earlier in the chapter, the label seems to lead to further social isolation, stigmatisation and victimisation. This seems to be because the nature of their social acts and social reputation attract increased stigmatisation from those occupying the same space, which exacerbates their already fragile positions.

> It's a term that's thrown about very lightly. Technically I suppose anyone that smokes crack is a crack head. That's the bottom line. Anyone that smokes on a regular basis but what it's normally tended to be thought of as a crack head when they've slipped down the ladder is when they've lost all respect for themselves and all they think about is the drug. That's the only thing they can think about from when they wake up in the morning until they pass out. They won't go to sleep. They'll stay out and stay out and stay out. In the rain – in all sorts of weather. You see them hanging around, they might be begging money 'Excuse me. Got 50p?' or 'Have you got a cigarette?' or 'Have you got a lighter?' They never have nothing. Any money that they get … they can be hungry but if they've got seven pounds they'll take a pound to get some chicken and chips or eight so you can make a stone and a stone won't stop you if you're hungry … What you've got to understand is that people get so desperate that they will do anything for crack, literally. They will steal. They will do sexual favours – sexually humiliate themselves and even sometimes a dealer who's bored and doesn't like someone will say 'okay you know what if you eat that rotten piece of bread in there I'll give you a loan for three or four pounds off' because he's bored … You've got to remember that a crack head will stand there and promise you their mother, their sister, whatever. They're going to get that money. They promise you. They'll come with a story. They're just waiting for the bank to open and it's all lies. They will hustle. They'll manipulate. They will trade on your weakness. I've known ones that have gone to the hospital and stolen TVs.
>
> (BD)

It seems that it is only in recovery in rehab – when crack users assess the self – that some concede to this label. No current crack user in the study admitted to being a 'crack head'. Here, Funky D reflects on how, having sought drug support services and rehab, she recognised that she was probably was a 'crack head' – having spent years denying it:

DAN: *What's a crack head?*

FUNKY D: *In the end I thought to myself 'Funky D, you're getting a crack head' and I could really see why people say people are a 'crack head' because before I used to say that I was a 'smoker'. Before I used to say I was just a smoker. I think a crack head – their priorities don't come first. Crack comes first or whatever choice of drug comes first.*

DAN: *So they smoke crack.*

FUNKY D: *You just live your life for crack. Remember you lose your kids. Not even your kids are important. Not even your mum's important. You've got to be a crack head. Your head is around crack. My head was around crack because all these things brought me to this stage* [in rehab] *because I'd lost my kids, my mum was fed up with me, I had to go and steal to go and support my habit. Everything I did revolved around crack. My friends had had enough of me because I got some bad shit. In the end I said to myself 'I'm not a crack head. I'm not that bad'. I fucking was. So there is progression.*

Particular cultural practices – associated with Low Life – poly-drug users (predominantly heroin and crack) and injecting drug users or 'junkies' (Simmonds and Coomber, 2009) are also stigmatised in the crack scene. Similarly, these practices are seen to symbolise a loss of all morals and lack of social control. In these excerpts, Philo and Baz reflected on looking down on the 'junkies' who inject heroin:

Yeah and there's a hierarchy, I mean, the whole drug-using world is very judgemental, you know, especially [interrupts himself] and I think one of the reasons for that is that anybody doing illicit substances particularly people that don't inject and look down on injectors because they've had to label this thing a danger in order they don't go there, so they say to anyone else that has stepped over that line. A lot of people are struggling with addictive substances, they try to convince themselves that they are in this place and they can get out and they're better than this person who is further down the hill, you know what I mean? And there's a lot of these sort of internal battles that affect the way in which they view others, or we view others or whatever, do you know what I mean? There were times when I always looked down on... not really down, but it was a place I didn't wanna go, you know, anybody sort of like giving up all pretence of normal life, because, you know I wanted to stay away from that, because it makes life more difficult for you, it's all associated with low life, isn't it? Any out of control drug use, you know. Drug users have the same values as everyone else, really.

(Philo)

I look down on the ones that take brown because I discriminate against them because it is like a hierarchy class. If you smoke weed, you are cool, crack, so so [in the middle], you take the brown stuff, that is the killer, it's over, you don't value life, that is the way I see it. You don't socialise with these people, they have different mentalities, these people are the thieves, they will have your shoes and that.

(Baz)

However, those who used both crack and heroin, and/or inject both drugs feel otherwise about this stigmatisation. Some said those applying the label to them are hypocrites and that their position is just as fragile as theirs. Ironically, having publically shown disdain for heroin use earlier in the chapter, here Cuz defends those who use crack as well as heroin:

DAN: *Some people I speak to say 'Oh I don't like to use heroin' but they do.*
CUZ: *Yeah you get a lot of it. They're liars, aren't they? That's bullshitters who aren't honest with themselves. They're just full of shit.*
DAN: *But it all comes back to this thing about people looking down on heroin.*
CUZ: *Yeah, of course, but they do take it.*
DAN: *Yeah. It's a complete contradiction.*
CUZ: *And if they saw me they'd say 'oh you fucking crack head' but you hypocrite. You're in exactly the same thing as I am.*

So, in essence, because of the potential stigma of the label, some crack users deny aspects of their crack use, while others deny their heroin use – because conceding to either label may have direct implications for attitudes to the self and identity (Maruna, 2001). Equally, when crack users recall some of the things they have done to get the drug, most feel guilty and ashamed. While only a few say they targeted vulnerable victims, others had provided various derogatory sexual favours for crack. Some like Pix continued using crack after being raped and physically abused while others like Firey A and Funky D neglected, and in some cases, abused their children. These experiences appear to compound individual feelings of uselessness and shame. In addition, many said, crack was used to numb these feelings and this seemed to increase fatalistic attitudes. Funky D described her actions after losing her children and investing further resource in a crack-using lifestyle:

When I think about it now, I targeted the man. I know he's got money and I want that money. That was all that was in my head. I could have gone and shoplifted and left the man alone, when I think about it now; but because I'd seen that money, I wanted that money, because I knew that that money was certain. Do you understand? I knew that money was there. He's got it and I want it, and I sat and waited for him. He came from the bank, he went into Iceland [food supermarket] and I sat there and watched for him to come out of that shop and followed him into the lift. I did 'it' [robbed him], and it's only afterwards now that I started worrying. That's when I started worrying.

(Funky D)

With this in mind, and despite being in recovery, the shame and guilt still seemed to weigh heavily on her mind because these experiences were reflexively visited. Others remained adamant that they were not prepared to let their reliance on crack lead to such acts. Gums related: 'It depends on the person. Some would not step over certain moral boundaries: I couldn't go up to [rob] a vulnerable person whether they're old or young or whatever.' It is widely agreed, however, that some users are beyond social repair and this, users say, is evident in how they are treated and how they interact in the crack scene.

> It is a community on its own [the crack heads] because they see they belong there, because they are not being judged, or if they are judged, they don't respond to it and they don't know how to respond. If you told me I was dirty and that I was wasted, it wouldn't matter, I am not there. I am detached but I have the company and that is all that matters, I don't care about family, friends, or anything.
>
> (Iverson)

Very often, this label, once applied, seems difficult to counter as it often carries significant weight throughout the social networks of the crack scene. The label is also associated with acts of violent crime, risk and sex behaviours. Contrary to popular perception, in the crack scene there is little kudos associated with such behaviours; if anything, these acts are generally frowned upon (Glaser, 1978):

MR LEE: *Yeah. I'm going to tell you something, you know. Don't forget people can get angry but they can get angry but people can just think bad things, yeah? And we do, we all think bad things, yeah? People can think bad things but I mean then, thinking bad things it's not bad is it?*

DAN: *No, no, just thinking it.*

MR LEE: *Right, you know when it's bad is when a person acts, ok?*

DAN: *When they do it?*

MR LEE: *Yeah. Tony Blair, any one of the big names, just name them. They think bad things like all of us [crack users], but thinking is not bad, man. It's when a person acts and surely I do think bad thinking but me, I'm not going to act, you know.*

DAN: *Yeah?*

MR LEE: *Do drug users do bad things to people, hurt people? No, drug users is not like that. No way. I wouldn't hurt nobody and the majority of my friends wouldn't hurt people. All of my friends who me smoke with. No them won't hurt people, just to get a fix or anything. No. Well maybe then I don't broaden my horizon to know a lot more drugs people but then I know so much drugs people, man.*

Crack user narratives indicate that such acts appear as symbols of degradation and stigma which may increase levels of shame among crack users. There seem to be certain places people don't want to go, but when they do, it may reinforce the individual and social stigma of their actions, their social and self-perception and, as a consequence, their identity. This also seems to be the case in the context of the environments crack users occupy – in particular, crack houses.

The crack house: signs of status or symbols of stigma?

> There are the high flyers, some people coming in [to the crack house] once a month, others come in on a Friday or Saturday, just like some people coming in with a shirt and tie and others have no jobs, stinking.
>
> (Iverson)

In general, it is difficult to typologise crack houses by particular behaviours and/or particular sets of crack users – whether they are recreational or heavy crack users – because the cultural pressures of the crack scene and crime control dynamics determine crack house operations (Briggs, 2010). Indeed, this study indicates that the crack house experience seems to relate to different structural, social and spatial narrative constructions:

> So the [crack] house ran like that for about six months. I had my friends – some could stay – there was about four/five of them, this was a one-bedroom flat you know with about five of us in it. So we had beds, we had settee, TV/video – four and five of us. Maybe it was three – the girl and the three geezers. They were the main ones to stay. So that ran like that for about six months plus you've got the people coming to the door buying and selling and going. Some people bought and came in – those they'd let – that was for about six months ... We used to have a laugh and a joke. We used to have deep conversations. We used to have the music on. Sometimes we'd smoke and we've got the telly on. It really was civilised.
>
> (Sneaks)

In the context of Sneaks' narrative, when times were good – the environment, the company, the crack – so too was the experience in the crack house. These environments don't seem to hold social stigma, but rather prestige and social status. This is not necessarily because they are socially or spatially superior but because the activities taking place in these environments are not perceived to be depraved or stigmatised by those involved. Moreover, the 'crack heads' as they see it, are not infecting their space. However, as crack careers evolve, and as some of these locations are closed down, crack users make choices to use other environments because access to the 'safe' establishments may become more difficult. Some crack users like Funky D are forced to improvise, try new places, build new relationships and take more risks in new environments. They may start to interact with others in different locations where more stigmatised social acts take place. Personal admissions of involvement in these stigmatised environments may confirm 'crack head' status and, for most, this seems difficult to accept.

Very few crack users feel attached to a crack house, and instead say they distance themselves from these locations – even though they use them. Some even deny that operations from their flat could be classified as a crack house (Briggs, 2010). On the one hand, they tend to do this to avoid community attention and to deter other potential social pollutants from encroaching on what 'they have'. On the other hand, they seem to do this to avoid a broader label being placed on their operations – both from the community and from crack scene players. For example, Dawg always used to deny his flat was a 'crack house', yet his crack-using associates felt otherwise. They had reason for such assumptions because Dawg invited all sorts of strangers to smoke any kind of drug in his flat at any hour of the day or night. When not in his flat, Dawg lingered around outside drug services trying to persuade others to part with drugs or to use drugs in his flat in exchange for drugs. Because of this, he was generally perceived as a 'ponce': someone who did not work hard for his drug money.

Because Dawg found it hard to earn money, he bartered out his flat in exchange for crack. However, other drugs, such as heroin or prescription drugs would also be alluring. The flat regulars were Blood, Big T, JC, and Bones. Big T and JC appeared only on social security payment days, if they could be persuaded by Dawg. Blood and Bones, however, often spent long overnight spells at Dawg's, making their money for crack and treating him to a 'few pipes'. The flat, however, was not exclusive in its occupancy because although Dawg said 'only a few knew', it was where I met Fuzz, Holt and Cheque, Brummie and Flea; all smoking and injecting crack and heroin in Dawg's premises.

At times, Dawg's flat did not display any outside social or drug-taking characteristics of a 'crack house'. Some days, there were no visitors; perhaps dealers were unavailable or Blood and Bones went visiting other crack-using locations. While Dawg regarded direct transactions with crack dealers in their flats as 'crack house operations', this view was not shared by Blood, Big T or JC. As we walked to a street deal, Blood declared that 'crack houses are places where people take crack – that's all. You don't have to have a dealer there.' Perhaps Dawg was just cautious about what might happen if too many people found out about his operations? (Because it had backfired in the past.) Or perhaps he was more conscious of what it would mean for his image if he was seen to be operating a crack house?

Other crack users are certainly concerned about image when it comes to the permissiveness of certain behaviours in crack houses. For some, injecting behaviours symbolise individual and social stigma in crack houses:

> I am thinking about the injecting. I am trying to think why people who use crack see their selves a cut higher than the normal junkie but if they are sitting in a room with someone who is sticking a needle in them – it kind of brings everyone down to their level and they can't have that. There is a lot of denial, like where crack is, where can we smoke a bit, 'we smoke a rock but we're not like them guys hanging around outside the tube station selling travelcards who is injecting in their groin.' Really there is no difference, they are both addicted to class A substances and they are destroying their lives. It is important for them to see their selves above these people that's why you can't do it in the crack house because you bring everyone down to that level.
>
> (Alwight)

In a similar example, Fam also denied that the daily and all-night crack-smoking sessions funded by organised credit-card fraud operations in his Victorian flat made it a 'crack house' (Chapter 1). Therefore, for individual purposes, denial of crack house operations seems to be associated with reducing community attention and pressure from other crack scene members but also appears to be associated with denial of the deviant label, because these venues are associated with stigma and shame. Conceding to the 'crack house' label may have some bearing on their individual identity and therefore it is of interest to deter such labels being applied. This is because crack users said crack houses are populated with the 'Low Life', 'ponces', 'crack heads' and 'diseased prostitutes' who do anything for crack. Someone who spent time in these crack houses had forgone all morals and was beyond social repair:

BD: *I'm a twenty-year crack user. I'm now in recovery. I'm attending a day programme. I've done everything from started out selling cocaine to, at my lowest point when I was actually living in a crack house.*

DAN: *Lowest point?*

BD: *Yeah. Well you don't get a lot lower than living in a crack house, trust me.*

And:

> I think they are real sordid, dangerous places. I feel very security conscious … People get down to their lowest instincts in the crack house. Stuff around violence, sex, anger, degradation especially, well both male and female. How addiction gets hold of these people that are in that environment. Seeing men that aren't gay perform blow jobs on men. I have seen women do the same thing on men for a £10 rock. I found it really degrading – I found the whole mentality of those places to be the lowest of the low.
>
> (Easy E)

While Fam did not consider his flat to be a crack house, he is quick to point out the kind of people who normally attend these venues. They are certainly not people like him:

> A crack house? It's just where most low life go up there. I try not to go to crack houses. I go to crack houses at night but I try not to stick with them. Most ones that I've been in are proper low, low places where as soon as you walk in they're like flies around shit because I think I keep myself nice and they've got this thing that all women do anything for it and basically I've been calling them bastards when they've got their thingies out. I've said 'fuck that' and there are girls that are doing that up there and it's disgusting. It's gross. Horrible place!
>
> (Fam)

Participation in the crack house life or the derogatory acts associated with it such as sex-for-crack exchanges, various physical and mental abuses, and violence seem to have implications for the inner core of the individual's identity (Fitzgerald, 2009). Those in rehab reflect on feeling ashamed of their actions in these environments – not only what they did as individuals but what they did to others. Throughout this interview with Madmax, he intermittently shook his head in disbelief at the things he had done to others while on crack:

> My first thought when I had a pipe was that I wanted a girl to perform for me and I can be honest, I made women do that. I get them high and was getting horny and then I would have more and would say 'what are you going to do for me now?' I started to get more devious. People would call me up and want £40 [rocks] then call me up and want £80 [rocks] and a freebie and I would say 'yeah, but you know you owe for that now' and I started to think 'I'm not giving you nothing for nothing'... male, female, whatever, don't matter if I don't know you, but with the women I could get sexual pleasures. I thought they could serve me. I went round this girl's house and she phoned and she only had £10 but she wanted to deal and I said 'I don't deal £10 stones no more' but my head I already have the game plan. I went there, she finished her pipe, and I am rolling a crack spliff and she is looking for it so she said 'please, until tomorrow' and I said 'I don't do that any more'. I was a demon, I treated her badly. She is in there, and I am horny because I have smoked a spliff so I said 'go in there and put something sexy on' and she was like 'what' and she had never done anything like this before. She went in there, I had a pipe, my cock is hard and I said 'you need to put that in your mouth'. And when she had, I didn't give her the rock, I treated her like a dog and threw the stone on the floor. I became very evil, it was like I was a fiend. As soon as I had a pipe around women, and I knew I could manipulate them, it wasn't all women but ones I knew I had the power over, I made them do things they did not expect to do.

Later in the interview, after he had put his head in his hands several times:

> I've been invited to all sorts of [crack] houses. Frank, who has recently passed away, had this very seedy, musty place. There had to be an exchange for a smoke [on the premises], there was a condition [to get in]. I used to bring women down there. One time, Frank asked me if he could ask my girl to suck his cock. I said 'you're having a laugh, bruv, this is mine'. And he was like 'go on, get her high so I can do things to her'. Then I ran out of fags, so I had to go to the shop, and then I got back to the house, he had given her a big pipe, and she was on him and I thought 'fuck you bitch', I didn't care. Through my stupidity, it hurts. I got her involved in crack.
>
> (Madmax)

Some like Madmax seem to internalise these feelings of guilt and shame (Bourdieu, 1984), and it is these compounded feelings (Box, 1981) that seem to make it difficult for crack users to make changes to their lives (Chapter 8).

Conclusion

This chapter shows that crack users seek to counter their socio-structural position (Goffman, 1959) by attempting to be responsible citizens who live normal lives (Bauman, 2007). However, despite some quest for intimacy (Giddens, 1991), in general, the social interactions that form the foundations of identity construction seem volatile and self-perpetuating. This is because crack users appear to be as much the victims as they are the perpetrators in the crack scene (Dunlap, 1992, 1995; Bourgois, 1995; Bourgois and Schonberg, 2009). Therefore, a conflict appears to arise between their individual quest to counter their position (Bauman, 2004), their individual needs (Preble and Casey, 1969) and their pursuit for intimacy and trusting social relations (Bourgois and Schonberg, 2009; Giddens, 1991). Indeed, many like Cuz struggle to manage this relationship. Indeed, once the label is applied (Black Eyes), it seems to attract further attention and stigmatisation (Becker, 1953; Young, 1971), the potential for victimisation (Bourgois, 1995) and seems to be an individual reflection that the 'self' has become increasingly 'spoilt' (Simmonds and Coomber, 2009).

Crack users seem to rely on a social image of themselves in the crack scene to confirm who they are (Cooley, 1964) and it is this maintenance of self image which seems to supersede all (Goffman, 1963). It is used, where possible, to counter the 'crack head' image (Pearson, 2001; Simmonds and Coomber, 2009); to deny particular practices and associations; or to deny use of particular places (Sykes and Matza, 1957). To do this, crack users seem to engage in social discourses in an effort to 'other the other' (Young, 2007). Those most vulnerable seem to become increasingly fatalistic, pessimistic and seem to manifest these feelings in their risky practices (Bourdieu, 1984; Farmer et al., 1996; Wilkinson, 2006). For most, the rational response to their structural circumstances (Evans, 2002; Giddens, 1984) is manifested in ongoing denial and increasing fatalism, and this seems to shape the person they have become (Becker, 1953; Chapter 4). Therefore individual decision-making and actions in these contexts are also a product of them (Bourdieu, 1984; Giddens, 1984). Despite this, many crack users speak of their intentions and attempts to 'get clean' (Maruna, 2001). After all, the majority of people with whom I spent this time did not want this lifestyle and took little long-term enjoyment from it.

Chapter 8

Ways out or ways down?

I was depressed because I wasn't with my children, because guilt and shame is a big part for me … The reasons why crack users avoid participation in services or drop out? I think that's self-worth – an individual not having any self-worth. Feelings of loneliness, I can't do this, I can't motivate myself.

(Firey A)

To enter the system is to enter a world of uncertainty, where one may be treated with exquisite passion one day and contempt the next; a world of hurry-up-and-wait, of double-binds and contradictions, where arbitrary and differential treatment, and myriad rules and regulations, triumph over the very purpose of the system itself.

(Liebow, 1993: 147)

Introduction

This chapter gives greater insight into the attempts crack users make to seek 'ways out' of their predicaments. First, the chapter looks at how appointments and meaningful engagement with drug support services are jeopardised by the day-to-day pressures of the crack scene (Bourgois and Schonberg, 2009; Chapter 5; Chapter 7; Malchy et al., 2008) and crime control dynamics (Aitkin et al., 2002; Chapter 6). The second part considers more indirect influences, which rest predominantly with the individual. Crack users do make active decisions to seek a way out but, all too often, their free will capacity – 'agency' hereafter – becomes eroded after self-motivated efforts towards change are consistently blocked (Evans, 2002; Giddens, 1984). While a few are able to make changes, what follows for most are self-rationalisations that their life is 'crack' (Maruna, 2001). For these people, continuing to take crack – and other drugs – seems the best thing to do in light of the unpromising long-term prospects (Booth Davies, 1997). For some, it is these experiences that perpetuate more fatalistic attitudes (Chapter 9; Mieczkowski, 1990) and redirect them into more entrenched risk practices (Lemert, 1967).

Those who manage to display enough commitment towards change, have to confront the 'crack head' identity (Neale et al., 2006; Simmonds and Coomber,

2009). This seems to be extremely difficult for many to accept because many are still in denial of their position (Goffman, 1963; Radcliffe and Stevens, 2008). For years, it seems, they have rationalised their past behaviours are 'down to the drugs' (Sykes and Matza, 1957) and they find it difficult for the 'self' to accept his/her actions (Maruna, 2001) – particularly when there is significant stigma and shame attached to what they have done (Chapter 7). The last part of the chapter is devoted to success stories: those who have, thus far, been able to 'get clean' despite these pressures.

The rocky road of drug support service engagement: Shake's appointments

The socio-structural pressures that surround the crack scene deter access to and hinder engagement with drug support services. This seemed especially apparent during one day I spent with Shake. He was homeless for the best part of the early fieldwork period. I often saw him next to a bank opposite the park. It had become somewhere people knew they could, within a day or so, connect with him. Initiatives to disperse street drinkers had him bundled into this category and he was frequently moved on to other areas in Rivertown. His daily life was characterised by a lifestyle around crack and other drugs. I was surprised when he told me one morning he had an appointment at Connections North – at the other end of Rivertown. This was because his local service – Connections Central – had expelled him after he had some disagreements with other clients. As a result, he had been referred to Connections North. On this cold, winter morning in January 2005, he was due at his appointment at 11am, which we later learnt when we got to the service was actually 10am. It was just before 10am when we met:

> Shake was clucking badly when I saw him first – his eyes were watering, his nose running and his hands shaking slightly. He held his stomach in pain. He had mustered up £10 and I let him use my phone to call the dealer. He tried one number and it failed so he called another and was told to walk up the road. In a change to his normal dealing routine, we walked round the corner towards a pub.
>
> (Field notes)

It seemed odd to see him scoring crack and heroin in such a well-to-do area. After about 10 minutes, I walked up the road – the dealer hadn't arrived. As Shake was waiting, he was joined by Gary, who had been released from prison a week ago. Gary was 'clean' and had been given a DTTO on condition that he report there five days a week, although, he said he was only expected two days a week for a 'swab and a chat'. They talked briefly about 'the best deals' in crack. As I returned, Shake introduced me and then the dealer pulled up in a white maintenance van. The van beeped, Shake leapt in, and was driven 50 metres down the road before getting out:

We left Gary and walked back up to town. I was looking at my watch and thinking 'he would never make his appointment' – it was about 10.15am and he hadn't even taken the drugs. He walked into McDonald's but stopped and introduced me to another, Kenny, who used crack 'here and there', so he said, and drank heavily. Shake disappeared for 20 minutes or so while I was talking to Kenny. It was kind of awkward because, having not met Kenny, he was sort of dumped on me.

(Field notes)

It was just after 10.30am when Shake reappeared from the toilets in a real mess. He could hardly talk properly or stand up, and almost fell mid-walk. We walked slowly to the bus stop and I agreed to cycle to Connections North to inform them he would be late. I arrived only ten minutes later at around 10.40am and I ran inside to re-arrange the appointment. It was about 10.50am when Shake arrived which meant he was 50 minutes late for his appointment. For some reason, he said, he got off the bus early to walk. He was in a muddle, clearly still affected by the crack and heroin:

He got out his appointment time card – which fell out of his diary loaded with drug dealer phone numbers; his eyes were half open and drool periodically seeped from his mouth. He was told, politely, that he could have an appointment tomorrow for 1.40pm with the doctor. He was sitting in the waiting room with me trying to speak clearly but he was still struggling from the crack and heroin but I wasn't sure why we were waiting other than to wait for his recovery. Maybe he would have to make a similar journey tomorrow?

(Field notes)

My intervention may have saved him from clocking up a 'missed appointment' – three would mean expulsion from the service – and also may have influenced his treatment by the staff – he considered some in the drug service to be unfriendly. However, he didn't make the next appointment and I didn't see Shake for the next three months. He was arrested and sent to prison. In prison, he managed to 'get clean' but on release faced similar problems of unstable housing and the social pressures of the crack scene. Some months later:

As I walked back to my bike, I passed the social security office and saw Shake – he was well, healthy and had put on weight. He said he had managed only to use drugs once since release from prison which I thought was impressive given the pressures ... Later that day, however, I saw him in his 'old area', outside the bank opposite the park. He looked desperate and was late for something. He asked me to look after some money. We argued and I eventually refused, persuading him to give it to his girlfriend. Some guy called Abdul started to linger in the background and I got the impression he was hanging around because he knew Shake had money. He managed to get rid of Abdul but, as we were about to get on the bus, two younger crack users whom Shake had met in prison, came up to him. They pestered him for drugs. Shake sent them along their way, turned to me and said 'they are like demons, they're all around me'.

(Field notes)

Shake's experience seems to show how a disorganised, unpredictable daily life-style around crack and heroin coupled with crack scene social influences (Chapter 5) have implications for engagement with drug support services. Furthermore, the pressures of the crack scene do not appear to diminish, despite efforts to get 'clean' in prison; the pressure clearly evident in Shake's last words. Displacement to different areas of Rivertown also feature in the narrative, as well as expulsion from his local service (Chapter 6). Indeed, some have 'good intentions' to get to their appointments with drug support services:

You have good intentions to go but you just don't get there [to drug support services]. The drug takes over. The addiction's so strong you can't leave it. Do you understand what I mean? You only plan to have one pipe before you go to this appointment but someone else comes around your house or you bump into someone else and then it's one thing for like a week but you know that already, don't you?

(Lively T)

For these reasons, it is difficult for crack users to maintain engagement with drug support services – not only because of the social pressures or but also because of the conditions which such services impose (Chapter 6).

Maintaining engagement: Silver's 'commitment' and Lady Di's predicament

Despite the entrenched nature of most crack users' lifestyles, they are expected to show commitment and take responsibility for themselves to seek a way out of their crack use (Chapter 2). This seemed to be particularly evident in the stories of Silver and Lady Di.

Silver had served a number of prison sentences for burglary and shoplifting. Since 2001, he had detoxed from crack and heroin three times but relapsed on all occasions. This wasn't, however, the whole story as he recalled how he disengaged from the service because a worker 'lied to him about possible prescriptions'. This broke the trust in the relationship. He continued to use crack and heroin until he was arrested and imprisoned again. He described prison as a 'slap in the face', but he did see a worker from Rivertown Referrals a week before his release. On his release to the community, he avoided crack for the first ten days. However:

I got out on a Friday, I rang up hostels that were available, saw my GP and then I made an appointment with my [worker] on Monday and he asked me if

I had thought about rehab and I said I hadn't used [drugs] and don't intend to … and because I had my family [to stay with], I said no. I then saw [another worker] the following week and just started using [crack], told him I hadn't – then the following week came in and told him I had used and that over each day it had been escalating day by day. The week after that I asked to go to detox.

After a few weeks in the community, Silver said he could see himself 'go down that slippery slope again'. Then, 'it started' he said. He started scoring over four-day intervals with 'a couple of guys' he met in prison. His crack and heroin use, initially sporadic after release from prison, then became more frequent. When he approached his worker with this pattern, he was told they needed to see 'a bit more commitment' from him. Meantime, to maintain some motivation to avoid social contact with other crack users, he spent a considerable amount of time looking through long lists of potential rehabs and made six selections. However, he was told that the local authority would not fund five of the six. In 2002, he was told:

They only funded six people a month to go though rehab. I didn't know whether it was the six most deserving cases or six people most at risk. I wasn't sure how they decided – the funding meetings were every Thursday and my case was a week after I had done this. I had to attend the interview and this woman would argue my case.

Rivertown's selection process, however, appeared to be related to the fact that some rehabs had lower success rates with Rivertown's crack users because they were 'high risk'. Consequently, workers tended to reject placements for crack users. Silver was told that the reason for this delay was that he was not using 'enough' crack and heroin to warrant funding through detox and rehab. He said this left him 'passing time' in a hostel which affected his motivation to get clean:

There is a big problem of housing. A lot of the hostels that people go into are just full of people using drugs. So if someone comes out of prison or anywhere with all the best intentions and willingness to stay drug free – put that person into a hostel and they are surrounded by people dealing and going out offending. You could be there six months to a year before you are re-housed by the council and the chances are you will start using and re-offending. The rooms are smaller than the cells and there is normally only room for a single bed. Most people know about where they might want to go – but when you get out, you have to apply, 6–8 weeks waiting. That's 6–8 weeks of you being bored and around people that are using [drugs] and offending.

(Silver)

He stayed there for two years. In December 2004, however, he got a place at a rehab but he left after three months, after disagreeing with the service philosophy of strict abstinence. By April 2005, the next time I saw him, he was smoking crack and heroin in a crack house. Perhaps he had not hit 'rock bottom'? There seemed to be some agreement among both drug workers and drug-using groups that one needed to hit 'rock bottom' before they were able to make changes to their lives. 'Rock bottom', however, seems to be entirely subjective and could mean the 'first night in a prison cell' for some, while it could mean 'homeless on the streets, injecting in the groin' for others. A few crack users seem to reason that they have not hit 'rock bottom' which acts as a rationalisation to continue to use crack. It may also serve to reduce their agency: 'I tried, but they said I couldn't' or 'they told me I couldn't qualify for treatment yet'. Indeed, some infer that there are still others 'worse off than them' which means they have not hit their 'rock bottom'. So, when Silver did show enough commitment to engage, he was asked for more. For others, continuing to show commitment is difficult as most have amassed significant health and social problems which require more effort to resolve (Chapter 2). It certainly requires them to attend different appointments at different times in different services, which by now, for most, is challenging (Chapter 6).

Lady Di exemplifies a similar story. At the time of interview, Lady Di was 33, and said she had been released from prison three weeks ago. She said she was homeless because a care plan had not been devised for her release. When faced with the prospect of street sleeping, she reluctantly sought refuge with her abusive ex-boyfriend, The Duke. She said he forced her to earn money for his drug habit and stole credit cards to raise the '£200 a day' he needed. The interview took place on the street as The Duke was looking for her in the social security office opposite:

LADY DI: *Yeah well what it is I came out of prison and I didn't have nowhere to stay so he's letting me stay with him but I've got to keep [support] his habit. I came out of jail clean [from drugs] but because I've gone to stay with him and I ain't got nowhere to go I've sort of got myself back on the gear again. I've got myself popping crack and that gear habit again within three weeks ...*

DAN: *Were you living with him before?*

LADY DI: *Yeah.*

CUZ: *Were you having a relationship with him before? Were you?*

LADY DI: *Yeah.*

CUZ: *You were together? You were an item?*

LADY DI: *Well yeah. Well before I went away [in prison] for the last six months – we weren't ... well I've been with him for three years and for two and a half years I was with him but for the last six months before I went away there was no sexual relationship because when you're on drugs and I'd end up hating him because I could see that he was using me.*

CUZ: *No, you saw what he was really like.*

LADY DI: *Yeah I saw him for what he was and I'd end up hating him. I'd say to him 'I'm using you, like your gear and your money and that but I'm only here because I've got nowhere else to go' but he hasn't got any shame. He don't care as long as he's getting his money and his gear. He ponces off of everybody. If it weren't me it'd be someone else.*

While she desperately wanted to leave, she said she had 'not had the time' to go to the homeless persons unit because 'as soon as you get up you're ill' [from the withdrawal of crack and heroin]. Even if she did go, she reflected she would have had to provide some ID or a birth certificate to register as homeless. She didn't have either document. Without the necessary paperwork, she said, this added to her worries:

> You need to go and get some money to get some gear [heroin], then you have a [crack] pipe and everything else – any plans you make to get anything done just goes out the window and you think 'I'll do it tomorrow' and tomorrow's the same. Every day's exactly the same.

She felt helpless and powerless:

LADY DI: *I've got no choice really because if I don't support his habit then I'm no use to him and I've got nowhere to live at the moment.*

CUZ: *I've told her what she's got to do.*

LADY DI: *I'm going to go down the homeless persons place. I'm going to go down there. It's just though when you get a roof over your head that's what it is – a drugs relationship – I get him gear and the house is quite clean and tidy and I can go there and I can ...*

DAN: *... wash and keep clean.*

LADY DI: *Wash and keep myself clean and get new clothes, cook something to eat and live like a normal person so to speak but I have to sort this habit out as well. And he's always ill. He has a bit of gear and he's still ill or he still wants another pipe. He's just been on the gear for 23 years.*

DAN: *How old is he?*

LADY DI: *He's nearly 40 so he's never going to get off the gear.*

DAN: *I guess when I say bully I mean does he beat you?*

LADY DI: *Yeah he does slap me about yeah, yeah.*

DAN: *So essentially you're supporting two habits?*

LADY DI: *Yeah and it's hard.*

DAN: *Is that part of the condition of you staying there?'*

LADY DI: *Yeah, oh definitely, yeah because I wouldn't have nowhere else to live.*

Indeed, The Duke was to be seen most days down at the social security office, 'poncing' and intimidating others for money or drugs. She had, however, tried to engage with Crack Service but the shutters were down:

LADY DI: *I've been to Crack Service and places like that.*

DAN: *And why are you not in Crack Service?*

LADY DI: *Because I'm getting methadone off of my doctor but I mean I'm on a prescription with my doctor of methadone and a bit of brown but I haven't tried to sort out the crack. I've tried to go places but – there's one place, it used to be a crack service but every time I've gone there it's been shut.*

In an absence of care plan and housing, Lady Di felt she had little other choice but to rely on the social networks of the crack scene. It was these very networks which, she felt, drained her motivation to make changes:

LADY DI: *You can't walk down the road without people [dealers] going 'here's my number, here's my number'. Do you know what I mean? If you look like you're on drugs. I don't think they always give The Duke the number. They don't give me the number because I don't look too bad at the moment.*
CUZ: [Walking back from social security office after being summoned over by The Duke] *He wants you to go over there.*
DAN: *He said what?*
CUZ: *To try and move it up a bit [hurry up]. He's from Scotland. He's Scottish so he's actually... she loves him.*
LADY DI: [sarcastically] *Yeah I love him so much I can't wait to leave him. Like I've told him to his face 'I'm using you'. Not meaning to be rude but it's no sexual relationship because drugs are the one and only thing in his life.*
CUZ: *Well that's his wife isn't it?*
LADY DI: *Yeah. It does more things than I would because I don't do anything anyway because I'm just using him as some way to live. I think the fucking price that I'm paying I could live with the rich. I could be living somewhere nice.*
CUZ: *Look at him staring.*
[THE DUKE STANDS ON THE OPPOSITE SIDE OF THE ROAD, STARING DIRECTLY AT LADY DI. HIS EYES AND BODY DO NOT SEEM TO MOVE FOR A FEW MINUTES]
LADY DI: *Oh god.*
CUZ: *No. He's looking at me for some reason. He's probably thinking I know that cunt's reputation [as popular with the women]. He's going to take her away from me.*
LADY DI: *When I came out of jail and it only takes three weeks to clean up and I'd really had enough when I came out and I said to him 'I don't want any gear' but where he's got no-one to earn his money he's worn me down. I'm thinking 'enough, enough, enough. Say no' but when you're around someone and you're living with someone.*
DAN: *He just kept on and on at you, yeah?*
LADY DI: *Yeah. In the end I just started taking it. So I've been taking it for a couple of weeks but my habit ain't that bad.*

Lady Di's repeated failed attempts also outline another interesting area: there are almost no references to personal responsibility or agency. Indeed, throughout the narrative, she says things like she had 'no choice'. Instead blame is placed on the pressures around her (Chapter 5) or the mechanisms designed to help her (Chapter 6). This seems to be for two reasons. First, because by blaming other pressures she neutralises personal responsibility for failure (Sykes and Matza, 1957). Second, it seems that in the instances where she had used her agency towards 'getting clean', there had been continual barriers. What therefore seems to happen is that, when continual free will attempts fail to materialise in perceived progress (Evans, 2002; Giddens, 1984), agency is eroded and, instead, blame is attributed to situational and social pressures, the services designed to help, and, once again, placed back on the drug (Maruna, 2001). For some, like Silver and Lady Di, this results in increased fatalistic feelings, personal inadequacy and shame, and continued crack use. In this quote, Cuz, who had tried to get some form of treatment in the past – albeit inappropriate for his poly-drug use – had called in to Connections North. He reasoned that he may as well try to get something which was better than 'nothing':

> When I first said to myself that I'd had enough going out there and stealing, I wanted some medication, like methadone. I knocked on the door and buzzed the buzzer in [Connections North] and said to them 'Is it possible for me to get onto methadone?' She said to me that I had to wait seven weeks! In the fifteenth week, they've sent me a letter saying that they want to see me but by then, I was doing burglaries so I was making a few pennies. They should help them when the person knocks on the door. He's asking for help. Take him, sit him down and listen to him. He's knocking on the door so that means – he's ready for something.
>
> (Cuz)

For Cuz, the waiting lists deterred him and the opportunity was lost, and he drifted back into drugs and crime. Even when he did receive the letter, this made little difference to his predicament because he had already been arrested. When he was offered services again in prison, he angrily rejected them because it did not reflect his ambition to 'get clean':

> It is too late, because I'm arrested now. I'm in the police station. I'm going to prison, so why all of a sudden – why are you coming into the cell to ask me about my drug problem? That's what I told them. 'You cunt. When I came knocking on your door when I was on the outside. You're telling me that you're going to send me letters in blah blah time and it took fucking fifteen weeks to fucking send me a letter, and now I've been arrested and I'm going to jail, you want to help me! Come on! It's all wrong. It's wrong. The way it's all planned is all wrong'.
>
> (Cuz)

Experiencing continual systemic barriers diminishes levels of agency which, in turn, seems to convince the individual that ways out are futile. Any self-promise of 'trying again tomorrow' also seems to be dangerous territory, which is why crack users, too often, seem to tell themselves 'fuck it' and continue in their lifestyles:

BD: *It almost discourages people because, you know what? People when they want to go into recovery, it's a short period of time that you've got when they think my life is shit. I need to do something about it. I need to get myself sorted out and then you're told that you need to get seen by a Substance Misuse Team. Well fuck that! 'Okay you've got an appointment. Come back in a week.' A week is a fucking eternity in a drug addict's life and on that day I've got fucking twenty quid and the last place I'm going to go is there and, if it's any other day apart from a social security day I'll probably be roped away anyway [exposed to social pressures] and I can't afford to get there.*

DAN: *So it's a window of opportunity?*

BD: *It's a window of opportunity and it's small and it's quite easy. Your addiction is very clever. If they tell you that it's going to take two weeks before they see you that's your perfect excuse – 'Oh I tried. I couldn't get in.' Bosh, fair enough! Fuck it! What am I meant to do? That's what happens.*

In this respect, crack users are very much using their free will to act. In addition, when their agency is denied, it also seems to reinforce the notion that 'crack is responsible for these problems' (Booth Davies, 1997); that they would not be in this position if it weren't for crack. For most, continual periods of crack use follow, which are coupled with revolving self-assessments that 'nothing can help'. Increasingly fatalistic attitudes toward the self can result in more self-destructive practices. Here, G, who at the time of the fieldwork was attempting to show commitment to one such drug support service, questioned the possible outcome of his current efforts based on his past experience some years back with Connections North:

DAN: *What's been your experiences with other services?*

G: *Yeah. If my memory serves me correct – I think it's Connections North.*

DAN: *Oh the prescribing place.*

G: *Admittedly this was two or three years ago and I wasn't impressed with them.*

DAN: *No. Why?*

G: *And I even had a go at them. I walked into that place. I found out the day that they had their walk-ins, their drop-ins and self-referrals and I went there one day crying out for help in the sense that I had a crack and heroin habit and I wanted to get off the gear. I even had money in my pocket. And I've gone in there and I left that place there with them telling me that I'd have to wait about six to eight weeks before I could get assessed.*

DAN: *Assessed? Shit.*

G: *I said 'thank you very much' and I walked off. I said 'It's alright. I'll go and buy some gear' and I've never been back but I have heard that it changed. I would expect it to change because the whole circuit's [crack scene] got worse so it stands to reason that they'd get some more staff or get some more help.*

In the subsequent period, G continued to binge heavily on crack and use heroin. When crack users have poor experiences of services, it helps them to reason that crack use is one viable option should the opportunity to use crack unexpectedly present itself.

After the appointment: crack binge opportunities

It was approaching 4pm and Babe still needed her methadone prescription from Connections Central. She couldn't collect it earlier because she was over the alcohol limit. She had tried to collect it at 10.30am but her breath registered at 65 – I am not sure which measurement it was. When she returned at 4pm, it was 47 but it needed to be under 35. She was advised to go and eat bananas and drink water. We left and I bought her both a banana and bottle of water, and we sat in a cafe. She complained about the drug workers because she said all they asked her was how she was and what drugs she had taken that week – that was all. She said they did very little for her and what she had done for herself, was all by herself. When we returned just before 5pm, she had managed to register 34 – and could therefore collect her methadone. We left and she cracked open a can of strong cider. Cuz advised her not to drink and take her pills because it would 'mong her out' but Babe knew this – she confessed that the pills did nothing for her apart from completely space her out. For some reason, she said she hadn't taken any pills since last Friday.

The time was about 5.05pm and we walked down the road from Connections Central and bumped into Clouds – one of Babe's friends. Clouds was 25, dressed quite well, new shoes, tight jeans and large fluffy jacket. Unlike others, she had a mobile phone. She was of normal weight and didn't look like your average crack user – she went on binges, she claimed and then said that she could often go without crack for a month or so.

As we walked down to the bank, she pulled up beside me while swigging at a can of extra strong cider. She was not afraid to talk about her experiences. She said her boyfriend was a crack dealer and that she had smoked away half of his stash. The relationship seemed strange. They both had a hostel place and they had been together for seven months. She claimed that, when she met him, she was clean from drugs but he had 'got her back on it [crack]'. I found it difficult not to judge his actions since she said he served up crack to his own brother. She said he always treated her to money, food and, of course, crack. What he didn't know, she said, was that she was smoking his crack stash away in large chunks. She then started bragging about how much crack she had smoked in a session. In one particular story, when she was being charged at the local magistrates', she had left during lunch to burgle three properties, made a couple of grand, returned to court where she picked up a fine and then sold all the goods and smoked a grand's worth of crack away in a night. She was very loud and colourful in her tone. At times, she seemed honest but didn't seem to make much sense. For example, she said to me she didn't take heroin but I overheard her confess in earlier conversations that she had recently taken it. She didn't consider herself a heroin user.

It was about 5.20pm that Shake staggered past and stopped to talk to me. He was dressed in a new coat which he had [shop]lifted because the nights were getting colder. We talked for a few minutes and he then disappeared with his girlfriend. While I had been talking to Shake, the other conversation had drifted towards crack and it turned out that Clouds had told the others [Cuz and Babe] about her boyfriend's stash. Suddenly, their faces lit up. Clouds invited us to her boyfriend's hostel room, where she said we would steal his crack and smoke it at Babe's.

I wheeled my bike and walked with them up the high street and took a left on to another road – it was dark at about 5.45pm. As we approached the hostel, Clouds explained how she had the keys to his room, but she didn't have the keys to her own room – where the crack was. Perhaps if the crack was found, she would be responsible for it? We got to the hostel and guests were allowed. I took my bike up to the third floor. Clouds had to go down to ask the management to let her in to her own bedroom to get the crack and left us to sit in the crack dealer's bedroom. I was praying he wouldn't come back. Clouds left, reassuring us of his 'good and harmless nature' but this did little to comfort me. She wasn't more than five minutes and returned with a chunk of crack the size of my palm, street value of about £1,000. It was clumsily wrapped in cling film. As she opened it up, it flopped into two bits which she had previously cut up.

Clouds put the TV on and asked us to sit on the bed while she cut it up. She then turned to us and said 'let's have a quick lick now'. The problem was she said her boyfriend was due back any minute. She told me I was to be her cousin 'Lorenzo' if he came in. I went along with it and as she started to cut up the crack, while Cuz and Babe huddled round on the floor. I remained sat on the bed as they all fiddled with the large amount of crack. However, the impending opportunity to smoke crack seemed to generate some excitement and petty squabbles:

CLOUDS: [To Babe] *Get some ash ready for me [to be able to prepare a crack pipe].*

DAN: [While looking at this large lump of crack] *How much is that worth?*

CLOUDS: *Quite a lot of money. A thousand pounds.*

DAN: [To everyone in disbelief] *And you're going to smoke all of it?*

BABE: *No. She's [Clouds] going to sort me some out until Thursday and then I'll pay her – even until tomorrow actually because I'll get my disability [social security benefit] hopefully.*

DAN: *That is just fucking unbelievable! Are you going to take one of the half blocks or are you going to ...?*

CLOUDS: *I'm going to split it. I ain't got no ash. That's two twenty [pound stones] there.*

CUZ: *No. That ain't two twenties.*

BABE: [To Clouds] *Fuck off you bitch. Don't try and scam us. I'm paying you Thursday so shut your mouth. You know you don't get nothing for nothing in this world.*

Because they had no pipes on them, they used extra-strength lager/cider cans they had been drinking from. They slightly dented the cans in half and with a Stanley knife (don't know where this came from), poked 7 or 8 holes half way across the can. They then put ash on the holes and put fairly large chunks of crack on the pipe (£20 stones). Clouds was the first to get her pipe ready, she seemed most keen. Cuz was worried he would go 'digi' because he preferred to smoke crack from foil rather than cans but we were in a rush to smoke it before the dealer came back. While Clouds smoked, her eyes widened slightly and her body gently wavered. She inhaled for about 30 seconds and she had managed to smoke the whole rock. She said nothing after piping and held the smoke in for about 20 seconds.

Cuz was next. He didn't go 'digi', as he put it, but he didn't seem to enjoy the buzz. Then Babe went. She took several deep breaths before she put the pipe to her lips, maybe to make sure she was relaxed and could draw a deep breath to smoke the crack. She relaxed herself and then came over to me and sat next to me on the bed. While she was talking to me, Cuz and Clouds packed away the crack; some dropped on the floor and Cuz took it without Clouds realising. Clouds clumsily wrapped up the rest of the crack in fresh cling film and mopped up the crack crumbs and put them into another bit of cling film.

Time was getting on and we wanted to leave – Cuz and I left as soon as he had smoked the crack. We walked outside. I wasn't sure of the implications of all this – how the dealer would react? Would he beat her? She said she had already smoked some of his crack stash away earlier that day. Cuz was congratulating himself at his swift move to steal some crack and told me he would sell it. Clouds and Babe then came downstairs with the large lumps of crack hidden and we walked to Babe's place. It was a flat in a relatively nice area. We entered through a glass door which led to a number of flats – Babe had a ground floor flat. The flat was relatively tidy, but there were no carpets and the curtains were pieces of cloth draped over the window. As we went in, the bedroom was to the left, the corridor was in front of me which led to the toilet, and the living room and kitchen were to the left.

Babe went straight to the living room and showed me a picture of her children – one, she said, was 17 and was smoking crack. Babe had, however, tried to get her off the drug. She said, 'to teach her a lesson', Babe made her daughter smoke £400 of crack in a session so she could be put off using the drug. Cuz then took the lead into the bedroom and Clouds followed. Babe and I were the last to enter. As we entered the bedroom, there was a huge old television in the corner and a very bouncy double bed. I sat in a rocking chair at the end of the bed.

Cuz started to prepare his foil, but again Clouds was the first to have her pipe ready – she had brought her glass pipe from the hostel. Cuz then started to smoke his crack from the foil. Babe, however, was taking a long time to prepare her pipe. She first of all cut the gauze from what looked like a packet you could buy in the shop. She spent about five minutes making sure she had cut the right amount of crack. She needed a fresh gauze, she said, as she needed to be able to inhale the crack smoke correctly. She showed me her pipe; the bottom of the small glass bottle had been knocked through – which was where you put your lips – and the top had black marks around the rim. She then held the gauze with some scissors while she burnt it with a lighter – I wasn't sure whether this process took this long as she was talking at the same time. She burnt the gauze for about five minutes at ten-second intervals before stuffing the gauze down the throat of the bottle – this took several minutes as well. Finally she melted the crack into the gauze itself – this was because she was about to turn the bottle upside down and it would have otherwise fallen out. This was very much unlike the rushed and clumsy process in the hostel.

I was surprised to then see her go to the bathroom to get the mirror – her 'buzz', she said, was to watch the smoke form in the bottle. She said it also helped measure how much crack she had left. She called me over to watch her over her shoulder in the mirror. I was a little worried I might ruin her buzz as she said liked to do this sort of thing by herself. While she was burning the crack, I watched the smoke gradually form in the bottle. It looked like a white cloud. Her eyes remained focused on the forming cloud. She didn't even blink. She inhaled slowly for about 25 seconds and when she pulled away, she slowly released the smoke. I sat down and smelt the remnants of Cuz's foil; it smelt like vanilla. Then he accidentally blew it in my face, but it was a nice smell I thought. Clouds then offered me a pipe, but I declined. I said it wasn't my thing – she was confused and asked me why I was hanging around with 'low life' like them but I said they weren't low life.

(Field notes)

There they stayed all night and finished the large lumps of crack that Clouds had stolen from her boyfriend. All this stemmed from a chance meeting after a drug agency appointment. This is, perhaps, why it does become a question of commitment. However, if like Silver earlier in the chapter, crack users can summon the commitment to seek continued support, the next barrier they encounter is facing up to themselves, their acts and their past. This process often starts with a series of assessments and perhaps counselling sessions where crack users are persuaded to 'take responsibility' for their drug use. This seems to be particularly difficult – arguably more difficult for crack users than heroin users – because of the high level of denial they appear to have developed about their crack use and the heavily stigmatised nature of their past actions. In addition, many seem unsure about the role crack use plays in their current drug use.

Denial: facing up to shame, stigma and the spoilt identity

Thus far, many crack users attribute their current circumstances to crack (Chapter 4) and, over time, seem to persuade themselves that an alternative identity is responsible for crack and the consequences of its use (Neale *et al.*, 2006). This identity seems to help to defer individual feelings of guilt and shame (Maruna, 2001). Indeed, if the hegemonic message of governmental institutions, the media, welfare and drug support agencies is that the crack 'does the destruction to the user', then it is highly likely that the people who use the drug will also ascribe a similar belief (Booth Davies, 1997). This also seems to aid the process of reducing the responsibility and agency of crack users. So, when they engage with drug support services or rehabs, they have to be persuaded that 'the alternative identity' that harboured their past, their criminality, and deviant acts was, in fact, themselves. Convincing the self that he/she is responsible for all these negative things becomes immensely difficult.

In the context of crack users, it seems that their level of denial is greater than other groups of drug users (Chapter 4) because, as they see it, the 'alternative identity' – or the drug – is responsible for their involvement in a higher proportion of criminal and stigmatised acts which contravene personal, social and cultural norms. What seems to make crack users different from heroin users is the level to which they engage in derogatory acts and high-risk behaviours (Chapter 2). In addition, for a few crack users in this sample, crack does not appear as problematic for them. Others cannot locate any recognisable pattern of use, can themselves see no visible 'side effects' and are convinced that there are others worse off than them – such as 'junky' heroin users (Chapter 7; Simmonds and Coomber, 2009):

> It's going to be harder with crack or rock addicts because remember as I said they are already in denial and they don't realise that they're just as bad as the heroin addict. They think they're one up. 'No, no, no I'm alright' because, well I'd say as much as 90 per cent of them wake up with no withdrawal symptoms or anything like that and they take that as a thing that they're better and they're not better. They have got a problem just like people who take brown. They have issues that need addressing. It's to get them to realise this and it's not going to be easy.
>
> (G)

Coming to terms with years of damaged feelings, victimisation and abuses, and personal acts of stigma seems to be too much for most. Even when in recovery, reflecting on 'the crack life' becomes difficult. In this conversation with Def Jam, a Jamaican woman in rehab during the fieldwork, she starts to reflect on crack-using practices. However, when the narrative drifts toward crack and crime, memories of using crack start to resurface. When they do, Def Jam attributes greater suffering to 'the crack' because she felt it led her down a more precarious drug-taking and risk-oriented pathway; and with it, she felt, went self-dignity and self-respect:

DAN: *Did you do white and brown together?*

DEF JAM: *Yes.*

DAN: *On the foil?*

DEF JAM: *Foil, yeah for a long time.*

DAN: *So pipe – then foil. Did you go up on the crack and down on the heroin?*

DEF JAM: *You can do both on the pipe as well?*

DAN: *Can you?*

DEF JAM: *Snowball they call it.*

DAN: *I didn't know you could do it on the pipe.*

DEF JAM: *Yeah.*

DAN: *What with a Martel bottle or with the plastic?*

DEF JAM: *A pipe with the gauze.*

DAN: *Yeah, but doesn't the brown fall through it?*

DEF JAM: *No. You just sprinkle a bit on the thing – on top. You put your coke on first then you just sprinkle a bit on.*

DAN: *Don't you melt the coke in?*

DEF JAM: *Yeah, you can sprinkle the heroin on top. You can do them both. I've had them both together.*

DAN: *How does that compare?*

DEF JAM: *It blows your head off. I don't want to talk about them things any more.*

DAN: *That's ok. We don't have to talk about it any more. That's fine. No, no. If you don't want to answer any questions don't worry.*

DEF JAM: *I don't really want to talk about drugs – smoking them.*

DAN: *That's fine. You do what you feel. I don't want to upset you …*

DEF JAM: *It just brought back …*

DAN: *… memories.*

DEF JAM: *Yeah.*

DAN: *Ok. What about the relationship between crime. Is there a difference between the crime you would commit if you had a crack habit and crime you would commit if you had a brown habit?*

DEF JAM: *Brown – that is a physical withdrawal. Ten pounds of brown can keep you satisfied for the day. Crack – that was when I went mad. I have got a [criminal] record. My record's upstairs. I have got a record like a book. They were trying to deport me and everything. I've been here [in the UK] since 1977 but, because of the crimes I've committed – I've committed too many crimes, it's a new thing they've brought out [legislation], and they tried to deport me. It didn't work out in the end. They said that I could stay but if I made any more crimes I'd be coming up in front of them again. I don't intend to anyway. With the crack, the man said to me when he looked at my record – the man from the Home Office – he said: 'This [criminal] record' he said 'it's like a long list. Tell me about the person behind this' and I thought 'You know something? If only you'd asked the first time you'd locked* me up and all those times I've been in prison. Why is it only now?' I did tell them but I was thinking 'why is it only now that they're asking these questions?' They should have been asking that at the beginning. Why is this person doing this?'

DAN: To stop it going that far?

DEF JAM: Yeah. From day one they should have been asking these questions not when I've been to prison from 1986 and I've probably been on the street [homeless] maybe four years out of those years. Lucky I was always in prison for Christmas. Right now I hate Christmas with all these decorations because I feel like I'm always in prison. It's not been a good time for me if I'm struggling. I'm putting in the effort but I'm struggling with it you know? Crack is worse than heroin. I don't care what anyone says. It is because with crack you want more and more and more and the thing is as well you don't even realise what you're doing to people until after you've done it because the crime that I was in for was an old guy you know? And I'm really ashamed to tell you.

DAN: If you don't feel comfortable ...

DEF JAM: No I'm just saying I feel ashamed to talk about it. Not just to you. I feel ashamed for myself in general but I have done it and I will say it. I'm not afraid to say it because I did it. He was pushing his wife in a wheelchair and I'd gone into the precinct to get some money because I was smoking crack and I'd seen him outside the bank counting his money and that was it. I just focused on that one man. I remember it you know and I sat and I waited for that man. He went into Iceland and I sat there waiting and I followed him into the lift and I robbed him in the lift. The man was on a heart machine and he could have died but he didn't thank God and that's through crack cocaine.

DAN: When you first started on crack were you just [shop]lifting?

DEF JAM: Shoplifting and prostitution but it escalated.

DAN: What to more violent ... ?

DEF JAM: Burglary, prostitution, street robberies.

DAN: As it progressed you started being a bit more violent?

DEF JAM: Yeah.

DAN: Are you sure you don't mind talking about this?

DEF JAM: No.

DAN: I mean what did it start with? Was it [shop]lifting first then sex work?

DEF JAM: Yeah. Shoplifting first but when I started shoplifting... I came from Jamaica so I wasn't born here ... my mum ...

DAN: She sent for you over here?

DEF JAM: Yeah – from Jamaica. She was here but I didn't know her because she left me when I was six months old and then I started going to school here. I'd see the girls at school [shop]lifting stuff and I started following them and it was just exciting so I done it. Then I started college and to look nice and to wear the clothes that were in and my mum weren't buying me the clothes that I wanted so I started shoplifting again but I used to get dressed at my friend's house, then change my clothes; dress up in the things that I wanted to dress in. Then I stopped. Then I started taking the drugs and I started again.

DAN: *With the sex work did that come about when you had ... were you known* [by the authorities]*?*

DEF JAM: *What happened was I was on the run* [from the police] *that's how that came about. The police wanted me. They wanted me for ... I done it one time* [sex work] *before that and then I stopped. Then when I started up full-time properly was when the police were looking for me and I didn't want to get caught. I was on the run for ages so I started doing prostitution.*

Ultimately, 'the crack', she felt, exposed her to further risk behaviours, making her more vulnerable 'on the street' – constantly looking for the next one pipe and engaging in unsafe sex. Over time, she said she lost weight, and took less care of her appearance and physical health. Even though she was in recovery once again, she said she didn't know 'how to feel' and had immense difficulty facing up to the past. Thus, in rehab, individuals must not only come to terms with the 'spoilt' nature of the self (Simmonds and Coomber, 2009) but also other areas of their past which they have had to try to block out. This was also the case for Firey A:

> For my colour, yeah, and also I was a fat child as well so I was black and fat and I really got it in the neck; not only from like peers at school but my siblings at home as well because I was the only one born in Britain. The rest of them were born in Jamaica so I was pretty slated. There are times when I've been pretty insecure about myself and I've had to reinvent myself and wear masks in order to get through life and I suppose that's where I am now today because the mask didn't stay up that well so I turned to drugs at the age of thirty-three.
>
> (Firey A)

Already damaged by racial abuse, the stigmatisation of having three children from three separate partners did not make the 'beautiful and young' Firey A feel 'sorry' for herself. Without the support of her family, she said she felt more 'frustrated'. Nevertheless, through these experiences she said she had lost trust in family, and men as providers in love and relationships, and was tired of her burdensome children who she compared to an 'albatross around her neck'. Feeling that she may have lost her youth, at 33, she said started a relationship with a 'not so nice guy' who was a 'closet crack smoker'. She was curious about his 'rave' lifestyle: 'I wanted some of that ... just soaking it all up really what I'd missed.' Given her limited financial circumstances, crack dealing through her boyfriend appealed as an alternative income opportunity. She said her boyfriend 'dented the profit margin' by smoking her 'stash'. He frequently boasted about the effects of crack with sex, and she became more curious and tried it because she didn't want to 'be responsible'. Within six months, her profit margins had disappeared. She said she became heavily reliant on customers who brought her stolen goods in exchange for crack. In this buoyant period, she reflected that:

Well we'd exchange clothes. They were shoplifters and that's how I basically lost everything because I would go and use with them. I did like the feeling. I enjoyed the feeling. I enjoyed the high. I enjoyed the buzz which, after that period, I never felt again. After that initial six months I was just chasing that buzz. I think that's what most users do but, by that time, I'd gotten involved with these people, was actually shoplifting myself, committing fraud. Those first six months it was like okay I had no responsibilities. I'd reinvented myself once again. I was like cropped blonde hair and really loud in appearance and the money was coming in. It was three hundred quid a day basically.

After several years in London, and under increasing pressure to care for maturing children, she reflected how she moved to another city in an attempt to 'get clean' and stayed with her parents. With both parents struggling for income, and increased economic pressure on her family, she said she tried prostitution to make money 'for the family' but kept it from them because of the stigma. Within three months, she 'was on the crack'. She felt 'ashamed to work in the city' so instead moved to a nearby town but she started to steal from her family. She then fled with her children to another town to 'work the massage parlours'. After two years, she tried a 'fresh start' in another city: her daughters, she said, were 'damaged' and 'had not forgotten' the whole experience. The housing waiting list was lengthy but she said she befriended another '[crack] user' and moved the family in and, again, within three months, was 'smoking again'. Increasingly desperate, she turned to more crime:

> I started taking things out of the house and started robbing them and, before I knew it, I was at a real low and attempted street robbery, aggressive street robbery and theft of persons and the police caught up with me and I got a twelve month sentence and I served six months. First I was in Holloway, then Styal, then finally Eastwood Park. I did the rehabilitation service in Styal prison and I was supposed to come to the rehabilitation service on 7th February last year [2003] but they transferred me to another prison and all my network, everything that I'd ever set up, all fell to bits and I was put back out on the streets.

This experience appeared only to compound her feelings and amplify feelings of guilt and shame:

> I felt like I was dying. I felt like I wanted to die – shame, guilt. I rang my children but I just couldn't stop [using crack]. I couldn't stop myself. I stole from my mother. Apart from stealing from shops and stuff I'd never ever stolen from another person before. I stole my mother's chequebook and within a month I emptied her account of like three thousand pounds. So I was running scared now. Everybody's looking for me. I went on a rampage. I just felt like a slab of concrete you know.

(Firey A)

Having lost her children – two to the care of her mother and one to social services – she found some refuge in a hostel, where she 'started using [drugs], scamming people and really getting dark and bullying people'. She said the hostel experience motivated her to 'badger and hassle' people for a place in a rehab, which was where I met her for several interviews. Despite engaging well with drug support services and showing strong will to 'get clean', she found it difficult to come to terms with her feelings. Halfway through the fieldwork period and her stay in rehab, she fled. The only worker who had been able to get 'past her façade' said she could not recover from the shame and guilt of her past actions. These challenges do not necessarily desist once crack users have been through rehab.

Success stories? BD and Easy E

> They [the government] haven't solved the problem and they are not willing and this is what the crux of the matter is – addiction depends on funding and the government don't really want to fund treatment for addiction – they say it as if they are doing something about it but they're not. Really is what they want to do is find out the solution – the solution is get people into treatment and offer them a different way of life and give them continued support to sustain that life – and it isn't about sticking ex-crack users on council estates. It isn't about saying we can fund you for six months, that's all we can fund you for. You are kind of giving an addict a one-shot-in-a-financial-year which a lot of councils do – they say they can only fund you once in a year, then the geezer will come out of treatment and relapse and he has to wait another x,y,z months before he can see if he can get funding.
>
> (Easy E)

This research and the respective literature show that very few crack users go through rehab and remain drug free (Chapter 2). Many in this study said they had been through rehab and either failed to complete or relapsed soon after completion. Many complain that the time they spent in rehab was too short – suggesting that to recover and come to terms with years (and in some cases decades) of drug abuse, physical and mental ailments, and practical problems would require the State to devote much more than six months to help them in their recovery. As crack users see it, these institutions have been constructed as the answer to their drug use problems – as well as a general resolution to all life's problems. Consequently, many have high expectations that going 'into detox' or 'getting rehab' will set them on the right track to recovery. For a few, this seems to work, but for most crack users in this sample it seems to be a false economy. Indeed, those that do complete rehab for the first time seem to have a naïve sense of their potential vulnerability:

> I had a bad scenario once. I came into some money legally. I put some away and I had a couple of grand around me and I was at one of those stages when

I thought 'I'm alright' [after going through detox and rehab]. I'd been clean for a while and I was walking down the road and I just got a trigger. I saw someone – a friend of mine – and I knew he had just scored – it was how he was moving. I knew he'd just scored. I said 'oi oi oi'. I had two hundred pounds on me and I thought 'Let me just go and have one [pipe]. That ain't nothing'. I smoked two grand in fourteen days.

(G)

These kind of slip-ups contribute to general negative perceptions of crack users as social failures, so the authorities may think it is not worth risking further investment in their recovery – that is, their reputation for failure outweighs the benefits of funding treatment. If they are given the chance, there is also the possibility that they will 'be irresponsible' and start using crack again, which is why professionals must determine who can show *commitment*. This is why, with all good intention, it comes back to a question of *commitment* on the part of the crack user and, with all the will in the world, if the crack user cannot be responsible and 'change their ways' then 'time is wasted'. One housing worker said:

The team will try to accommodate them [crack users] but the time is wasted when people receive accommodation and then decide not to live there or don't pay the bills, especially when there is other more committed people waiting to get into housing.

(NACRO worker)

Once crack users learn that neither drug support nor rehab, housing or other welfare support systems can offer the magic bullet to resolve their crack use – and other problems – many reason crack use to be a normative, rational option. Indeed, Booth Davies (1997: 35) shows that 'all things considered, therefore, pressing the lever' – which in this context would be taking crack again – 'seems the best thing to do despite the unpromising long-term prospects implied by the environment'. In fact, there seems to be little guarantee for those who do complete rehab that they will survive without crack and other drugs. Here, BD reflects on the seven-month engagement process having been homeless, using crack and out of contact with drug support services. Engaging and accessing services, as he suggests, requires navigating overcrowded temporary accommodation, waiting lists and appointment systems (Chapter 6).

BD: [You need a place] *so that when you go in there and say I have an addiction you can see a substance misuse team, you can be assessed, you can be told there and then whether funding is available and there and then when a place will be ready for you. It took me seven months to get into this day programme because I was homeless at the time and they won't take you when you're homeless and living on the street because they say you need a stable base so that means you then have to get a hostel, get into your hostel, be stable in your hostel, continue to go to see*

Crack Service to show them that you're committed and do all these things now while you're waiting for a place and then you go for your interview and then you might have to wait three or four weeks after your interview before you're offered a place. So seven months is a long time. You've got to be pretty committed and people that are committed don't have seven months and, in those seven months, you risk the chance of being nicked [sent to prison] and in which case you're almost back to square one again.

DAN: *Yeah. So you're saying there needs to be a place where there's a lot of different other services there where people have a ...*

BD: *One-stop shop, yeah.*

DAN: *Is that the only thing you can foresee that would help people with this kind of addiction? Like you say they'll find excuses to use you know?*

BD: *Yeah, but like I said also the State puts some real barriers in your way.*

DAN: *Like what?*

BD: *Like I said. The fact that you need to have somewhere to live, the fact that there are so few hostel places available for most people that are that far down [have so many problems]. You see you have to get to the bottom before you can get back up but, if you're at the bottom it's very hard to get back up because finding accommodation now in London – which is one of the requisites that you need now before you can go into a day programme – is difficult.*

Crack users are quick to complain about the social and structural barriers but few are able to identify the individual barriers that may prevent them from making progress. This is because, in most cases, their agency has been eroded. Even if crack users manage to generate funding for rehab, they encounter significant power dynamics with others in the same stage of recovery. Some, like Silver, may also disagree with the service philosophy. Others encounter old adversaries or, because they are still coming to terms with facing up to the past, seek to portray themselves as 'better off' than their recovering counterparts. Those that surpass these stages must then wait for stable housing. They do this in hostels where they face the day-to-day pressures of the crack scene and continual reminders of their former lifestyle (Chapter 5):

There's just not that many areas that I can imagine myself going and living in, and knowing that one day I'm not going to walk out my door and see someone that I know, and 'Oh, I didn't know that you lived here'; and it goes around the bush telegraph, 'Oh, [name] got a flat down there.' It's not going to be long before somebody's in the area scoring, and like 'I've just bought a bag from around the corner. Is it all right if I have a dig in here?' I just don't want it. So the idea is that I just want to get away from all of it.

(Silver)

In many cases the few who manage to stay clean from crack are housed back in the very areas they used to occupy as 'crack users'. This presents them with daily tests of their commitment to stay drug free. After going through rehab three times, Alwight was allocated accommodation on the same estate where he started using crack – except this time, he was housed next to a crack house. He saw it as almost therapeutic:

DAN: *How do you feel, having been through rehab and living in these areas – do you feel temptation?*

ALWIGHT: *You see what goes on there – it is not attractive to me. I don't really feel tempted no – no I don't. It is kind of difficult. Sometimes when I am lying in bed and I know there is crack house next door and somebody knocks on the door and they go in and I might sit there and think – that person there is probably smoking a crack pipe and I might start getting physical feelings of euphoria or that but, by and large, I think that life is shit and I am glad I am not living that life any more. If I choose to go into one of them places I probably will be back on it and I don't want that to happen. I have lived that life – it reminds me of how it was before me.*

Conclusion

This chapter shows how social and cultural pressures (Chapter 5) and structural barriers (Chapter 6) influence intentions to seek a way out (Shake). The same forces present day-to-day barriers to attending appointments and meetings but also sustaining such engagement (Babe, Silver and Lady Di). Few are able to show meaningful commitment for sustained periods – quickly learning of the limitations and contradictions of service configuration (Chapter 6) and reason crack use to be a rational option (Booth Davies, 1997). They remain, in most instances, at the mercy of the crack scene (Chapter 5). This is important because crack users do show genuine individual intentions to resolve crack use – and other problems – but their motivations, it seems, become weakened when continual social (Chapter 5) and structural (Chapter 6) barriers are experienced (Giddens, 1984). They reconcile that 'they tried' but the mechanisms for support were not forthcoming. This seems to increase the tendency for fatalistic thinking, low self-esteem and low self-respect (Chapter 7). They may reflect on their position in the crack scene and their failed attempts, and feelings of shame (Giddens, 1991) may coincide with increasingly risky or dangerous drug use (Bourdieu, 1984; Farmer *et al.*, 1996).

If, however, crack users muster up the required commitment, they are encouraged to acknowledge that it was 'self' – not the crack – which was responsible for their criminal and stigmatised actions (Maruna, 2001). Suddenly, the self is asked to shoulder all of life's losses (Dunlap, 1995); the shame of the past and the stigma associated with the individual's deviant and criminal acts (Chapter 7; Maruna, 2001). In drug support services and rehab, crack users are persuaded to concede to the 'spoilt' identity (Simmonds and Coomber, 2009) yet many rationalise that their lives deteriorated significantly as a consequence of crack and this, they reconcile, perpetuated their involvement criminal and deviant acts. Because these acts hold significant amounts of stigma and break personal, emotional, individual, social and cultural codes (Chapter 2), it becomes more difficult for many to come to terms with them. Although a few battle through the power dynamics of rehab (Briggs, 2007; Weppner, 1981), they are then often thrust back into drug-using hostels while they wait for accommodation (Waterson, 1997), and these are most likely to be in areas where crack and other drugs are present (Chapter 2; Chapter 6). The penultimate chapter of this book seeks to merge the literature, the theoretical framework, with the research findings. Recommendations for policy and practice follow a conclusion.

Chapter 9

Discussion and conclusion

Introduction

This book has examined crack users' addictions and the realities of their lives. Ethnographic methods were used over nine months in 2004/05 with these people in south London. While there has been other ethnographic research with crack users in the UK (Parker *et al.*, 1998), this is the first ethnographic study of its kind that has attempted to describe how crack careers evolve and the socio-structural context of crack-using practices; the interactions among crack users in crack houses and across the crack scene; and how they interplay with socio-structural processes. Therefore the study provides new insights into the nature of crack use in the UK. This penultimate chapter of the book is devoted to discussion of the findings in the context of existing literature and the theoretical framework. Recommendations for policy and practice also follow.

Contributions to current literature

This UK study complements other work undertaken by American (Agar, 2003; Bourgois, 1995; Williams, 1990) and Canadian researchers (Malchy *et al.*, 2008) in the context of crack. It sought to understand why crack users are perceived to be the most problematic drug-using group in the UK and why they continually fail in treatment settings (Weaver *et al.*, 2007). UK studies in the context of crack have tended to explore crack use as a consequence of deterministic processes with the actors involved perceived as victims of the drug (Chapter 2; Reinarman and Levine, 1997). However, this study seeks to connect 'background factors' and 'network explanations' of crack use with individual decisions made in the context of crack use and participation in the crack scene. Furthermore, the research also builds on identity work (Maruna, 2001; Neale *et al.*, 2006; Simmonds and Coomber, 2009) in the context of crack use. This is important given that many UK studies either seem to be concerned with 'crack users failing to engage with services' or overemphasise the drug 'consuming' the user.

Theoretical contribution

A number of theoretical perspectives have been used in this book to help understand the socio-structural position of crack users, and the macro and micro forces
which shape their daily lives (Chapter 3; Malchy *et al.*, 2008) and crack careers
(Falck *et al.*, 2007; Hser, 2002). An interactionist perspective helps to understand
why crack users remain clandestine about their operations; precisely because they
are considered to be deviant and illegal. Indeed, sociology of deviance theories
prove useful in locating how identity shifts occur (Matza, 1964) in the context of
the reciprocal interactions crack users make in relation to social institutions such
as law enforcement agencies and drug support services (Becker, 1953; Chapter
3; Ray, 1964). Of equal importance is the concept of the socially constructed self
(Cooley, 1964) because, as identity tensions arise throughout crack careers, the
mechanisms of the crack scene influence attitudes and practices (Singer, 2001;
Young, 1971). In particular, the marginalising nature of the environments in
which crack users use also appears to influence their identities (Chapter 3; Duff,
2009) and attitudes to their sense of self (Rhodes *et al.*, 2005).

Theories of political economy also help to understand what shapes crack users'
decisions and attitudes (Chapter 3). A political economic perspective helps to
explain why particular urban areas are exposed and vulnerable to high levels of
crack use (Agar, 2003; Wacquant, 2002), but also how the restructuring of urban
life and public space seems to take place at the expense of problematic populations such as crack users (Marez, 2004). Policymakers, governments, and media
(Reinarman and Levine, 1997; 2004) enforce the notion that crack users pose a
potential threat to communities and their way of life (Chapter 2; Seddon, 2008)
and this contributes to a hegemonic rhetoric that positions crack as the primary
problem among these groups (Reinarman and Levine, 1997; 2004), rather than as
a deep-rooted symbol of marginalisation and structural violence (Bourgois, 1995;
Bourgois and Schonberg, 2009).

This study makes use of these perspectives because they appear to offer insight
into how these powerful macro forces are experienced, and are manifested in
day-to-day, cultural practices (Bourgois *et al.*, 1997). The way in which crack
users internalise cultural systems and macro processes seems to reflect a form
of symbolic violence (Bourdieu, 1984). In this respect, key themes from this
research mirror those from other studies on social oppression, structural violence
and marginalisation, which illustrate how stigma, shame and fatalism become
characteristics of crack users and their day-to-day lives (Chapter 7).

The study locates these micro interactionist and macro political economic
processes against a 'risk society' perspective (Beck, 1992; Giddens, 1991; Lupton,
1999). As with the political economy framework, this perspective shows why there
is considerable community fear and anxiety associated with populations such as
crack users (Seddon, 2008). Yet this work shows there is nothing to fear from
these people. If anything, it emphasises the desire crack users show, like any late
modern individual, to seek a coherent biography (Bauman, 2007) under precarious

circumstances (Young, 2007). However, the nature of the social, structural and environmental conditions under which they survive seems to jeopardise ontological security and the continuity of the self. Indeed, an inadequate life biography may highlight feelings of inadequacy, moral failing and shame (Giddens, 1991). This seems particularly the case for crack users in this study (Chapter 7).

The concept of reflexivity is useful because it explains why crack users struggle to make lifestyle changes because, when internalised feelings and stigmatised past actions are reflexively revisited, most struggle to come to terms with them (Maruna, 2001). The work also shows that they want to be responsible for their health (Petersen, 1997; Rimke, 2000) but many find it difficult when their free willed intentions are continually denied. This is why responsibilisation theories associated with Beck and Beck-Gernsheim (2002) are also important to consider.

Methodological innovations

This study builds on other ethnographic studies undertaken in the context of crack users (Anderson, 1990; Bourgois, 1995; Parker *et al.*, 1998; Sterk, 2002; Williams, 1990). There have been continual calls for the lived experience of problematic drug users to be given greater consideration in the UK. It is acknowledged that this is a short study in contrast to US ethnographies but such a study was a significant time period for UK-funded ethnographies especially in light of national and local funding restrictions and ethical barriers associated with this kind of fieldwork. No comparison is made against heroin users because this group has already attracted significant attention. The study does not claim to account for all crack-using groups but those that I was able to contact in this time period, in this area who permitted me access to their experiences.

I sought to adopt a critical realist perspective and acknowledge my presence in interactions, interviews and observations. I had to live a life that was alien to me to do this research (Inciardi, 1995). I acted in ways that were both risky and unsavoury to gain acceptance, but I had a clear purpose. I tried not to collude, and acted with sympathy and humanity (Fetterman, 1989) when the people I was with were in real trouble (Bourgois and Schonberg, 2009). The nature of my presence and the difficulties I experienced at times seem to aptly reflect the nature of the crack scene, especially the problems I experienced with Cuz. To ensure I was representing as well as possible this particular culture, I showed Dawg, Blood, Cuz and Fam my reports, discussed emerging findings and undertook follow-up interviews. These people were always put first in my study, and regardless of my research agenda, their safety, their confidentiality and our relations were always most important to me.

Local knowledge in Rivertown

Historically, epidemiological studies have struggled to capture the number of crack users in Rivertown; in particular, those out of contact with drug support services. This is undoubtedly related to the transient nature of their lifestyles (Al-Rahman *et al.*, 2007) and the restrictive methods previously used to gather such data (Chapter 2). This study does not pretend to be quantitatively representative but reveals key aspects about crack users' lives and experiences that can be useful for local policymakers.

The study shows why crack users are particularly difficult to retain in local drug services and, despite local concerns that it was a problem specific to crack users (Chapter 3), to some degree, the policies, systems and protocols which the local authority and other institutions had strategically devised also impinge on crack users and their attempts to make changes (Chapter 8). Similarly, service configuration has, for some years, failed to adapt to crack users' needs because drug service configuration in the context of crack users has been historically poor and methods of engaging crack users almost non-existent. The research shows that coercing crack users into treatment does not seem to be beneficial – despite an increased policy shift towards this ideology towards the end of the fieldwork (Chapter 6).

Indeed, scaling back investment from the agencies that seem to provide the most beneficial support does not bode well for the future of drug support configuration in Rivertown. Sadly, when the final report for the project was delivered, Rivertown authorities continued to retract support and treatment for problematic drug users – including crack users. Despite completing a report with recommendations, to date, it is difficult to identify how this research has actually translated into effective local policy – especially when the primary service which is charged with helping crack users (Crack Service) continues to reduce its opening times and flexibility. Instead, increasing numbers of crack users are funnelled through statutory services that have more stringent conditions attached to engagement (Reuter and Stevens, 2008).

Crack use and crack careers

The bulk of previous research appears to have separated different aspects of crack use from its social context (Chapter 2). Furthermore, much of the understanding of these areas has come from the US. UK literature on pathways into crack use tends to bundle risk factors together with no explanation as to how they interact. The literature on the physical and mental health consequences of crack use also fails to connect to social processes. A broader understanding of crack use was necessary to consider how broader emotional, social, cultural and structural features encompass crack use and how they are interconnected. Therefore, this study sought to provide a greater understanding of how what might be seen as 'stand-alone' attributes such as mental health, risk and sex behaviours interact with crack careers.

This study also brings a greater understanding to crack-using patterns in the UK, and, in particular, to crack binges. The crack binge appears less a feature of the 'drug' driving the individual to use more crack (Home Office, 2002; Lindsell,

2005) or located within a linear stage toward crack addiction (Ford, 2004), but instead appears at various points in the crack career and is shaped more by social relations, structural conditions (Bourgois, 1995), their pressures and the emotions of the user (Briggs, 2010). Good examples of this are Cuz's crack binges which followed his misinterpretation of a hostel letter and evolving relations with Babe in Chapter 7, and when Cuz and Babe met Clouds in Chapter 8, which led to an all-night crack binge. Equally, the binge can quickly alter the trajectory of the crack career and have detrimental consequences for engagement with welfare and drug support services.

Previous UK research shows little understanding on pathways into crack use (Chapter 2). Indeed, for some, the initial decision to use crack seems to relate to increasing prevalence of a consumer society (van Ree, 2002) set against the normalisation of drug use (Parker *et al.*, 1998; Pearson, 2001). This study highlights two main pathways – recreational and established – which seem to evolve through a mediation of social, cultural and structural forces in reciprocal exchanges. Mediating pathways into crack use are individual decisions against social-structural and contextual influences, which together seem to play a part in the decision to use crack and subsequent decisions to continue to do so (Evans, 2002).

Narratives of early, recreational crack use indicate some temporary stability/ excitement away from mundane life and pressing work, family and personal issues (Blackman, 1995). Yet crack use remains secret; not only because of the potential stigma attached to it (Becker, 1953) but because of the social shame it could cause the user if their actions are discovered (Lemert, 1951). Such attributes may be 'deeply discrediting' because of the 'special discrepancy between virtual and actual social identity' – between the person one seems to be and the person one could be proven to be (Goffman, 1963: 3). What follows, it seems, is a shift in interaction with various structures and social groups, which also act to shape the trajectory of the crack career and the identity of the crack user. So the process of becoming a crack user is one through micro-social interactions made against various structures that generate meaning over time (Giddens, 1984). The study shows, therefore, that crack users are not necessarily passive subjects at the mercy of the drug but more active decision-makers (Miles, 2000) who play a role in their own identity constructions (Bauman, 2007).

However, as areas of their lives start to change, the decisions they make to continue to use crack often only seem to perpetuate their circumstances. When the deviancy of their actions is discovered, this appears to act as catalyst for further identity shifts (Lemert, 1951). This is a key stage in the process of becoming a crack user, because most tend to respond through further denial of their position and, increasingly, make use of a façade that can show the conventional world that everything is under control (Goffman, 1963). This seems to be done to deflect feelings of shame and guilt thereby averting responsibility for their actions (Sykes and Matza, 1957).

Recreational users jeopardise work, family and responsibility (Matza, 1964) and, as this identity appears to be confirmed through contact with crime control agencies via various degradation ceremonies (Garfinkel, 1956; Maruna, 2001), crack users increasingly seem to interact with others in the crack scene, which also serves to confirm their identity (Matza, 1969). Many start to see themselves as powerless victims and blame the 'drug' for life's mishaps. Indeed, continual emphasis is placed on crack as the instigator of their misery which has a dual function because a) it permits the self to continue to use crack and b) it reduces personal responsibility for decisions and actions. Crack is instead associated with another identity and the narratives throughout the book support this. This has been examined in the context of heroin (Maruna, 2001) but this study shows how these processes take place in the context of crack.

Furthermore, the study seems to show the importance of how shame and denial (Goffman, 1963) build throughout the crack career (Falck et al., 2008) and how they are reflexively visited when crack users have 'lost everything' or exhausted all support structures (Cohen and Stahler, 1998). Importantly, this only seems to amplify individual feelings of shame, and has consequences for how they feel about themselves.

The cultural sphere of the crack scene

This work provides an intimate account of the interactions of the UK crack scene. To date, such an understanding of these relations in the context of crack remains limited to the US (Anderson, 1990; Bourgois, 1995; Sterk, 2002; Williams, 1990) and Canada (Malchy et al., 2008). Indeed, despite the numerous studies on crack markets in the UK (Chapter 2), no study seems to highlight how priorities are given to particular groups/individual crack users (Chapter 5). This study indicates how certain benefits seem to be available to high-earning crack users (High Society), which, in turn, affect their access to crack supply. The interactions among this group seem to be generally different from those which take place among the lower end of the crack scene (Low Life). Conversely, these Low Life groups and individuals seem to be more vulnerable to violence, victimisation and manipulation. Therefore the study builds on current knowledge by suggesting that access to crack supply is dependent on hierarchal position – which is, in part, why most consider it important to sustain an image of themselves (Chapter 7).

While these clusters are not necessarily static and crack users can move temporarily in and out of each group, it seems more difficult for crack users occupying the lower end of the crack scene to escape their position. This appears to be linked to the crack career: the difficulty in maintaining a wage for crack seems linked to increasing physical and mental problems, feelings of isolation, lack of trust and paranoia (Chapter 7). Those at the upper end of the crack scene – or who reflect on time in this sphere – tend to reflect on more positive crack-using narratives in safe and secure environments (Sneaks and BD), while those at the lower end appear more paranoid and anxious about their crack use and the environments in which it takes place (Shake). This is because these environments, as crack users construct it, are more insecure (Fitzgerald, 2009). It is here where the culture of the crack scene seems to mediate the experience of crack or the crack 'buzz' (Singer, 2001).

As crack careers deteriorate, so too, it seems, do hierarchical positions. At the same time, however, the importance of maintaining the crack-using experience increases because it means much more for the individual to maintain it (Giddens, 1990, 1991; Lasch, 1985) – that is, crack use has become, for most, a central feature of day-to-day life (Preble and Casey, 1969). For some, this fall from grace can increase feelings of shame and anxiety, which is why attribution is placed on the 'drug' for significant life changes (Booth Davis, 1997). Therefore, in the crack scene, most crack users further deny their position and attempt to make the most of their crack 'buzz' for which they have 'worked' all day. Any disturbance or threat of intrusion heightens feelings of insecurity and hopelessness (Rhodes *et al.*, 2007). Indeed, one coping mechanism some develop which may deflect feelings of shame and difference is to develop normative, emotional barriers when using crack. Contrary to other research (Chapter 2), some become desensitised to using crack in public, which also allows some like Cuz and Gums to avert individual feelings of shame if they are in public view or if someone intrudes on their activities. Others, like Shake, however, don't seem to develop such a framework and are far more vulnerable, as their crack-using experiences – as they construct them – are more directly affected by socio-structural and environmental conditions (Duff, 2007).

The study also indicates that crack user identity construction also takes place in the cultural milieu of the crack scene (DeCorte, 2001; Rhodes *et al.*, 2007) and its environments (Duff, 2009; Zinberg, 1984) through reciprocal, interactional processes (Duff, 2007; Evans, 2002). This occurs in public settings, temporary accommodation and crack houses (Parkin and Coomber, 2009). A good example of this is how Funky D experienced identity shifts, over time, as she started to interact with different crack-using partners and environments (Chapter 7). Indeed, these environments seem to have a strong influence on crack user identities, because they may amplify individual levels of shame, anxiety and insecurity (Rhodes *et al.*, 2007).

Contrary to other UK research on crack houses (Chapter 2), this study considers UK crack houses less as static structures attributed to specific acts (Burgess, 2003; Webster *et al.*, 2001) but rather as fluid structures (Inciardi, 1995) which are shaped by the social dynamics of the crack scene, social control mechanisms and individual subjective experiences of using crack in these environments at different points in the crack career. For some, early in the crack career, the crack house seems to be a comfortable place but, for many, this view changes as most start to use more crack and spend more time in the crack scene. In turn, they seem to start to associate the crack house with stigmatised activities to neutralise their fragile position (Sykes and Matza, 1957).

Indeed, social experiences for Low Life in these environments seem to become embedded in everyday crack user practice (Friedman *et al.*, 1998). This study shows how the crack house environment impacts on attitudes and behaviours. In these environments, individual anxieties and insecurities seem to become exacerbated by the crack-taking experience which, in turn, seems further amplified by the pressured situational, social and structural conditions (Zinberg, 1984). This pressure seems to jeopardise individual ontological security (Giddens, 1991).

For example, the book shows the psychotic state or 'crack psychosis' – experiencing a heightened state of awareness as a consequence of taking crack ('wired' or 'prang') – may not necessarily only be a result of an 'overuse of crack' as current UK literature suggests (Chapter 2). This study shows that, for some, this particular state of being high on crack seems to interplay with the fear and insecurity of interruption of the crack 'buzz', perceived threats from other drug users, the potential for police intervention, and the impending diminishment of crack supply. Some, like Shy H in Chapter 7, are wanted by the authorities, and by operating in unstable circumstances, taking illegal drugs in unpredictable environments, experience an amplification of personal insecurity and feelings of mistrust.

For example, when taking crack in crack houses, some like Halle and Tooth seem to be able to 'lock/zone' out, others are paranoid (Funky D), some are violent (Iverson), while some talk incessantly (Dawg), and some remain silent (at times Cuz, Fam). However, continual exposure to crack houses seems to impact on individual behaviours and attitudes, and many learn quickly that they are unfavourable places, and instead seek increasingly solitary conditions to take crack. This is, in the main, because they fear and mistrust others. This has implications for how they see themselves in society and in the crack scene – often bereft of both worlds which makes them harder to reach, or hidden.

The political economy of crack users

This work builds on existing research that makes use of political economic perspectives in the context of crack (Bourgois, 1995; Bourgois and Schonberg, 2007; Chapter 2; Marez, 2004). This study shows that the pharmacological effect of crack use needs consideration against individual experiences, micro-interactional contexts and crack-using environments, and political economic processes (Bourgois, 1995). Together, these features shape the 'crack-using experience'. It shows that crack scene dynamics appear affected through the political economy of crime control agencies and aggressive social policies designed to eradicate problematic/visible street drug users (Chapter 2) – just as we were asked to 'move on' when outside St Peter's Drop-In (Chapter 6). Indeed, unlike previous UK work with problematic drug users (Chapter 2), this study shows how these macro processes play a part in the transience of crack users (Aitkin et al., 2002) and this radically impacts on crack users' interactions, practices, the environments in which crack is used, and the way in which crack is experienced (Rhodes, 2002). Indeed, this study highlights how social control mechanisms contribute to the aetiology of crack-using spaces, in particular, the crack house (Chapter, 8; Duff, 2009). Consider the experiences of Shake and Dawg.

Indeed, these macro forces seem very much evident in narratives and observations of the crack-using experience (Chapter 6). Such cultural practices appear to be internalised and are reproduced resulting in paranoia, manipulation, risk and sex behaviours, violence and victimisation (Bourdieu, 1984). Sadly, it also seems that some agencies designed to help crack users are, to some extent, also involved in the political economy of their socio-structural position (Bourgois, 2003). This is evident through some drug support services' reluctant collusion with law enforcement agencies and local authorities.

In addition, this study supports other work that suggests that crack users have poor experiences of drug support and treatment services (Chapter 2). However, this study brings to light further processes which impact on crack users. First, service configuration does not appear to honour the complexities of this client group – probably because many are asked to engage when they have hit 'rock bottom' – when their problems are likely at their most complex (Dorn and South, 1985; Henkel, 1999). In addition, some may lie to services about their crack use just to qualify for a treatment which may not necessarily benefit them (methadone) – nevertheless, many rationalise this to be the only route out for them when there is no specific crack treatment (Donmall et al., 1995).

Second, during the fieldwork, there was a reduction in direct access to crack services despite increased investment in the 'crack problem'. Third, to manage the increasing number of clients coming through the treatment system, priority is given to the low-risk drug users, meaning crack users rarely qualified for housing/ funding for drug treatment. In this study, crack users are considered 'high risk' because of their poor retention rate and this results in further discrimination by workers who seem reluctant to fund them for treatment (Parkin, 2008). Instead, crack users like Ish are persuaded to deny their crack use to get forms of support.

When crack users continually experience these barriers, which seem to continually block progress, many develop increasingly fatalistic feelings (Chapter 8). Therefore, with all good intention, the configuration of drug support services also seems to be involved in these processes of social exclusion (Aitkin et al., 2002). The study shows that the support seems to be out of sync with crack users' lifestyles, which is perhaps why many crack users find it difficult to navigate the panoply of requirements to seek change (Chapter 2). Therefore it is, perhaps, unsurprising that under these conditions that most reason that crack is the only viable solution (Young, 1971). With a life increasingly restricted to the crack scene, crack users look for ways to live responsibly in an effort to retain some respect.

Deployment of the self in the crack scene

This book shows that crack users seek to counter their socio-structural position (Goffman, 1959) by attempting to be responsible citizens who live normal lives (Bauman, 2007). Similarly, they also strive for intimacy (Bourgois and Schonberg, 2009). However, the social interactions of the crack scene are volatile and self-perpetuating (Dunlap, 1992), which creates a conflict between their individual quests to counter their position, their individual needs and their pursuit for intimacy and trusting social relations. Indeed, what seems to supersede relations is the maintenance of self image (Goffman, 1963). Some, like Cuz, struggle to manage this relationship (Chapter 7).

Indeed, crack users rely on a social image of themselves in the crack scene to confirm who they are (Cooley, 1964). Deployment of image determines hierarchical arrangement in the crack scene, but for most it becomes difficult to maintain (Chapter 5). A 'good' image seems to carry some form of self-respect and self-worth as well as social status, and is attained, to some extent, through othering. A 'bad' image carries stigma, attention and potential victimisation in the crack scene. Discourses of othering establish these bad images, facilitate denial of an individual's position, but are also used, where possible, to counter the 'crack head' image, to deny particular practices, associations or use of particular places (Sykes and Matza, 1957). Indeed, because crack users enforce a social expectancy to be responsible for themselves (Bauman, 2004; Petersen, 1997; Rimke, 2000), behaviours such as begging, injecting, extreme violence and derogatory sexual acts are generally frowned upon (Glaser, 1978). These are acts of social stigma. Engaging in such behaviours or being known to engage in them may result in being labelled as 'crack head', a 'ponce' or even, by some, 'Low Life'. So people often go out of their way to deny they do/did certain behaviours; that they are not this sort of person. This may explain the ambiguities between who and what is considered to be stigmatised behaviour/practices/associations/places – because essentially everyone is saying 'every type of behaviour/practice/association/place is stigmatised' (Simmonds and Coomber, 2009).

The Low Life are heavily stigmatised. Other crack users, such as BD and Iverson, consider them redundant (even though they themselves may display similar behaviours/practices to the Low Life). My work shows that narrative constructions of 'crack head' seem to be in the context of the other person who is perceived to be 'worse off' than they are. However, as we have seen with Black Eyes in Chapter 7, once the label is applied, it may attract further attention and stigmatisation, the potential for victimisation and may be an individual reflection that the 'self' has become increasingly 'spoilt' (Simmonds and Coomber, 2009). When the realities of the 'spoilt identity' start to become more evident through crack scene labelling, individual mental and physical fragility, increasingly socio-structural forces seem to take a more direct role in symbolic practices of crack users (Bourdieu, 1984). These people appear more paranoid and anxious, seek isolated conditions to use crack, and, consequently, most seem to become increasingly fatalistic. They manifest these feelings through further damaging drug use practices/risk behaviours (Farmer *et al.*, 1997; Wilkinson, 2006) – some perhaps still in denial of their position. They become hard to reach, hidden populations.

Similarly, participation in 'crack houses' is also associated with low-status social acts and even those in the crack scene frown on them (Chapter 7). These places are generally considered the 'lowest of the low'. The crack house, in particular, is associated with stigma because it might mirror their social standing in the crack scene, and bring about more attention and labelling. Perhaps some, like Dawg and Fam, reason that it is best to deny association with the crack house because of social stigma attached to it. The social acts in these places, while part of the cultural norms of the crack scene, also seem to contravene deep-rooted individual conceptions of behaviour which is why many deny association with them and/or involvement in those acts in these places – even though they may have taken part in them. Consider Madmax's reflections in Chapter 7. In essence, this seems to form part of the wall of denial that crack users construct to neutralise and rationalise their behaviours (Booth Davies, 1997; Sykes and Matza, 1957).

Ways in, ways down, but ways out?

The book shows that crack users do try to seek changes (Booth Davies, 1997; Haines et al., 2009) yet socio-cultural pressures and socio-structural barriers influence intentions to seek a way out (Shake). For people like Silver and Lady Di, these forces present day-to-day barriers to attend appointments but also exacerbate difficulties in sustaining that engagement (Malchy et al., 2008). Crack users have fleeting contact with drug support services because, for many, crack does not appear problematic. For most, it is not used in any recognisable pattern, has no visible 'side effects', as they see it, and on assessment, some struggle to quantify how much they use or the role it plays in their drug-using repertoire (Chapter 2). Furthermore, they may feel they need to lie about crack use to get various forms of welfare support (Chapter 6).

Crack users are expected to be responsible for themselves and find ways of resolving their crack use and life predicaments (Bauman, 2007); they are asked to show commitment and perhaps rightly so. Local service provision is limited, and, in the face of diminishing funding across Rivertown (Chapter 3), filtering out the committed may be the only way to ensure progress for some. However, if crack users cannot show a high level of commitment towards life changes (Chapter 7), they are not considered 'ready for change' – a psychological treatment philosophy of Prochaska and DiClemente (1986) which seems to sideline entrenched social and emotional problems (Young, 2002). However, this medical model appears to generically respond to any drug user in the same way and, as this study shows, for many crack users this has less relevance, thereby unwittingly contributing to the political economy of their social suffering (Chapter 2).

This work also shows that crack users seem to be rarely considered/prioritised for rehab because they are considered to be 'high risk'. This appears to perpetuate their situation, perhaps leading most, like Silver, to the conclusion that there is little chance for a 'way out' (Singer, 2001), thereby extending their crack career (Falck et al., 2008). This may be exacerbated by reducing the volition of service attendance (Stimson, 2000), which, in turn, may diminish free will decisions to make changes. With fragile commitment levels and increasing practical and health problems, most feel more powerless and fatalistic about the chances of change and this exacerbates personal feelings of shame and distance (Bourgois, 1995, 2003).

As the literature suggests (Chapter 2), few are able to show meaningful commitment for sustained periods. Some quickly learn of the limitations of service configuration (Chapter 6) and have continual engagement problems, which dents personal agency, and most reason continued crack use as a viable solution. They remain, in most instances, at the mercy of crack scene pressures (Chapter 7). This is important because crack users do show genuine individual intentions to resolve crack use – and other problems – (Bauman, 2007) but their motivations, it seems, gradually erode when continual barriers are experienced (Giddens, 1984). They reconcile that 'they tried' but the mechanisms for support were not forthcoming. When the already fragile individual realises that he/she is totally reliant on him- or herself to change, this seems to increase the tendency for fatalistic thinking, low self-esteem and low self-respect (Bourdieu, 1984). Consequently, some may make further reflections on their position in the crack scene and internalise feelings of shame and guilt. Some, like Tattoo, may engage in increasingly risky and dangerous drug use practices. In addition, failed attempts to 'get clean' are reflexively visited (Giddens, 1991), which may also contribute to this isolation and social distance (Farmer et al., 1997).

If, however, they manage to muster up the required commitment, they are encouraged to acknowledge that 'crack' was not responsible for their criminal and stigmatised decisions and actions (Maruna, 2001). Such facts seem contradictory because, for so long, they have attributed their problems 'down to the crack' but suddenly the self is asked to shoulder life's losses, the shame of the past, and the shame associated with the individual's stigmatised and criminal acts (Chapter 8). In drug support services and rehab, crack users are persuaded to concede to the 'spoilt identity' (Neale et al., 2006; Simmonds and Coomber, 2009). Many, however, consider crack use to be the cause of the increased misery in their lives and crack, they reconcile, perpetuated their involvement in criminal and deviant acts. Because these acts hold significant amounts of stigma across society and in the crack scene, and break personal, emotional, individual, social and cultural codes (Chapter 2), it becomes more difficult for people like Firey A, Madmax and Def Jam to come to terms with them.

This work shows that there are also further tests of character ahead. Some battle through the power dynamics of rehab and are then often thrust back into drug-using hostels while they wait for accommodation which may be in areas where crack and other drugs are present (Chapter 7). When some discover how difficult it is to re-enter mainstream society on the terms of the State, they fail (Chapter 8). Repeated attempts continue to diminish agency and, once again, most feel increasingly helpless about their chances (Chapter 2). Because they are expected to be responsible for their own 'steps toward change' (Beck and Beck-Gernsheim, 2002), they feel increasingly inadequate when they fail and these feelings do not seem to disappear easily (Bauman, 2007). A few, like BD and Alwight do complete treatment yet still face crack scene pressures. Indeed, there is always the chance they may also be approached by dealers with offers of crack and other drugs – Lady Di and even myself at times! – or by other crack users (Shake in Chapter 5) because they used to use crack or look like a 'crack head'.

Conclusion

This study offers some reasons why crack careers are difficult to break. Continual barriers to making changes seem to dent personal agency, and feelings of distance and fatalism start to develop. Indeed, some are persuaded to engage when they are 'ready', often when they hit 'rock bottom', before any intervention begins. However, 'rock bottom' is a subjective concept and many remain in denial that they have not reached this stage, telling themself that there is always someone worse off than them. So by the time many crack users approach services with some commitment, practical problems, as well as physical and mental health problems, have deteriorated significantly. As individual failings and structural issues become absorbed as personal character deficits, self-destructive behaviours become more entrenched. For most, crack use, shame and fatalism have become mutually reinforcing. Moreover, as individuals, for many years, they are used to interacting in discourses of denial, attribute the most significant problems to 'crack' and many have become too ashamed of their past, their actions and, therefore, find it extremely difficult to 'take responsibility' for their actions and face up to the 'spoilt identity'. It is these experiences that likely explain why crack users are considered to be the hardest to reach and most difficult drug-using group to retain and treat in drug support services. If there is to be any serious progress toward helping such populations, then a number of recommendations need to be considered for service configuration and structural change.

Recommendations for policy

Drug support service configuration

The current response to problematic drug use, it is suggested, either tends to offer a generic range of services to a limited number of clients or targeted services to a specific client group (Fox et al., 2005; Lupton et al., 2002). Part of the problem is that there has been a shift from the practical matters of recovery such as housing, social care and benefit support to an 'overemphasis on the treatment of addiction' (Audit Commission, 2004; Fox et al., 2005). This has meant a significant reduction in the time the State will fund drug users in treatment (Briggs, 2007). Therefore, crack users will first need to be consulted on how best to configure crack services (see Boyd et al., 2008).

Although many services do not have sufficient funding or staff to cope with the demand and offer immediate treatment or care to every client, some thought could be invested into creative ways to manage applications and minimise the despondency which results from being put on a 'waiting list'. Crack users should be able to engage with the service of their choice regardless of where they are staying. It is clear, however, that for this inclusive approach to be realised, funding streams may need to be re-structured. One option would be for services to offer emergency treatment to all those who present themselves, then to pass crack users over to other services in a manner designed to minimise the risk of disengagement – for example, outreach worker taking crack user to new service; joint assessment and risk-assessment protocols; joint prescribing protocols; speedy and effective communication systems between substance misuse services; information-sharing protocols.

Crack users express a sense of fatalism and hopelessness about entrenched crack use. Without mentoring and practical assistance, getting to housing departments, organising the paperwork and ID necessary to find a job and apply for benefits or services, managing their money and their tenancies, are all seen as daunting tasks. Therefore advocacy and mentoring could be provided through outreach teams to ensure that crack users are monitored and supported in temporary accommodation/flats/houses – similar to that used in the US and Canada (see Fischer *et al.*, 2006; Haydon *et al.*, 2005). Advocacy and practical support could be provided for crack users – for example, with making appointments, paying bills. Heavy crack users generally need to be monitored and supported more often in their tenancies than other individuals. Outreach workers and Rivertown Housing floating-support workers could 'double up' on monitoring their clients.

It is clear that future crack service provision will need to approach crack users, rather than expect crack users to approach them (for good practice see Malchy *et al.*, 2008). Within this, staff attitudes need to be more consistent towards crack users (Chapter 2). Such support should offer inducements to engage so crack users return to the service. Moreover, service workers must expect the dip in/drop out pattern of engagement, and structure services around it with contingency plans – for example, providing high-intensity services when crack users are in contact, and lower-intensity contact and empathetic follow-up (including harm-minimisation advice, brief interventions and practical assist-ance) when they drop out of contact. Involving stabilised crack users in devising strategies and systems for local services would help them develop needs-led and client-centred responses.

Drug support services should be open in the evening and weekends, to cater for crack users seeking help outside office hours (see Stöver, 2002). While some services in Rivertown offer condoms and injecting equipment, this is limited and there could be more efforts to offer more innovative and creative harm-reduction tools. 'Crack packs' with lip balm, a comb, toothbrush and toothpaste, vitamins, condoms, etc., would be ideal – and some form of safe crack pipe if one could also be devised – and could be used as engagement incentives. Successful engagement programmes in the US and Canada have offered something of value to crack users (Booth *et al.*, 2003; Higgins *et al.*, 1993; Malchy *et al.*, 2008; Wechsberg *et al.*, 1993). Services could usefully provide harm-minimisation and awareness advice about the 'pranged' or 'wired' state. This could include: how long the experience may likely last; cognitive techniques for managing it; and consult crack users to develop strategies to avoid this state.

Structural change

Historically, multi-disciplinary treatment for drug users in the UK has been provided sequentially. In order to solve their problems related to mental health, physical health, finances, employment, education, childcare and housing and drug reliance, crack users must themselves negotiate the bureaucracy and criteria of each service provider independently (Chapter 2; Chapter 8). The result is often frustrating as the qualifications for inclusion in one service depend on satisfying the criteria for another (see Fox *et al.*, 2005). Many drug users, but crack users in particular, are often not able to organise their lives to keep appointments, make phone calls and complete the paperwork necessary to navigate these tasks in the right order to qualify for housing, medical care, counselling, etc (see Chapter 8; Dorn and South, 1985; Henkel, 1999). Crack users need competent case managers who can advocate directly for users and help them to get the most out of the various services, and/or instant access 'one-stop-shop' centres that would house representatives from all services and government departments.

Similarly, the onus on drug support service engagement needs to be balanced equally between the criminal justice system and community drug settings (Stimson, 2000). Because many cannot access drug support services when they may be 'in crisis', their genuine motivation for change is not reflected when they are put on lengthy waiting lists or offered treatment in custody. This, as I have shown, angers them and contributes to distance (Chapter 6). Furthermore, crack users need to be distinguished from cocaine users in policy documents because they are from different social groups (see EMCDDA, 2007; Williamson *et al.*, 1996). By awkwardly bundling the two together in government and treatment policy documents, and also in service delivery (Chapter 6), provision design is skewed. An appreciation of the different groups, their attitudes and practices should bring about appropriate drug treatment design.

The 'free will' medical model of Prochaska and DiClemente (1986) endorsed by the NTA may need some reconsideration in the context of crack users. The model treats crack users as culpable adults responsible for their own actions. Some commentators suggest that such a model shifts responsibility for treatment failures on to the drug user (see Holt, 1967; Sterne and Pittman, 1965). Such a medical treatment philosophy focus on addiction is only partially successful because of a limited view of the reasons why people use drugs (Young, 2002). This study shows that this treatment ideology does not seem to work well with crack users. This is not to say they should not be responsible, because this study shows they do attempt to make decisions towards change. The problems arise when continual attempts fail; and this erodes hopes for change (Chapter 8). Many become engaged in more risky drug and sex behaviours and feel fatalistic about change. Their circumstances, in most cases, become increasingly complex and entrenched which means more commitment is needed for them to engage. When they cannot summon the 'free will' to get to appointments, or maintain housing, they feel greater personal shame and hopelessness. Drug service philosophies need to consider this pattern to establish better ways of ensuring people do not sink into this state.

Drug service philosophy therefore needs to offer greater appreciation of structural inequities of problems with engagement such as poverty, homelessness, unemployment and lack of social support (see Pauly, 2008), the social pressures of the crack scene which also inhibit engagement and the individual barriers which develop the crack career. In order to sustain change, crack users need alternatives to crack use, which will require governmental institutions to better provide opportunities for recovering crack users and help instil the motivation to pursue them. Some consideration also needs to be given to the spatial design of prevention and support programmes if they remain situated and controlled among surplus populations in relatively controlled settings with lack of opportunities and little upward mobility – such as temporary housing (Waterson, 1997).

Chapter 10

Epilogue
The field lives on

Introduction

This final chapter charts some of the moments in which I have met some of the participants since the fieldwork finished in the summer of 2005. Sadly, I am not in touch with anyone but these short exchanges say something about the scene in which some continue to participate and my position outside these dynamics. The difficulty I have is that I know what goes on in this world, and delicate feelings and emotions now surface very quickly in such moments. You will also see that, over the years, I have also come to encounter similar populations around the world. The way I see these groups seems to relate to my experiences with the people I met in Rivertown during 2004/5 because they gave me an awareness which I now can't seem to disengage. Though not intimate, my moments with these groups are also included in this chapter because I feel this says something about the world we live in and the world they live in. So in writing this book, I hope you now have a greater insight into the world they live in so you can reflect on the world we live in.

April 2006: ongoing transience

I am in Oxford Street, central London. I move around the hustle and bustle of busy shoppers. For some reason shoppers, unlike commuters, don't have that automatic ability to avoid each other – maybe because it is Saturday and they have relaxed that automatic-pilot mode which would normally help them weave in and out of oncoming people traffic. Consequently, I find myself making stealthy manoeuvres just to avoid fatal head-on collisions with busy shoppers. I am looking for the least-populated shop to buy some clothes. I spot one across the road and start to cross; perhaps more cautious of the cyclists than the buses or taxis. As I cross I look to my right, and between the flood of people, I see a figure limping in the centre of the road about 100 metres away. He doesn't seem to be crossing but walking along the central reservation. I halt mid-walk and stare for a moment. As I start to walk towards him, I recognise the limp, the hair, the heavily inscribed body – it is Tattoo. What is he doing here? As I start to pick up my pace towards him, I remember that I left my girlfriend on the other side of the road and deviate back to my shopping responsibilities.

October 2006: everyday questions at drifting relations

Some months later, I am back in the Rivertown. I stop by the café where I used to interview crack users. I think about going in and decide a poorly made cup of tea would be the perfect way to reminisce. I sit in the same place I sat last year, at the back of the café where no one could hear our conversations of crack, crime and violence. The same Polish waitress serves me and I sit looking out of the window. Suddenly, there is a commotion outside. It is a tall man in a raincoat waving off a shorter man who is shabbily dressed. I think perhaps the shabby-looking man is giving the respectable-looking man some hassle. A potential robbery? My mind continues to explore the possibilities until the man with the raincoat turns around. It is Dawg. I leap out of my chair and go outside to talk to him. As I come out, the shabbily dressed man starts to meander off into the distance and Dawg stands there wiping something off his raincoat. As before, he is smartly dressed in a pin-stripe suit – his non-drug user image. However, other aspects of his demeanour seem to confirm he is high as a kite. His eyes are wide, and his hands fidget as he mops his brow frantically. 'Dan, alright mate,' he says nervously and smiles. As his mouth widens, the large scar across his cheek melts into the contours of his face. As we talk about the weather, his flat and the others, he impatiently steps from side to side. When I ask about Blood, his speech stutters, he tries to change the subject and makes an excuse to leave.

March 2007: a distant memory among the humdrum

I am drinking with some friends in the north of Rivertown, relaxing after a week at work. There is a typical Friday-night buzz; many in the pub look relieved to be living their leisure time now. I have been here since 3pm, and seen workers by their hundreds leave the supermarket opposite with wine bottles in one hand and mobile in the other. They stride as fast as they can with their iPods hammering out music at deafening levels. The music seems to motivate most to hurry urgently for the train home so they can sit on the sofa to relax; no doubt to watch some reality bollocks about how miserable other people's lives are so they can feel better about themselves. The pub is already busy and, unlike the others around me, I am drinking a diet coke. We all sit outside so that the only one of the six in our party who smokes can do so. By 6pm, I have had a pint or two and turn around to make for the toilets. I then see two familiar faces – it is Fam and Twitch. Fam is very inconspicuously sifting through a wallet – which I suppose he has just stolen – because when I approach him, he hides it like schoolchild would hide a stolen sweet. His face is sweaty and his nose is dripping. Twitch looks slightly fearful and hides behind the short figure of Fam. Our conversation goes a little like this:

DAN: *Fam, Fam, Twitch, how are you?*

FAM: [Looking confused and vacantly into my face] *Who are you, mate?*

DAN: *Are you serious, you don't recognise me?*

FAM: [Looking at Twitch] *Er …*

DAN: *I used to come down to your place, you know, down south. What are you doing up here?*

FAM: *Are you the bloke…*

TWITCH: *Yeah, he used to come up to us … you was doing that thing?*

FAM: [Unconvincingly agreeing] *Yeah, yeah* [as if he recognises me].

TWITCH: *You was asking us them questions, you …*

DAN: *Yeah, the research, you do remember.*

FAM: *YES, mate, I remember …* [doubting himself now] *a little bit.*

DAN: *Well, anyway it's great to see you.*

TWITCH: *Yeah, funny how time flies.*

I wasn't too disappointed; particularly because I knew Fam struggled to remember things on a day-to-day basis. We arrive at the topic of his son and his eyes start to well with tears. In the years since the fieldwork had concluded, he says his son had been excluded from school and was involved with a local gang.

August 2007: reinforcing shame and stigma?

When I encountered Blood two years after the fieldwork had concluded in 2007, I felt completely broken. I don't write this to compare my situation to his circumstances but the short exchange cut me in half emotionally. Maybe because he was the youngest person using crack and I had hoped that, of everyone I met, he would the one who would most likely escape his situation. While I wait for a bus, I see Blood approach people in the queue for money. It feels like those moments when you are about to encounter someone who you haven't seen for a while and can't summon the correct means to greet them. I don't normally have this problem but this is certainly how I was feeling. As he moves down the line, people seem to realise he is begging and their responses quickly become robotic and automatic. In fact, no one gives him any money. He tries to avoid me at first and continues in another queue that has evolved elsewhere. With little thought to how this may make him feel, I go over to him.

Believe it or not, he still has the same jumper from two years previously. His clothes have accumulated numerous bloodstains and he smells pretty bad. He didn't ask me for money. Probably feeling ashamed of his position, he just looks down and never once looks me in the eye. Perhaps I look stupid, after all everyone else who has dismissed him is now staring at me trying to make conversation with him. I reach in my pocket and insist he take my money for food or something. He moves his head up but looks past me, and, after several distant looks into the horizon and relentless hand-waving gestures, he reluctantly accepts my offer. I concede this may have been careless but I am human; I guess it shows just how much these people meant to me. I can't remember what I said as I left, I started to feel pretty bad. When I got on the bus, I just broke down in tears; probably because I knew Blood was still in that brutal world in which I spent some time.

March 2009: working out of difference and working for acceptance?

I walk out of Embankment underground station in the unseasonal wintry weather. As I walk out, I meet Silver selling the *Big Issue*.[1] The last time I saw him, in 2005, he was smoking crack and heroin in a crack house. He stands like Michelangelo's David – except with one arm loaded with *Big Issue* magazines and the other holding a scruffy roll-up cigarette. He impatiently taps his right foot and his wide-hemmed jeans, waistcoat and wincing smile make him look like a villain from a spaghetti western. His hair is longer, and slightly more silver. The fact he is selling the magazine may represent some steps towards recovery; it may mean he has some accommodation otherwise he would not be able to be a licensed distributor of the *Big Issue*. I start to hope he has come out of that lifestyle as hundreds of questions fill my head. I smile and approach to say hello but, before we can get into a conversation, he is interrupted by some representative from the *Big Issue*, who has been lingering at the side of the road. Silver apologies and excuses himself to speak to his new boss. I walk away while Silver continues to receive some training on how best to sell the magazine. When I return a few hours later in the hope of speaking to him, he has left.

July 2009: surviving in another world

I had forgotten just how large Paris Gare du Nord was, yet still it managed to instil wonder in me. This is where I met Alex, a policeman. Now Alex stands with a very military haircut next to the ticket office in his perfectly-ironed police uniform. He aggressively chews gum and talks to someone on his earpiece. Alex also has a large, muzzled Alsatian which he struggles to control. By the time I get to the front of the queue to buy 'dix billets', Alex and his dog have moved on. I walk to my platform where I see a man slumped in a heap on a seat. He seems to be asleep and has a brown bag near his foot. He is not dressed well and his ragged clothes hang awkwardly off his decrepit body. Suddenly our friend Alex appears nearby and his dog starts to violently bark at the slumped man. Alex starts to speak French but when he realises the man is not responding, he starts to shout at the slumped man 'No sleeping here'. His dog, which has been well-behaved towards the 'normal citizens', continues to leap and bark at the man. Eventually, the man comes out of his slump and, while protesting his innocence, slowly gets up from his place, his steps frail and intermittent. Alex walks off shaking his head with his dog barking back at the old man.

During the day, I see them on the streets begging for money. One man doing this seems respectful so that I acknowledge him when I say I have 'no change'. Another, while forcibly pressing a radio next to his ear, just stares at me through his rough grey, soiled beard and bushy eyebrows. As I walk out of the metro, however, there is another. He has one leg and is in a wheelchair. He is sand-wiched between a trendy café and a fish market on St Germain. I watch for about 10 minutes and few people look at him as he calls out for some money. In an effort to make an impression, he wheels himself toward a woman finely dressed in purple – well purple was the main colour theme. With one hand cupped, the other tries to shift the wheelchair a few yards forward. He barely moves a foot forward but it seems to disturb the woman's intended path; not that he was near her or anything. She quickly sidesteps to her left out towards the edge of the pavement. Her concentrated face just about remains intact despite a slight grimace. Luckily, the unsightly event is over for her as quickly as it had evolved. The man, clearly used to this reaction, already starts to locate a potential other.

By now, I am used to seeing these people in most metro stations. Day or night, they mostly seem to wedge themselves between the seats and the wall. No one is near them. Of all the seats free on the platform, it is those near these men. Indeed, they are all men and they are all old. They all wear improvised clothing, which overlaps their bodies in any way possible. Some don't seem to move for hours. Those accustomed to their presence have learnt not to look and stare but there may still be moments when they can glance; when they can be reminded of their own fortune but remain confused and perhaps sympathetic at other people's desti-tution. Walking down on to the platform of St Michel Notre Dame, there is one exchange between a young Parisian girl and a man sandwiched between the wall and the seats on the other side of the platform. Those who are near the man refrain from looking. As the train comes on into the station, the young girl looks on at him from the opposing platform. Her gum chewing slows momentarily as she stares at the man. Her eyebrows start to assume a frown but the sound of the train closing in appears to remind her of which world she is in. She resumes the rhythmic action of her gum chewing and starts to bob her head to the music.

November 2010: collective othering

The New York metro has lengthy, low-ceiling platforms. As I descend into the humid heat of the subway, I cannot fathom the temperatures it reaches in summer – and this is winter. The noise and vibrations of the oncoming train create a welcome backdraft as the train loudly shuttles into the station. As I get on the subway, I look for the map to direct me where to get off. The train is about half full and I am trying to understand why so many wear sunglasses on the subway in winter. In the absence of seats, I stand – happy to look around. The train is barely half full and most are comfortably seated. A few minutes into the journey, a man enters through the end doors of the carriage. He is dressed in black trousers with a few stains, a loose shirt and a jacket. At first, he has trouble with the door, which causes some attention towards him. The passengers quickly look away as if to assist in potential embarrassment. As he enters, he trudges up and down the carriage. He starts to speak: 'This ain't no joke man, could happen to anyone, anybody man.' He has to shout because of the noise of the train. As he plods through the main part of the carriage, people's eyes start to descend to the floor. Some continue to stare in front of them, as if to pretend that this slow figure is not there and is not speaking loudly. Those with sunglasses on seem well-placed to avoid eye contact. The man continues to trudge up and down the carriage: 'I had a job once, like you, like all of you. Could happen to anybody, man,' he shouts. He shakes his head; perhaps at his situation or the lack of interest in his situation. The crowd look blankly into nothing. Conversations cease. For fear of interaction? For fear of confrontation? For fear of involving themselves in an interaction which may bring them unnecessary attention and stigma for their intervention? I think to myself that I would like to say something because I like to engage but it is not the norm. 'Just a dollar, just to get something to eat, come on, fuck's sake man,' he says, but no one responds. He walks past people and their attention is either fixed to the floor or the fact he has passed does not seem to stir their attention. He seems to be looking for eye contact but the train folk, probably to avoid emotional response, continue to ignore him.

My reaction echoes those around me and I feel I am clearly also involved in this united disregard. Because by signalling our collective neglect of his words, his presence and his being, we symbolically declare our position on his difference from us while simultaneously maintaining our shared response. Our lack of collective interaction – instead our collective response to ignore him – does not help. He disappears into the next carriage but comes back soon after – perhaps after little luck there as well. He looks up and down the carriage and revisits us: 'This ain't no fucking joke man, could be any one of you.' But his words seem to bounce off the other passengers. They seem used to people like him.

November 2010: the outsider, peeping in, and then looking out

When the plane lands late in San Francisco after a five-hour flight from New York, my wife and I are eager for some food. We jump in the taxi and head for the city centre. The driver seems chatty and seems to think we are worried as we pass the Tenderloin area of the city – which is reputed to be the red light and principal drug-using area. We are not concerned per se but completely surprised at the overt nature of begging and drug-using activity. He tells us 'Don't worry man, it is a safe city now.' I personally have every confidence it is. After we have checked in, we decide to take a walk around to get some dinner. The receptionist tells us to head for the centre of town and not to stray but gives no reasons for this. Within a few minutes of leaving the hotel, we are approached by quite damaged men; some in wheelchairs, some with no teeth, some with little clothing and others with a combination. Unlike their British counterparts, their attempts to earn money are mobile and proactive – even if they are quite immobile.

On one such occasion on our way back from dinner, a man by the sidewalk limps up to us: 'You got a dolla, frien?' I look at him and say 'I'm afraid not'.

The irony, of course, is that I do have a little change but it is completely meagre – perhaps a quarter. I ask myself: Would it help? Is it enough? Would it be insulting? Perhaps noting that it was unusual for me to respond and noting my different accent, he then limps after me – dragging his right foot along the floor at my swift-walking pace. I know that if I slow, I will almost certainly have to enter into a lengthy exchange so I continue at my pace. When he speaks, I can't quite understand him as he seems to have severely damaged his tongue and he has about three teeth. The conversation goes a little like this:

JAMAICAN MAN: *Whe you fro, frien?*
DAN: *London.*
JAMAICAN MAN: *I' rom amaica, man. Come on, help me out.*
    [CONTINUING TO WALK, I LOOK INTO HIS EYES. I GET LOST IN WHAT I WANT TO SAY
    BECAUSE THE INTERNAL DILEMMA HAS STARTED EATING AWAY AT ME]
DAN: *Ok, we are at our hotel. Do take care.*

No doubt I sound patronising and it burns me inside when he says as I walk in 'not even a dolla, frien?' I realise that perhaps it makes sense for the majority to avoid eye contact and interaction because it makes for confrontation and awkward exchanges. It is in their interest to ignore these people, not because they don't care – although some may not – but to ensure they do not enter into interaction because this could expose their conscience to social suffering through social inter-action processes which, in a way, may affect them quite significantly. There may certainly be problems if they do.

Generally people do not seem to be troubled by all this activity. Even overt placards of 'I have HIV AIDS' and stories of suffering seem to have little impact on the public and almost all walk straight past without a glance. One lady sits there with one such banner, has no legs, and crouches in her wheelchair. A few nights later, we walk out to dinner. I am quite used to this now and am quite happy to at least acknowledge these people. However, as we cross the road, we see a rich-looking lady pass some coins to an old man who has clearly won her over with his little paper cup. Not content with her generous offering, as she sees it, he persists – because she seems to smile as if to suggest 'I did my bit'. He then follows, holding the cup out to her for more. The lady seems to feel guilty and fishes around again, however, the situation is further complicated when another man sees that this lady seems to be handing out these financial gifts. He approaches her with his paper cup. Suddenly, the husband becomes frustrated. What was a passing gesture of goodwill has now created more atten-tion and the husband tries to hurry his wife along. Attention not only from the homeless men but also those walking past – it seems now a potential moment of embarrassment as the woman tries to politely fend off two homeless men. She seems frustrated because her husband is upset and now, having entered into some interactional exchanges, she now finds it difficult to manage the situation. Will this deter her from further acts of goodwill?

I ponder all this over a few glasses of wine that evening. However, it is not long before I am reminded of events.

That night, around 10pm, I am channel flicking and, among the endless number of religious and shopping channels, I come across the 'comedy duo' on Paramount. I lie down on the bed hoping for some entertainment and within a few minutes, I am disappointed as the double act start to mock the local homeless:

COMEDIAN 1:   *My mom thinks the new LA fashion is like trampy homeless.*
COMEDIAN 2:   [Sarcastically] *Oh that's right, let's pick on the homeless.*
COMEDIAN 1:   *It's ok, they aren't watching, they're homeless.*
COMEDIAN 2:   *Even if they are they can't hear because they are watching through the shop window* [Audience roar with laughter].
COMEDIAN 1:   *Is it cold outside, homeless? I have lots of money and I'm inside on TV, homeless* [Audience in hysterics].

In disgust, I turn the TV off.

January 2011: discourses of denial?

I am walking briskly from Charing Cross underground station after a guest lecture at Coventry University. To get to the mainline station, one has to go through an underground passage. It is a renowned place for homeless people to sleep and beg. I am in some hurry, conscious of the potential to catch a train at 19.32. It is 19.28. As I walk to the escalator, I glance down to my left at a man begging – I normally do this in any case. As I look closer, I recognise the face and it is Ish – he is hiding beneath a stained sleeping bag and a long beard. He has been homeless for nine months. I stoop down to talk to him – I must look like some charity case but if only people knew that I knew this man. He immediately remembers me: 'You're the guy who used to come to the hostel that time', he says. He smiles to reveal more gaps in his teeth; his eyes still look in opposing directions. This is quickly followed up by: 'I'm not using no more crack, not for nine months.' I don't know what to say because the last person likely to make judgements on his crack use is me. I end up saying 'Well the main thing is you are alive.'

He keeps looking down at the floor and struggles to look at me. I ask if he was in contact with anyone from the hostel and he says 'long time, long time, many years – not seen none.' I ask where he sleeps and he says: 'I would sleep with my girl in Camden but I have an ASBO there so just hang around here now.' The context is awkward and my open-ended questions are increasingly met with closed answers. Our exchange is coming to a natural end and we run out of conversation. I feel uncomfortable talking to him in my suit, which may reinforce my normality and his difference. I leave a few pounds and say I hope to see him again. I miss my train but who cares? Instead, I stand on the platform and my thoughts start to meander. We've all seen people like Ish – they aren't likely to concede they take drugs when they are begging for money, are they? Look at the way everyone's eyes divert to the floor when people like Ish sit by the sidewalk or get on trains to ask for money? People don't want to hear they are using drugs and even if we ask people like Ish, they will deny it. I miss another train but who cares?

April 2011: where are you?

In the years since the fieldwork, I have not managed to be reunited with Cuz – the person with whom I had my closest contact. I asked my publisher, Julia Willan at Routledge, for an extra month to see if I can locate him. While part of me is curious to document 'the story since', really I just want to know he is alive and well. When I start to phone around all the drug agencies in Rivertown, I don't quite know how to frame my request for information on his whereabouts or even to be put in contact with him. Almost all the staff I ask for don't work in the services any more. When I try to explain the motive for the phone call to the new staff, it is met with automatic responses such as 'that's confidential information' and 'we cannot allow you access to the names on our files'. This, I concede, is fair enough but the mundane and drawn tones of staff members really bother me. My phone calls are redundant and I take to the streets, asking around at old places where we used to hang out. Perhaps it is futile because either no one seems to know him or no one knows where he is. With little other than my memories, I am left to reflect over observation notes and transcripts of our relationship:

> You've opened your eyes! That's why I respect you because you're willing to come out here, that's what I keep saying to everybody, you're willing to come out here and see – not take it [crack] – because a lot of people see this life, what we're doing, and they have to take it, but you ain't. You've gone another way and you're willing to sit down with us and see what it is happening, how it is, and I respect that. I really do, because a lot of people to find out about this shit have to start smoking it and I respect you because you can sit there and watch other people smoke.
>
> (Cuz)

Notes

Chapter 1

1   A term meaning to trick other drug users out of money/drugs.

Chapter 2

1   Crack users in this study refer to this as 'prang'.
2   Selective recommendation sampling is a form of purposive sampling which uses the participant as the 'vehicle and engine' for sampling via recommendation or advice.

Chapter 4

1   A spoon is used to 'cook' or 'mix' drugs in preparation for injection.

Chapter 10

1   The Big Issue is a charity that helps the homeless by employing homeless people to sell a magazine. The homeless people get some share of what they sell.

References

Abercrombie, N., Hill, S. and Turner, B. (1994) *The Penguin Dictionary of Sociology*, London: Penguin.

Adler, P. (1985) *An Ethnography of Drug Dealing and Smuggling Communities*, New York: Columbia University Press.

Agar, M. (1986) *Speaking of Ethnography*, Beverly Hills, CA: Sage.

Agar, M. (2003) 'The story of crack: Towards a theory of illicit drug trends', *Addiction, Research and Theory*, 11(1): 3–29.

Ahern, J., Stuber, J. and Galea, S. (2007) 'Stigma, discrimination and the health of illicit drug users', *Drug and Alcohol Dependence*, 88: 188–96.

Aitkin, C., Moore, D., Higgs, P., Kelsall, J. and Kerger, M. (2002) 'The impact of a police crackdown on a street drug scene: Evidence from the street', *The International Journal of Drug Policy*, 13: 193–202.

Al-Rahman, A., Craig, D. and Lamour, P. (2007) *Crack User and Carer Consultation*, London: NTA.

Anderson, E. (1990) *Streetwise: Race, Class and Change in an Urban Community*, Chicago: University of Chicago Press.

Arnull, E., Eagle, S., Patel, S. and Gammampila, A. (2007) *An Evaluation of the Crack Treatment Delivery Model*, London: NTA.

Atkinson, P. and Hammersley, M. (1994) 'Ethnography and Participant Observation', in N. Denzin and Y. Lincoln (Eds), *Handbook of Qualitative Research,* Thousand Oaks: Sage, pp. 249–61.

Audit Commission (2004) *Drug Misuse 2004 – Reducing the Local Impact*, London: Audit Commission.

Bailie, R. (2003) *Tackling Crack in Rivertown*, Rivertown Drug and Alcohol Action Team and Rivertown PCT Report.

Bauman, Z. (2004) *Wasted Lives: Modernity and its Outcasts,* Cambridge: Polity Press.

Bauman, Z. (2007) *Liquid Times: Living in an Age of Uncertainty*, Cambridge: Polity Press.

Beck, U. (1992) *Risk Society: Towards a New Modernity*, London: Sage.

Beck, U. and Beck-Gernsheim, E. (2002) *Individualisation*, London: Sage.

Becker, H. (1953) 'Becoming a Marihuana User', *American Journal of Sociology*, 59 (November): 235–43.

Becker, H. (1963) *Outsiders: Studies in the Sociology of Deviance,* London: Free Press.

Becker, J. and Duffy, C. (2002) *Women Drug Users and Drug Service Provision: Service Level Responses to Engagement and Retention*, London: Home Office.

Belenko, S. (1993) *Crack and the Evolution of Anti–Drug Policy*, Westport, CA: Greenwood Press.

Bennett, T. (2000) *Drugs and Crime: The Results of Second Developmental Stage of the NEW-ADAM Programme, Home Office Research Study No. 205*, London: Home Office.

Bird, S., Hutchinson, S. and Goldberg D. (2003) 'Drug-related deaths by region, sex and age-group per 100 injecting drug users in Scotland, 2000–01', *Lancet*, 362: 941–4.

Blackman, S. (1995) *Youth: Positions and Oppositions – Style, Sexuality and Schooling*, Aldershot: Avebury Press.

Boland, P. (2008) 'British Drugs Policy: Problematising the distinction between legal and illegal drugs and the definition of the "drugs problem"', *Journal of Community and Criminal Justice*, 55(2): 171–87.

Booth, R.E., Crowley, T.C. and Zhang, Y., (1996) 'Substance abuse treatment entry, retention and effectiveness: out-of-treatment opiate injection drug users', *Drug Alcohol Dependence*, 42: 11–20.

Booth R., Kwiatkowski, C. and Chitwood, D. (1999) 'Sex related HIV risk behaviours: Differential risks among injection drug users, crack smokers and injection drug users who smoke crack', *Drug and Alcohol Dependence*, 58: 219–26.

Booth, R., Corsi, K. and Mikulich, S. (2003) 'Improving treatment to methadone maintenance among out-of-treatment drug users', *Journal of Substance Abuse Treatment*, 24: 305–11.

Booth Davies, J. (1997) *The Myth of Addiction*, Amsterdam: Harwood Academic Publishers.

Bourdieu, P. (1984) *Questions de sociologie*, Paris: Les Editions de Minuit.

Bourdieu, P. and Wacquant, L. (1992) *An Invitation to Reflexive Sociology*, Cambridge: Polity.

Bourgois, P. (1989) 'In Search of Horatio Alger: Culture and Ideology in the Crack Economy', *Contemporary Drug Problems,* 16(4): 619–49.

Bourgois, P. (1995) *In Search of Respect: Selling Crack in El Barrio*, Cambridge: Cambridge University Press.

Bourgois, P. (2002) 'Anthropology and epidemiology on drugs: The challenges of cross–methodological and theoretical dialogue', *International Journal of Drug Policy*, 13: 259–69.

Bourgois, P. (2003) 'Crack and the political economy of social suffering', *Addiction, Research & Theory*, 11(1): 31–7.

Bourgois, P. and Schonberg, J. (2007) 'Intimate apartheid: Ethnic dimensions of habitus among homeless heroin injectors', *Ethnography*, 8(1): 7–31.

Bourgois, P. and Schonberg, J. (2009) *Righteous Dopefiend*, Berkeley: University of California Press.

Bourgois, P., Lettiere, M. and Quesada, J. (1997) 'Social misery and the sanctions of substance abuse: Confronting HIV risk among homeless heroin addicts in San Francisco', *Social Problems*, 44: 155–73.

Bovaird, T. (2004) *Tackling Drug Supply: Effective Partnership Notes*, London: Home Office.

Box, S. (1981) *Deviance, Reality and Society*, London: Holt, Rinehart and Winston Ltd.

Boyd, C. (1993) 'The antecedents of women's crack cocaine abuse: Family substance abuse, sexual abuse, depression and illicit drug abuse', *Journal of Substance Abuse Treatment*, 10: 433–8.

Boyd, C. and Mieczkowski, T. (1990) 'Drug use, health, family and social support in crack cocaine users', *Addictive Behaviours*, 15: 481–85.

Boyd, S., Johnson, J. and Moffat, B. (2008) 'Opportunities to learn and barriers to change: Crack cocaine use in the Downtown Eastside of Vancouver', *Harm Reduction Journal*, 5(34): 1–12.

Brain, K., Parker, H. and Bottomley, T. (1998) *Evolving Crack Cocaine Careers*, London: Home Office Findings 85.

Brecht, M., Huang, D., Evans, E. and Hser, Y. (2008) 'Polydrug use and implications for longitudinal research: Ten-year trajectories for heroin, cocaine and methamphetamine users', *Drug and Alcohol Dependence*, 96: 193–201.

Brenner, N. (2004) *New State Spaces: Urban Governance and the Rescaling of Statehood*, Oxford: Oxford University Press.

Brewer, D., Hagan., H., Sullivan, D., Muth, S., Hough, E., Feuerborn, N. and Gretch, D. (2006) 'Social structural and behavioral underpinnings of hyperendemic hepatitis C virus transmission in drug injectors', *Journal of Infectious Diseases*, 15; 194(6): 764–72.

Briggs, D. (2007) *Evaluation of the One Day At A Time Drug Rehabilitation Facility*, London: Hope Worldwide.

Briggs, D. (2010) 'Crack cocaine users: Ways in, ways down, but ways out?' *Safer Communities*, 9: 9–21.

Briggs, D., Rhodes, T., Marks, D. and Kimber, J. (2009) 'Injecting drug use, unstable housing and the scope for structural interventions in harm reduction', *Drugs, Education, Prevention and Policy*, 15(5): 436–50.

Buchanan, D., Tooze, J. A., Shaw, S., Kinzly, M., Heimer, R. and Singer, M. (2006) 'Demographic HIV risk behaviour and health status characteristics of "crack" cocaine injectors compared to other injection drug users in three New England cities', *Drug and Alcohol Dependence*, 81: 221–9.

Burgess, R. (2003) *Disrupting Crack Markets: A Practice Guide*, London: Home Office.

Butler, J. (1990) *Gender Trouble*, New York: Routledge.

Carroll, K., Rounsaville, B., Gordon, L., Nich, C., Jatlow, P., Bisignini, P. and Gawin, F. (1994) 'Psychotherapy and pharmacotherapy for ambulatory cocaine abusers', *Archives of General Psychiatry*, 51: 177–87.

Child, P., Edmunds, M. and Joseph, I. (2002) *Substance Misuse Treatment Needs in a London Borough*, London: Rivertown DAT.

Chitwood, D., Rivers, J. and Inciardi, J. (1996) *The American Pipe Dream: Crack Cocaine and the Inner City*, London: Harcourt Brace Publishers.

Cohen, E. and Stahler, G. (1998) 'Life Histories of Crack-Using African American Homeless Men: Salient Themes', *Contemporary Drug Problems*, 25(2): 373–97.

Cohen, E., Navaline, H. and Metzger, D. (1994) 'HIV-risk behaviors for HIV: A comparison between crack-abusing and opioid-abusing African-American women', *Journal of Psychoactive Drugs*, 26: 233–41.

Connolly, P. and Healy, J. (2004) 'Symbolic violence, locality and social class: The educational and career aspirations of 10–11-year-old boys in Belfast', *Pedagogy, Culture and Society*, 12: 15–32.

Cooley, C. (1964) *Human Nature and Social Order*, New York: Schocken Books.

Cornish, J. and O'Brien, C. (1996) 'Crack cocaine abuse: An epidemic with many public health consequences', *Annual Review of Public Health*, 17: 259–73.

Cregler, L. (1989) 'Adverse health consequences of cocaine abuse', *Journal of National Medical Association*, 81(1): 27–39.

Crum, R., Lillie-Blanton, M. and Anthony, J. (1996) 'Neighborhood environment and opportunity to use cocaine and other drugs in late childhood and early adolescence', *Drug and Alcohol Dependence*, 43: 155–161.

Cusick, L., Martin, A. and May, T. (2003) *Vulnerability and Involvement in Sex Work*, London: Home Office Research Study 268.

Dackis, C. and O'Brien, C. (2001), 'Cocaine dependence: A disease of the brain's reward centers', *Journal of Substance Abuse Treatment*, 21(3): 111–17.

Dale, A. and Perera, J. (1994) *A Situational Assessment of Substance Misuse in a London Borough*, London: London Centre for Research on Drugs and Health Behaviour.

Darke, S., Topp, L. and Kaye, S. (2001) *Drug Trends Bulletin–Illicit Drugs Reporting System: December 2001*, Sydney: National Drug and Alcohol Research Centre.

Davis, R. and Lurigio, A. (1996) *Fighting Back: Neighbourhood Anti-Drug Strategies*, Thousand Oaks, CA: Sage.

DeCorte T. (2001) 'Drug users' perceptions of "controlled" and "uncontrolled" use', *International Journal of Drug Policy*, 12: 297–320.

Denison, M., Paredes, A., Bacal, S. and Gawin, F. (1998) 'Psychological and psychiatric consequences of cocaine', in Tarter,. R., Ammerman, R. and Ott, P. (Eds) *Handbook of Substance Abuse: Neurobehavioral Pharmacology*, New York: Plenum Press.

Donmall, M., Sievewright, N., Douglas, J., Draycott, T. and Millar, T. (1995) *National Cocaine Treatment Study: The Effectiveness of Treatments Offered to Cocaine/Crack Users*, Manchester: University of Manchester Drug Misuse Unit and Community Health Sheffield NHS Trust.

Dorn, N. and South, N. (1985) *Helping Drug Users*, London: Gower.

Dovey, K., Fitzgerald, J. and Choi, Y. (2001) 'Safety becomes danger: Dilemmas of drug use in public space', *Health and Place*, 7: 319–31.

Doyle, L. (1979) *The Political Economy of Health*, London: Pluto Press.

Duff, C. (2007) 'Towards a theory of drug use contexts: Space, embodiment and practice', *Addiction, Research and Theory*, 15: 503–19.

Duff, C. (2009) 'The drifting city: The role of affect and repair in the development of "Enabling Environments"', *The International Journal of Drug Policy*, 20: 202–8.

Dunlap, E. (1992) 'Impact of drugs on family life and kin networks in the inner city African American single-parent household', in A. Harrall and G. Peterson (Eds) *Drugs, Crime and Social Isolation: Barriers to Urban Opportunity*, Washington DC: Urban Institute Press.

Dunlap, E. (1995) 'Inner-city crisis and drug dealing: Portrait of a drug dealer and his household', in S. MacGregor and A. Lipow (Eds) *The Other City: People and Politics in New York and London*, New Jersey: Humanities Press.

Dunlap, E. and Johnson, B. (1992) 'The setting for the crack era: Macro forces, micro consequences (1960–1992)', *Journal of Psychoactive Drugs*, 24: 307–21.

Dunlap, E., Benoit, E., Sifaneck, S. and Johnson, B. (2006) 'Social constructions of dependency by blunt smokers: Qualitative reports', *International Journal of Drug Policy*, 17: 171–82.

Duster, T. (1970) *The Legislation of Morality: Law, Drugs and Moral Judgment*, New York: Free Press.

Edlin, B., Irwin, K. and Faruque, S. (1994) 'Intersecting epidemics – crack cocaine use and HIV infection among innercity young adults', *New England Journal of Medicine*, 331: 1422–7.

Edmunds, M., Hough, M. and Urquia, N. (1996) *Tackling Local Drug Markets. Crime Detection and Prevention Series, Paper 80*. London: Home Office.

Edmunds, M., May, T., Hearnden, I. and Hough, M. (1998) *Arrest Referral: Emerging Lessons from Research, Drug Prevention Initiative Paper No. 23*, London: Central Drug Prevention Unit, Home Office.

Edmunds, M., Hough, M., Turnbull, P. and May, T. (1999) *Doing Justice to Treatment: Referring Offenders to Drug Services*, London: Home Office.

European Monitoring Centre for Drugs and Drug Addiction (EMCDDA) (2007) *The State of the Drugs Problem in Europe*, Lisbon: European Monitoring Centre for Drugs and Drug Addiction.

Evans, K. (2002) 'Taking control of their lives? Agency in young adult transitions in England and Germany', *Journal of Youth Studies*, 5: 245–69.

Falck, R., Wang, J., Siegal, H. and Carlson, R. (2004). 'The prevalence of psychiatric disorders among a community sample of crack cocaine users. An exploratory study with practical implications', *Journal of Nervous and Mental Disorders*, 192: 503–7.

Falck, R., Wang, J. and Carlson, R. (2007) Crack cocaine trajectories among users in a midwestern American city', *Addiction*, 102: 1421–31.

Falck, R., Wang, J. and Carlson, R. (2008) 'Among long-term crack smokers, who avoids and who succumbs to cocaine addiction?', *Drug and Alcohol Dependence*, 98: 24–9.

Farmer, P. (1997) 'On suffering and structural violence: A view from below', in A. Kleinman, V. Das, and M. Lock (Eds) *Social Suffering*, Berkeley, CA: University of California Press.

Farmer, P., Connors, M. and Simmons, J. (1996) *Women, Poverty and AIDS: Sex, Drugs and Structural Violence*, Monroe, Maine: Common Courage Press.

Faruque, S., Edlin, B., McCoy, C., Word, B., Larsen, S., Schmidt, D., Von Bargen, J. and Serrano, Y. (1996) 'Crack cocaine smoking and oral sores in three inner-city neighbour-hoods', *Journal of Acquired Immune Deficiency Syndromes*, 13(1): 87–92.

Fernandez, J. (2002) Ethnic presentation in a London drug clinic: The value of examining case studies, Unpublished report.

Fetterman, D. (1989) *Ethnography: Step by Step*, London: Sage.

Finestone, H. (1957) 'Cats, kicks and color', in H. Becker (Ed.), *The Other Side*, New York: Free Press.

Firestone, M., Kalousek, K. and Fischer, B. (2006) *Crack Cocaine: Fact Sheet*, Ottowa: Canadian Centre on Substance Abuse.

Fischer, B. and Coghlan, M. (2007) 'Crack use in North American cities: The neglected "epidemic"', *Addiction*, 102: 1340–1.

Fischer, B., Monga, N. and Manzoni, P. (2005) 'Differences between co-users of cocaine and crack among Canadian illicit opioid users', *Sucht*, 51: 217–24.

Fischer, B., Rehm, J., Patra, J., Kalousek, K., Haydon, E. and Tyndall, M. (2006) 'Crack across Canada: comparing crack and non-crack users in a multi-city cohort of opioid and other street drug users', *Addiction*, 101: 1760–70.

Fitzgerald, J. (2009) 'Mapping the experience of drug dealing risk environments: An ethnographic case study', *International Journal of Drug Policy*, 20: 261–9.

Fitzgerald, J. and Threadgold, T. (2004) 'Fear of crime in the street heroin market', *International Journal of Drug Policy*, 15: 407–17.

Fitzgerald, J., Dovey, K. and Choi, Y. (2004) 'Health outcomes and quasi-supervised settings for street injecting drug use', *International Journal of Drug Policy*, 15: 247–57.

Fletcher, A., Bonnell, C., Sorhaindo, A. and Rhodes, T. (2009) 'Cannabis use and safe iden-tities in an inner-city school risk environment', *International Journal of Drug Policy*, 20: 244–50.

Ford, C. (2004) *Guidance for Working with Crack Cocaine Users,* London: NTA.

Fountain, J., Bashford, J., Winters, M. and Patel, K. (2003) *Black and Minority Ethnic Communities in England: A Review of the Literature on Drug Use and Related Service Provision*, London: NTA.

Fox, A., Khan, L., Briggs, D., Rees–Jones, N., Thompson, Z. and Owens, J. (2005) *Throughcare and Aftercare: Approaches and Promising Practice in Service Delivery for Clients Released from Prison or Leaving Residential Rehabilitation*, Home Office Online Report, London: Home Office.

Friedman, S., Jose, B., Stepherson, B., Neaigus, A., Goldstein, M., Mota, P., Curtis, R. and Ildefonso, G. (1998) 'Multiple racial/ethnic subordination and HIV among drug injectors', in M. Singer (Ed.), *The Political Economy of AIDS*, Amityville, NY: Baywood Publishing Co.

Fryer, R., Heaton, P., Levitt, S. and Murphy, K. (2005) Measuring the impact of crack cocaine, Unpublished report.

Garfinkel, H. (1956) 'Status degradation ceremonies', *American Journal of Sociology*, 77: 697–705.

Garland, D. (2008) 'On the concept of the moral panic', *Crime, Media and Culture*, 4: 9.

Giddens, A. (1984) *The Constitution of Society: Outline of the Theory of Structuration*, Cambridge: Polity Press.

Giddens, A. (1990) *The Consequences of Modernity*, Cambridge: Polity Press.

Giddens, A. (1991) *Modernity and Self Identity*, Cambridge: Polity Press.

Glaser, B. (1978) *Theoretical Sensitivity: Advances in the Methodology of Grounded Theory*, Mill Valley: Sociology Press.

Goffman, E. (1959) *The Presentation of Self in Everyday Life*, Garden City, NY: Doubleday Anchor.

Goffman, E. (1961) *Asylums: Essays on the Social Situation of Mental Patients and Other Inmates*, New York: Doubleday.

Goffman, E. (1963) *Stigma: Notes on the Management of Spoiled Identity*, Englewood Cliffs, NJ: Prentice-Hall.

Gold, M. and Millner, N. (1997) 'Criminal activity and crack addiction', *International Journal of Drug Policy*, 29: 1069–78.

Goldstein, P. Brownstein, H. Ryan, P. and Bellucci, P. (1989) 'Crack and Homicide in New York City: A Conceptually Based Event Analysis', *Contemporary Drug Problems*, 16: 651–67.

Golub, A. and Johnson, D. (1996) 'The crack epidemic: Empirical findings support an hypothesized diffusion of innovation process', *Socio-Economic Planning Sciences*, 30 (3): 221–31.

Goodenough, W. (1967) 'Componential analysis', *Science*, 156: 1203–9.

Gossop, M., Griffiths, P., Powis, B., Strang, J. (1994) 'Cocaine: Patterns of use, route of administration and severity of dependence', *British Journal of Psychiatry* 164: 660–4.

Gossop, M., Marsden, J. and Stewart, D. (2001) *NTORS after five years: Changes in substance use, health and criminal behaviour during the five years after intake*, London: Department of Health.

Gossop, M., Marsden, J., Stewart, D. and Kidd, T. (2002) *The National Treatment Outcome Research Report*, London: National Addiction Centre.

Greater London Alcohol and Drug and Alliance (GLADA) (2004) *An evidence base for the London crack cocaine strategy*, London: GLADA.

Grella, C., Anglin, M. and Wugalter, S. (1995) 'Cocaine and crack use and HIV risk behaviours among high-risk methadone maintenance clients', *Drug and Alcohol Dependence*, 37: 15–21.

Haines, R., Poland, B. and Johnson, J. (2009) 'Becoming a "real" smoker: Cultural capital in young women's accounts of smoking and other substance use', *Sociology of Health and Illness*, 31: 66–80.

Hall, T. and Hubbard, P. (1998) 'The entrepreneurial city: New urban politics, new urban geographies?' *Progress in Human Geography*, 20: 153–74.

Hamid, A. (1990) 'The Political Economy of Crack-Related Violence', *Contemporary Drug Problems*, 17: 31–78.

Hammersley, M. (1992) *What's wrong with ethnography? Methodological explorations*, London: Routledge.

Harocopos, A., Dennis, D., Turnbull, P., Parsons, J. and Hough, M. (2003) *On the Rocks: A Follow-Up Study of Crack Users in London*, London: South Bank University.

Hasaan, C. and Prinzleve, M. (2001) *Support Needs for Cocaine and Crack Users in Europe*, Hamburg: University of Hamburg.

Hatsukami, D. and Fischman, M. (1996) 'Crack cocaine and cocaine hydrochloride: Are the differences myth or reality?', *Journal of the American Medical Association*, 276: 1580–8.

Hawkins, J., Catalano, R. and Miller, J. (1992) 'Risk and protective factors for alcohol and other drug problems in adolescence and early adulthood: Implications for substance abuse prevention', *Psychological Bulletin*, 112: 64–105.

Hay, G., Gannon, M., MacDougall, J., Millar, T., Eastwood, C. and McKeganey, N. (2006) *Estimates of the Prevalence of Opiate Use and/or Crack Cocaine Use (2004/05) for the London Region*, London: Home Office.

Hay, G., Gannon, M., MacDougall, J., Millar, T., Eastwood, C. and McKeganey, M. (2007) *National and regional estimates of the prevalence of opiate and crack or cocaine use 2005/06: A summary of the key findings*, London: Home Office.

Haydon, E., Chorny, Y. and Fischer, B. (2005) *Crack use and public health (with a specific focus on hepatitis C): Epidemiology, risk factors and interventions, Final draft report*, Ottawa: Public Health Agency of Canada.

Health Protection Agency (HPA) (2008) *Shooting up: Infections among injecting drug users in the United Kingdom 2007 – An update: October 2008*, London: HPA.

Hellawell, K. and Trace, M. (1998) *Tackling Drugs to Build a Better Britain: The Government's Ten-Year Strategy for Tackling Drugs Misuse*, London: Her Majesty's Stationery Office.

Henkel, Y. (1999) '"The Problem With..." Young People, Drugs and Homelessness', *Parity*, 12 (8): 3–4.

Hickman, M., Higgins, V., Hope, V., Bellis, M., Tilling, K., Walker, A. and Henry, J. (2004) 'Injecting drug use in Brighton, Liverpool and London: Best estimates of prevalence and coverage of public health indicators', *Journal of Epidemiology and Community Health*, 58: 766–71.

Hickman, M., Hope, V., McDonald, T., Madden, P., Brady, T. and Honor, S. (2006) HCV prevalence and injecting risk behaviour in multiple sites in England in 2004, unpublished paper.

Higgins, S., Budney, A., Bickel, W., Hughes, J., Foerg, F. and Badger, G. (1993) 'Achieving cocaine abstinence with a behavioral approach', *American Journal of Psychiatry*, 150: 763–9.

Holstein, J. and Gubrium, J. (1997) 'Active interviewing', in D. Silverman (Ed.) *Qualitative Research: Theory, Method and Practice*, London: Sage.

Holstein, J. and Gubrium, J. (2000) *The Self We Live By: Narrative Identity in a Postmodern World*, New York: Oxford University Press.

Holt, W. (1967) 'The concept of motivation for treatment', *American Journal of Psychiatry*, 123(11): 1388–95.

Home Office (2002) *Tackling crack cocaine: A national plan*, London: HMSO. (Ref DSD14).

Hope, V., Hickman, M. and Tilling, K. (2005) 'Capturing crack cocaine use: Estimating the prevalence of crack use in London using capture–recapture with co-variates', *Addiction*, 100: 1701–8.

Hope, V., Kimber, J., Vickerman, P., Hickman, M. and Ncube, F. (2008) 'Frequency, factors and costs associated with injection site infections: findings from a national multi-site survey of injecting drug users in England', *BMC Infectious Diseases*, 8(1):120.

Howard, A., Klein, R., Schoenbaum, E. and Gourevitch, M. (2002) 'Crack cocaine use and other risk factors for tuberculin positivity in drug users', *Clinical Infectious Disease*, 35: 1183–90.

Hser, Y. (2002) 'Drug use careers: Recovery and mortality', in S.P. Korper and C.L. Council (Eds) *Substance use by older adults: Estimates of future impact on the treatment system*, (DHHS Publication No. SMA 03–3763, Analytic Series A–21) (pp. 39–59). Rockville, MD7 Substance Abuse and Mental Health Services Administration, Office of Applied Studies.

Hser, Y., Anglin, M.D., Grella, C., Longshore, D. and Prendergast, M. (1997) 'Drug treatment careers: A conceptual framework and existing research findings', *Journal of Substance Abuse Treatment*, 14, 543–58.

Hunter, G., Donoghoe, M. and Stimson, G. (1995) 'Crack use and injection on the increase among injecting drug users in London', *Addiction*, 90: 1397–400.

Inciardi, J. (1995) 'Crack, crack house sex, HIV risk', *Archives of Sexual Behaviour*, 24(3): 249–69.

Inciardi, J., Pottieger, A. and Surratt, S. (1996) 'African Americans and the Crack–Crime Connection', in D. Chitwood, J. Rivers and J. Inciardi (Eds) *The American Pipe Dream: Crack Cocaine and the Inner City*. Fort Worth: Harcourt Brace College Publishers.

Jackson-Jacobs, C. (2002) *Refining rock: Practical and social features of social control among a group of college-student crack users*, Federal Legal Publications.

Jayne, M., Holloway, S. and Valentine, G. (2006) 'Drunk and disorderly: Alcohol, urban life and public space', *Progress in Human Geography*, 30: 451–68.

Johnson, R., Gerstein, D., Pach, A., Cerbone, F. and Brown, J. (2002) *HIV risk behaviours in African-American drug injector networks: Implications of injection-partner mixing and partnership characteristics*, New York: NIDA.

Kessler, R.C., K.A. McGonagle, K., Zhao, S., Nelson, C., Hughes, H., Eshleman, S., Wittchen, H. and Kendler, K. (1994) 'Lifetime and 12–month prevalence of DSM–III–R psychiatric disorders in the United States', *Archives of General Psychiatry*, 51: 8–19.

Kessler, R., Nelson, C., McGonagle, K., Liu, J., Swartz, M. and Blazer, D. (1996) 'Comorbidity of DSM-III-R major depressive disorder in the general population: results from the US National Comorbidity Survey', *British Journal of Psychiatry Supplement*, 30: 17–30.

Klee, H. and Morris, J. (1995) 'Factors that Characterize Street Injectors', *Addiction*, 90: 837–41.

Kleinman, A., Das, V. and Lock, M. (Eds). (1997) *Social Suffering*, Berkeley: University of California Press.

Kleinman, P., Miller, A., Millman, G., Woody, T., Todd, J., Kemp, J. and Lipton, S. (1990) 'Psychopathology among cocaine abusers entering treatment', *Journal of Nervous and Mental Disease*, 178(7): 442–7.

Laposata, E. and Mayo, G. (1993) 'A review of pulmonary pathology and mechanisms associated with inhalation of freebase cocaine ("crack")', *American Journal of Forensic Medicine and Pathology*, 14: 1–9.

Lasch, C (1985) *The Minimal Self: Psychic Survival in Troubled Times*, London: Norton.

Latkin, C., Mandell, W. and Vlahov, D. (1996) 'The relationship between risk networks patterns of crack cocaine and alcohol consumption and HIV-related sexual behaviours among adult injection drug users: A prospective study', *Drug and Alcohol Dependence*, 42(3): 175–81.

Leibow, E. (1993) *Tell Them Who I Am: The Lives of Homeless Women*, New York: Penguin Books.

Lemert, E. (1951) *Social Pathology*, New York: McGraw–Hill.

Lemert, E. (1967) *Human Deviance, Social Problems and Social Control*, Englewood Cliffs, NJ: Prentice–Hall.

Leonhardt, K.K., Gentile, F., Gibert, B.P. and Aiken, M. (1994) 'A cluster of tuberculosis among crack house contacts in San Mateo County, California', *American Journal of Public Health*, 84: 1834–6.

Levine, R., Walsh, C. and Schwartz, R. (1996) *Pharmacology: Drug Actions and Reactions*, 5th edn. London: Parthenon Publishing Group.

Lindsell, H. (2005) *Underground: An Analysis of Lewisham's Crack Cocaine Market*, London: Lewisham Drug Strategy Team.

Logan, T. and Leukfeld, C. (2000) 'Sexual and drug use behaviours among female crack users: A multi-site sample', *Drug and Alcohol Dependence*, 58: 237–45.

Ludwig, W. and Hoffner, R. (1999) 'Upper airway burn from crack cocaine pipe: Screen ingestion', *American Journal of Emergency Medicine*, 17(1): 108–9.

Lupton, D. (Ed.) (1999) *Risk: New Directions and Perspectives*, Cambridge: Cambridge University Press.

Lupton, R., Wilson, A., May, T., Warburn, H. and Turnbull, P. (2002) *Drug Markets in Deprived Neighbourhoods, Research Findings 167*, London: Home Office.

Malchy, L., Bungay, V. and Johnson, J. (2008) 'Documenting practices and perceptions of "safer" crack use: A Canadian pilot study', *International Journal of Drug Policy*, 19: 339–41.

Marcos, M., García M. and de Alba Romero, C. (1998) 'Cocaína: actuar es posible', *Formación Médica Continuada en Atención Primaria*, 5: 582–9.

Marez, C. (2004) *Drug Wars: The Political Economy of Narcotics*, Minneapolis: University of Minnesota Press.

Maruna, S. (2001) *Making Good: How Ex-Convicts Reform and Rebuild Their Lives*, Washington, DC: American Psychological Association Books.

Matza, D. (1964) *Delinquency and Drift*, New York: John Wiley and Sons.

Matza, D. (1969) *Becoming Deviant*, Englewood Cliffs, NJ: Prentice Hall.

Matthews, R., Easton, H., Briggs, D. and Pease, K. (2007) *Assessment of the Outcomes of Anti-Social Behaviour Orders*, London: Polity Press.

May, T., Edmunds, M. and Hough, M., (1999) *Street Business: The Links Between Sex and Drug Markets, Police Research Series 118*, London: Home Office Policing and Reducing Crime Unit.

May, T., Duffy, M., Few, B. and Hough, M. (2005) *Understanding Drug Selling in Communities. Insider or Outsider Trading?* York: Joseph Rowntree Foundation.

May, T., Cossalter, S., Boyce, I. and Hearnden, I. (2007) *Drug Dealing in Brixton Town Centre*, London: Lambeth DAT.

McBride, D. and Rivers, J. (1996) 'Crack and crime', in D. Chitwood, J. Rivers and J. Inciardi (Eds) *The American Pipe Dream: Crack Cocaine and the Inner City*, London: Harcourt Brace.

McClanahan, S., McClelland, D., Abram, K. and Teplin, K. (1999) 'Pathways Into Prostitution Among Female Jail Detainees and Their Implications for Mental Health Services', *Psychiatric Services*, 50(12): 1606–13.

McCoy, C., Lai, S., Metsch, L., Messaih, H. and Zhao, M. (2004) 'Injection drug use and crack smoking: Independent and dual risk behaviours for HIV infection in drug use and HIV behaviours', *AEP*, 14(8): 535–42.

McElrath, K. and Jordan, M. (2005) *Drug Use and Risk Behaviours among Injecting Drug Users*, Belfast, Northern Ireland: Department of Health, Social Services and Public Safety.

McMahon, J. and Tortu, S. (2003) 'A potential hidden source of hepatitis C infection among non-injecting drug users', *Journal of Psychoactive Drugs*, 35: 455–60.

Mieczkowski, T. (1990) 'The operational styles of crack houses in Detroit', *Drugs and Violence: Causes, Correlates and Consequences*, Research No. 103, New York: NIDA.

Miles, S. (2000) *Youth Lifestyles in a Changing world*, Philadelphia: Open University Press.

Miller, J. (1995) 'Gender and Power on the Streets: Street Prostitution in the Era of Crack Cocaine', *Journal of Contemporary Ethnography*, 23(4): 427–52.

Moore, D. and Dietze, P. (2005) 'Enabling environments and the reduction of drug-related harm: Re-framing Australian policy and practice', *Drug and Alcohol Review*, 24(3): 275–84.

Morgan, J. and Zimmer, L. (1997) 'The Social Pharmacology of Smokable Cocaine', in C. Reinarman and H. Levine (Eds), *Crack in America: Demon Drugs and Social Justice*, Berkeley: University of California Press: 131–170.

Morris, K. (1998) 'Seeking ways to cocaine addiction', *Lancet*, 352: 1392.

Murphy, E., Devita, D., Lui, H., Vittinghoff, E., Leung, P. and Ciccarone, D. (2001) 'Risk factors for skin and soft-tissue abscesses among injection drug users: A case–control study', *Clinical Infectious Diseases*, 33: 35–40.

National Institute on Drug Abuse (NIDA) (2004) *Crack and Cocaine*, New York: NIDA.

NIDA (2005) *NIDA Info Facts: Crack and Cocaine*, New York: NIDA.

National Treatment Agency (NTA) (2002) *Treating Crack/Cocaine Dependence*, London: NTA.

NTA (2007) *Statistics for Drug Treatment Activity in England 2006/07: National Drug Treatment Monitoring System*, London: National Treatment Agency for Substance Misuse.

Navarro, V. and Muntaner, C. (2004) *Political and Economic Determinants of Population Health and Well-being*. Amityville, NY: Baywood.

Neale, J., Godfrey, C., Parrot, S., Tompkins, C. and Sheard, L. (2006) *Barriers to the Effective Treatment of Injecting Drug Users*, London: Department of Health.

Nelson, L. (1999) 'Bodies (and spaces) do matter', *Gender, Place and Culture*, 6: 331–53.

O'Connor, J. (2004) '"A Special Kind of City Knowledge": Innovative Clusters, Tacit Knowledge and the "Creative City"', *Media International Australia incorporating Culture and Policy*, 112: 131–49.

O'Malley, P. (2008) 'Experiments in risk and criminal justice', *Theoretical Criminology*, 12(4): 451–69.

Ottaway, C. and Erickson, P. (1997) 'Frequent medical visits by cocaine-using subjects in a Canadian community: An invisible problem for health practitioners', *Journal of Substance Abuse Treatment*, 14: 423–9.

Page-Shafer, K., Cahoon-Young, B., Klausner, J., Morrow, S., Molitor, F. and Ruiz, J. (2002) 'Hepatitis C virus infection in young, low-income women: The role of sexually transmitted infection as a potential cofactor for HCV infection', *American Journal of Public Health*, 119: 1017–28.

Parker, H. and Bottomley, T. (1996) *Crack Cocaine and Drugs-Crime Careers, Home Office Research Findings No. 34*, London: Home Office.

Parker, H., Eggington, R. and Bury, C. (1998) *New Heroin Outbreaks Amongst Young People in England and Wales, Crime Detection and Prevention Series*, London: Home Office.

Parker, H., Aldridge, J., Eggington, R. (2001) *UK Drugs Unlimited: New Research and Policy Lessons on Illicit Drug Use*, Basingstoke: Palgrave.

Parker, R. and Aggleton, P. (2003) 'HIV and AIDS-related stigma and discrimination: A conceptual framework and implications for action', *Social Science and Medicine*, 57: 13–24.

Parkin, S. (2008) 'Public Injecting and Symbolic Violence: A Perspective Obtained from Practices Observed within a (UK) Local Authority', *Addiction Research & Theory*, 17(4): 390–405.

Parkin, S. and Coomber, R. (2009) 'Informal sorter houses: A qualitative insight into the shooting gallery phenomenon in a UK setting', *Health and Place*, 15: 981–9.

Pauly, B. (2008) 'Harm reduction through a criminal justice lens', *International Journal of Drug Policy*, 19: 4–10.

Payne-James, J., Wall, I. and Bailey, C. (2008) 'Patterns of illicit drug use of prisoners in police custody in London, UK', *Journal of Clinical Forensic Medicine*, 12: 196–8.

Pearson, G. (2001) 'Normal drug use: Ethnographic fieldwork among an adult network of recreational drug users in London', *Substance Use and Misuse*, 36(1): 1–28.

Perlman, D., Salomon, N., Perkins, M., Yancovitz, S., Paone, D. and Des Jarlais, D. (1995) 'Tuberculosis in drug users', *Clinical Infectious Diseases*, 21: 1253–64.

Petersen, A. (1997) 'The New Morality: Public Health and Personal Conduct', in O'Farrell, C. (Ed.), *Foucault: The Legacy*, Kelvin Grove: Queensland University of Technology.

Polsky, N. (1969) *Hustlers, Beats and Others*, London: University of Sussex Press.

Porter, J., Bonilla, L. and Drucker, E. (1997) 'Methods of smoking crack as a potential risk factor for HIV infection: Crack smokers' perceptions and behavior', *Contemporary Drug Problems*, 24: 19–347.

Power, R. (2002) 'The application of ethnography, with reference to harm reduction in Sverdlovsk Russia', *International Journal of Drug Policy*, 13(4): 330.

Preble, E. and Casey, J. (1969) 'Taking Care of Business: The Heroin User's Life on the Street', *International Journal of Addiction*, 4:1–24.

Prochaska, J. and DiClemente, C. (1986) 'Toward a comprehensive model of change', in Miller, W. and Heather, N., (Eds). *Treating Addictive Behaviors: Processes of Change*, New York: Plenum Press.

Provine, D. (2006) 'Creating racial disadvantage: The case for crack cocaine', in R. Peterson, L. Krivo and J. Hagan (Eds) *The Many Colours of Crime*, New York and London: New York University Press.

Punch, M. (2005) 'Problem drug use and the political economy of urban restructuring: Heroin, class and governance in Dublin', *Antipode*, 37: 754–72.

Radcliffe, P. and Stevens, A. (2008) 'Are drug treatment services only for "thieving junkie scumbags"? Drug users and the management of stigmatised identities', *Social Science & Medicine*, 67:1065–73.

Ray, M. (1964) 'The cycle of abstinence and relapse among heroin addicts', in H. Becker (Ed.) *The Other Side*, New York: Free Press.

Regier, D., Narrow, W., Rae, D., Mandersheid, R., Locke, B. and Goodwin, F. (1993) 'The de facto U.S. mental and addictive disorders service system', *Archives of General Psychiatry*, 50: 85–94.

Reinarman, C. and Levine, H. (Eds) (1997) *Crack in America: Demon Drugs and Social Justice*. Berkeley: University of California Press.

Reinarman, C. and Levine, H. (2004) 'Crack in the Rearview Mirror: Deconstructing Drug War Mythology', *Social Justice*, 31(1–2): 182–99.

Reuter, P. and Stevens, A. (2008) 'Assessing UK drug policy from a crime control perspective', *Criminology and Criminal Justice*, 8: 461–82.

Rhodes, T. (2002) 'The risk environment: A framework for understanding and reducing drug–related harm', *International Journal of Drug Policy*, 13: 85–94.

Rhodes, T., Stimson, G., Crofts, N., Ball, A., Dehne, K. and Khodakevich, L. (1999). 'Drug injecting, rapid HIV spread and the "risk environment", *AIDS*, 13: S259–S269.

Rhodes, T., Singer, M., Bourgois, P., Friedman, S. and Strathdee, S. (2005) 'The social structural production of HIV risk among injecting drug users', *Social Science and Medicine*, 61: 1026–44.

Rhodes, T., Briggs, D., Kimber, J., Jones, S. and Holloway, G. (2006) *Visual Assessments of Injecting Drug Use*, London: National Treatment Agency for Substance Misuse.

Rhodes, T., Briggs, D., Kimber, J., Jones, S., Holloway, G. (2007) 'Crack–heroin speedball injection and its implications for vein care: Qualitative study', *Addiction*, 102(11): 1782–90.

Rimke, H. (2000) 'Governing citizens through self—help literature', *Cultural Studies*, 14: 61–78.

Rivertown DAT (2003) *Tackling Crack in Rivertown*, London: Rivertown DAT.

Rivertown Primary Care Trust (2004) *A Proposal for Developing a Local Enhanced Services for Patients who Misuse Drugs*, London: Rivertown Primary Care Trust.

Rose, G. (1993) *Feminism and Geography*, Minneapolis: University of Minnesota Press.

Ross, T. (2002) 'Using and dealing on Calle 19: A high risk street community in central Bogotá', *International Journal of Drug Policy*, 13: 45–56.

Rubin, V. and Comitas. L. (1975) *Ganja in Jamaica: A Medical Anthropological Study of Chronic Marihuana Use*. The Hague, Paris: Mouton.

Safer Rivertown Partnership (2004a) *Tackling Drug Related Crime Through Treatment*, London: Safer Rivertown Partnership.

Safer Rivertown Partnership (2004b) *Adult Drug Treatment Plan 2004/2005*, London: Safer Rivertown Partnership.

Sangster, D., Shiner, M., Patel, K. and Sheikh, N. (2001) *Delivering Drug Services to Black and Minority Ethnic Communities, DPAS Paper 16*. Home Office report, London: Home Office.

Schwandt, T. (2001) *Dictionary of Qualitative Inquiry*, 2nd ed. Thousand Oaks: Sage.

Seddon, T. (2006) 'Drugs, Crime and Social Exclusion: Social Context and Social Theory in British Drugs-Crime Research', *British Journal of Criminology*, 46(4): 680–703.

Seddon, T. (2008) 'Dangerous liaisons: Personality disorder and the politics of risk', *Punishment and Society*, 10(3): 301–17.

Sherman, L. (2004) 'Research and Policing: The Infrastructure and Political Economy of Federal Funding', *ANNALS of the American Academy of Political and Social Science*, 593: 156–78.

Shifano, F. and Corkery, J. (2008) 'Cocaine/crack cocaine consumption, treatment demand, seizures, related offences, prices, average purity levels and deaths in the UK (1990–2004)', *Journal of Psychopharmacology*, 22: 71–9.

Sievewright, N., Donmall, M., Douglas, J., Draycott, T. and Millar, T. (2000) 'Cocaine misuse treatment in England', *International Journal of Drug Policy*, 11: 203–15.

Simmonds, L. and Coomber, R. (2009) 'Injecting drug users: A stigmatised and stigmatising population', *International Journal of Drug Policy*, 20: 121–30.

Singer, M. (2001) 'Toward a biocultural and political economic integration of alcohol, tobacco and drug studies in the coming century', *Social Science & Medicine*, 53: 199–213.

Singer, M. (2003) 'Imprisoning AIDS', *Newsletter of the AIDS and Anthropology Research Group*, 15: 1–2.

Small, W., Kerr, T., Charette, J., Wood, E., Schechter, M. T. and Spittal, P. (2006) 'Impacts of intensified police activity on injection drug users: Evidence from an ethnographic investigation', *International Journal of Drug Policy*, 17: 85–9.

Sparks, R., Girling, E. and Loader, I. (2001) 'Fear and everyday urban lives', *Urban Studies*, 38(5–6): 885–98.

Spijkerman, I., Van Ameijden, E. J. and Mientjes, G. (1996) 'Human immunodeficiency virus and other risk factors for skin abscesses and endocarditis among injection drug users', *Journal of Clinical Epidemiology*, 49(10): 1149–54.

Sterk, C. (1988) 'Cocaine and HIV seropositivity' [Letter] *Lancet* 1, 1052–3.

Sterk, C. (2002) 'Drug research: ethnographies or qualitative works?', *International Journal of Drug Policy*, 14: 127–30.

Sterne, M. and Pittman, D. (1965) 'The concept of motivation: A source of institutional and professional blockage in the treatment of alcoholics', *Qualitative Journal of Study of Alcohol*, 26: 41–57.

Stimson, G. (2000) 'Blair declares war: The unhealthy state of British drug policy', *International Journal of Drug Policy*, 11: 259–64.

Stitzer, M. and Chutape, M. (1999) 'Other substance use disorders in methadone treatment: Prevalence, consequences, detection and management', in Strain, E.C., Stitzer, M.L. (Eds), *Methadone Treatment for Opioid Dependence*, Johns Hopkins University Press, Baltimore, MD, pp. 86–118.

Story, A., Bothamley, G. and Hayward, A. (2008) 'Crack cocaine and infectious tuberculosis', *Emergency Infectious Disorder*, 14:1466–9.

Stöver, H. (2002) 'Crack cocaine in Germany – Current state of affairs', *Journal of Drug Issues*, 32(2): 413–42.

Substance Abuse and Mental Heath Services Agency (SAMHSA) (1995) *Preliminary estimates from the 1994 National Household Survey on Drug Abuse*, Rockville, Maryland: US Department of Health and Human Services.

Sykes, G. and Matza, D. (1957) 'Techniques of neutralization', *American Sociological Review*, 22: 664–70.

Taylor, I., Walton, P. and Young, J. (1973) *The New Criminology: For a Social Theory of Deviance*, London: Routledge.

Thorpe, L., Ouellet, L., Levy, J., William, I. and Monterroso, E. (2000) 'Hepatitis C virus infection: Prevalence, risk factors and prevention opportunities among young injection drug users in Chicago, 1997–1999', *Journal of Infectious Diseases*, 182: 1588–94.

Tortu, S., McMahon, J., Pouget, E. and Hamid, R. (2004) 'Sharing of noninjection drug-use implements as a risk factor for hepatitis C', *Substance Use & Misuse*, 39: 211–24.

Tourigny, S. (2003) Importing lessons from US city streets: Unexpected shifts in drug use patterns, Conference paper given at Trends and Options: An international conference on alcohol and other drugs.

Turnbull, P., McSweeney, T., Webster, R., Edmunds, M. and Hough, M. (2000) *Drug Treatment and Testing Orders: Final Evaluation Report*, London: Home Office.

Turnbull, P. and Webster, R. (2007) *Supervising Crack-Using Offenders on Drug Treatment and Testing Orders*, London: NTA.

Turning Point (2005) *The Crack Report*, London: Turning Point.

UK Drug Policy Commission (UKDPC) (2008) *Reducing Drug Use, Reducing Re-offending*, London: UKDPC.

Unger, J., Kipke, M., De Rosa, C., Hyde, J., Ritt-Olson, A. and Montgomery, S. (2006) 'Needle-sharing among young IV drug users and their social network members: The influence of the injection partner's characteristics on HIV risk behavior', *Addictive Behaviors*, 31: 1607–18.

United Nations Office on Drugs and Crime (UNODC) (2007) *2007 World Drug Report*, Vienna: UNODC.

Usdan, S., Schumacher, J., Milby, J., Wallace, D., McNamara, C. and Michael, M. (2001) 'Crack cocaine, alcohol and other drug use patterns among homeless persons with mental disorders', *American Journal of Drug and Alcohol Abuse*, 27(1), 107–20.

van Beek I., Dwyer R. and Malcolm A. (2001) 'Cocaine injecting: the sharp end of drug related harm', *Drug and Alcohol Review*, 20: 333–42.

van Ree, E. (2002) 'Drugs, the democratic civilising process and the consumer society', *International Journal of Drug Policy*, 13: 349–53.

Van Swaaningen, R. (2005) 'Public safety and the management of fear', *Theoretical Criminology*, 9(3): 289–305.

Venkatesh, S. and Levitt, S. (2000) '"Are We a Family or a Business?" History and Disjuncture in the Urban American Street Gang', *Theory and Society*, 3(29): 427–62.

Wacquant, L. (2002) 'Scrutinizing the Street: Poverty, Morality and the Pitfalls of Urban Ethnography', *American Journal of Sociology*, 107: 1468–532.

Wacquant, L. (2004) 'Decivilizing and demonizing: The social and symbolic remaking of the black ghetto and Elias in the dark ghetto', in S. Loyal and S. Quilley (Eds) *The Sociology of Norbert Elias*, Cambridge: Cambridge University Press.

Waldorf, D., Reinarman, C. and Murphy, S. (1991) *Cocaine Changes: The Experience of Using and Quitting*, Philadelphia, PA: Temple University Press.

Waninger, K. and Thuahnai, S. (2008) 'Use of lemon juice to increase crack cocaine's solubility for intravenous use', *Journal of Emergency Medicine*, 34 (2): 207–11.

Ward, J. (2010) *Flashback: Drugs and Dealing in the Golden Age of the London Rave Scene*, Cullompton: Willan.

Waterson, A. (1997) 'Anthropological research and the politics of HIV prevention: Towards a critique of policy and priorities in the age of AIDs', *Social Science and Medicine*, 44 (9): 1381–91.

Weaver, T., Charles, V., Madden, P. and Renton, A. (2002) *Co-morbidity of Substance Misuse and Mental Illness Collaborative Study (COSMIC): A Study of the Prevalence and Management of Co-Morbidity amongst Adult Substance Misuse and Mental Health Treatment Populations,* London: Imperial College.

Weaver, T., Hart, J., Rutter, D., Metrebian, N. and Chantler, K. (2007) *Summary of the NECTOS Study of Specialist Crack Services,* London: NTA.

Webster, R. (1999) *Working with Black Crack Users in a Crisis Setting: The City Roads Experience,* London: City Roads.

Webster, R. (2001) *An Assessment of the Substance Misuse Treatment Needs of Young People in the London Borough of Rivertown,* Rivertown DAT: London.

Wechsberg, W., Dennis, M., Cavanaugh, E. and Rachal, J. (1993) 'A comparison of injecting drug users reached through outreach and methadone treatment', *Journal of Drug Issues,* 23: 667–87.

Weppner, R. (1981) 'Status and role among narcotic addicts: Implications for treatment personnel', *International Journal of Offender Therapy and Comparative Criminology,* 25: 233–47.

Wilkins, L. (1964) *Social Deviance: Social Policy, Action and Research,* London: Tavistock.

Wilkinson, I. (2006) 'Health, risk and "social suffering"', *Health, Risk and Society,* 8: 1–8.

Williams, T. (1990) *Crackhouse: Notes from the End of the Line,* New York: Penguin.

Williamson, S., Gossop, M., Powis, B., Griffiths, P., Fountain, J. and Strang, J. (1996) 'Adverse effects of stimulant drugs in a community sample of drug users', *Drug and Alcohol Dependence,* 44: 87–94.

Withers, N.W., Pulvirenti, L., Koob, G.F. and Gillin, J.C. (1995) 'Cocaine abuse and dependence', *Journal of Psychopharmacology,* 15 (1): 35–7.

Woods, S., Sorscher, J., King, J. and Hasselfeld, K. (2003) 'Young adults admitted for asthma: Does gender influence outcomes?', *Journal of Women's Health,* 12: 481–5.

Young, J. (1971) *The Drugtakers,* London: Paladin.

Young, J. (2007) *The Vertigo of Late Modernity,* London: Sage.

Young, M., Stuber, J., Ahern, J. and Galea, S. (2005) 'Interpersonal discrimination and the health of illicit drug users', *American Journal of Drug and Alcohol Abuse,* 31: 371–91.

Young, R. (2002) *From War to Work: Drug Treatment, Social Inclusion and Enterprise,* London: Foreign Policy Centre.

Ziek, K., Beardsley, M., Deren, S. and Tortu, S. (1996) 'Predictors in a follow up in a sample of urban crack users', *Evaluation and Program Planning,* 19(3): 219–24.

Zinberg, N. (1984) *Drug, Set and Setting: The Basis for Controlled Intoxicant Use,* Connecticut: Yale University Press.

Zule, W., Flannery, B., Wechsberg, W. and Lam, W. (2003) 'Alcohol use among out of treatment crack using African American women', *American Journal of Drug and Alcohol Abuse,* 28(3): 525–44.

Index